Broadband Network Analysis and Design

For a complete listing of the *Artech House Telecommunciations Library*, turn to the back of this book

Broadband Network Analysis and Design

Daniel Minoli

Bell Communications Research, Inc.
New York University

Artech House
Boston • London

Library of Congress Cataloging-in-Publication Data

Minoli, Daniel, 1952–
Broadband Network Analysis and Design/Daniel Minoli
Includes bibliographical references and index.
ISBN 0-89006-675-2
1. Broadband Communication systems—Design. I. Title.
TK5102.5.M55   1993
621.382—dc20

93-12353
CIP

British Library Cataloguing in Publication Data

Minoli, Daniel, 1952–
Broadband Network Analysis and Design.
Includes bibliographical references and index.
I. Title.
621.382
ISBN 0-89006-675-2

© 1993 ARTECH HOUSE, INC.
685 Canton Street
Norwood, MA 02062

International Standard Book Number: 0-89006-675-2
Library of Congress Catalog Card Number: 83-12353

10 9 8 7 6 5 4 3 2

621·38
MIN

For

Gino, Angela,
Anna,
Emmanuelle, Emile and Gabrielle

. . . pero' mi accorgo che mal ponno sfogar rade, operose
rime il dolor che deve albergar meco. . .
Foscolo, Odi, MDCCCIII

Contents

Preface

Users have witnessed an accelerated introduction of new networking technologies in the past five years. Unfortunaly, usable network design tools, textbooks, and techniques, which might assist users discriminate between cost savings that the new services might possibly afford and high-pressure "hype," have not kept up with these developments. In the rather austere climate of the times, users should be punctilious in their pursuit of cost-effectivness over unnecessary or marginal capabilities that only exhibit "great efficiency" in the trade press and in multicolor sales brochures.

The 1990s is the decade of broadband services, from megabits per second (such as Switched Multimegabit Data Service) to gigabits per second (so-called gigabit networks). Given the relatively high cost of these technologies when compared to 9.6 kbps services (the data communications staple for the past quarter of a century), design methodologies should be applied to demonstrate actual cost-effectiveness that would satisfy any internal or external auditor. Broadband affords economy-of-scale, particularly for large backbone applications. For example, 1 T1 is cheaper than 24 DS0s; 1 T3 is cheaper than 28 DS1s; 1 STS3-c is cheaper than 3 STS-1s. However, the judicial use of analytical methods to design such networks remains critical.

Of course, all techniques, models, formulas, and approaches described in this text are equally applicable to narrowband services. However, the cost implications are more critical at broadband; therefore, the implied theme of this book is for broadband networks. For example a 1,000-mile dedicated voice-grade line costs approximately $900 per month; the cost of a same-distance T1 line is about $9,000 per month. If a manager who is installing voice-grade private lines miscalculates and installs 11 instead of the 10 lines that are needed, it will be a $10,000 a year mistake. But if the manager installs 11 T1 lines instead of the necessary 10, the mistake will cost ten times more at $100,000 each year.

This textbook aims at familiarizing the reader with a number of available network design techniques including: financial tools, linear programming, game theory, forecasting, queueing theory, traffic engineering, relaxation theory, optimization, quality-of-service analysis, and other methods. Topological and tariff aspects of network design are not covered because they normally depend directly on technology/communications service. For a complete assessment of the underlying technological aspects of broadband networks, the reader is refered to two companion texts: (1) *Telecommunication Technologies Handbook* (Artech House, 1991), which describes communications technologies such as wireless, satellite, microwave and fiber transmission, local area networks, metropolitan area networks, networks of private PBXs, and messaging networks; and (2) *Enterprise Networking* (Artech House, 1993), which provides a detailed survey of network technologies such as fractional T1, T1, switched T1, T3, SONET, frame relay, cell relay, BISDN and SMDS.

This text can serve as a one-semester graduate course in contemporary network design studies, particularly when a pragmatic perspective is desired. The material is currently used at Rutgers University and New York University, at which the author has taught for several years.

Acknowledgments

Ron Leighton, U S WEST Advanced Technologies, supplied Chapter 6 and is hereby thanked for this major contribution.

Mr. R. Egan, U S WEST Advanced Technologies, is thanked for his inspiration for this text and for the encouragement provided over a period of several years.

Mr G. Louit, NYNEX Sciences & Technologies, and Mr. R. Woodrow, NYNEX TRG, under whose tutelage some portions of this material came to light, are also thanked.

The following individuals are also thanked for their moral support of this undertaking: Dick Vigilante, New York University; Gail Allen, Rutgers University; Lance Lindstrom, DataPro Research Corporation; Tony Rizzo, Network Computing Magazine; Joanne Dressendofer, IMEDIA; and Ben Occhiogrosso, DVI Communications. Additionally, I thank G. H. Dobrowski, S. M. Walters, J. E. Holcomb, and J. J. Amoss of Bellcore.

This book does not reflect *any* policy, position, or posture of Bell Communications Research or the Bell Operating Companies. The writing of the book was not funded by Bellcore or by the Bell Operating Companies. All ideas expressed are strictly those of the author, developed over 18 years of network design activities. Data pertaining to the public switched network are based on the open literature and were not reviewed by the Bell Operating Companies. Vendor products, services, and equipment are mentioned solely to document the state-of-the-art of a given technology; the information has not been verified with vendors. No material contained in this book should be construed as a recommendation of any kind.

Bell Communications Research places value on understanding the data-communications environment in order to assist clients in developing suitable network-based data services. Consequently, Bellcore did support this undertaking in spirit, and I take this opportunity to express my appreciation for the moral encouragement provided by Bellcore, in general, and Mr. Walters, in particular. During the recent past, through projects at Bellcore, I have been involved with applying the new high-speed digital services to large commercial data users. Some material in Chapter 1 is based on one such project.

Daniel Minoli
April 1993

Chapter 1
Introduction

1.1 THE NETWORK DESIGN ENVIRONMENT

Corporate communication managers are under continual pressure to modernize their networks. This pressure is generated not only by business imperatives, but also by the availability of new communication services. The goal of this book is to identify analytical tools that enable end-users to evaluate the cost-effectiveness of the new broadband networking technologies within the context of their enterprisewide networks. These services include switched T1/DS1, fractional DS3, synchronous optical network (SONET), frame relay, switched multimegabit fata service (SMDS), and cell relay (also known as asynchronous transfer mode or ATM), among others [1]. A small design mistake can be very costly for a firm, particularly when it entails relatively expensive services [2]. Hence, there is a renewed interest in optimal network design with the advent of broadband. The techniques described in this text also are applicable to traditional networks.

The increased obsolescence rate of underlying technologies complicates the network design task. Traditional master-slave mainframe networks are being replaced by distributed peer-to-peer local area networks (LAN) [3]. Communications managers also must deal with varying network design objectives. Different objectives may lead one to employ different network topologies, technologies, and architectures. Typical objectives might be to: minimize cost, maximize profit, and minimize down time. Clearly, these criteria are not necessarily compatible with each other (for example, a network built to minimize the cost will probably not maximize reliability and quality of service), yet a compromise is sought.

Tariffs associated with services tend to change rather quickly. Data communications managers have a chronic problem getting up-to-date, clear, machine-readable tariff information on communications services they might want to use, particularly given the plethora of new services. Such information includes recurring charges, potential discounts, and installation charges. A design may involve the use of 50 or more items of such information for each of several services that the designer may want to compare or analyze from a sensitivity standpoint. Service availability information (i.e., the central offices (COs) that support specific services) can be difficult to obtain, especially when the designer is looking at many remote sites. Sometimes, the trade press leads users to believe that just because a carrier has announced a certain service, it is available at all 1,000 COs the carrier might have (there are about 20,000 COs in the United States); in fact, the service may be available in only one or two COs in the carriers' territory.

High-capacity digital private networks are becoming larger and more complex. To plan a network, the designer must know the number of remote sites, hubbing locations, media types (i.e., voice, data, messaging, video, or image), traffic characteristics, types of applications, required network/equipment redundancy, the response time required to support workforce productivity, interface issues (particularly in multinational environments), network management requirements, type or preference of equipment available, and carrier services available at the various locations.

Network designers would welcome computerized tools that can assist in the design of a network according to user objectives. Unfortunately, not enough computer-based tools are available that incorporate the new services enumerated above. There are two major on-line design and tariff services markets [4]: (1) network design and analysis services provided by external companies, and (2) computer-based systems that can be used to perform optimization. The first component of the market, spearheaded aggressively by systems integrators, was estimated to be $700M in 1991 and predicted to grow to $3B by 1996 (a 35% compounded growth in five years). The increased interest in outsourcing is a stimulus to firms offering network design services. The second component of the market, network design tools, was estimated to be $28M in 1991 and predicted to grow to $46M by 1993. There are 5,000 network design/analysis tools installed today, with a potential market of 30,000 sites for medium and large companies [4]. (The market is larger if one includes LAN design and telecommunications networks.) Three categories of suppliers provide carrier and design information: publishing firms (e.g., CCMI/United Communications Group, Telco Research, and Datapro), providers of on-line network design tools (e.g., Network Management Inc, Contel, and GTE), and consultants, particularly systems integrators (e.g., BBN, KPMG Peat Marwick, Andersen Consulting, EDS, and value-added networks).

1.2 WHAT YOU WILL FIND IN THIS BOOK

The goal of network design as a discipline is to enable the establishment of a cost-effective infrastructure that meets the applications' throughput requirements as well as the users' response time needs. Once a communication service or set of services has been selected based on a variety of considerations, one performs financial, queueing, traffic engineering, topological, and tradeoff analyses in order to achieve the targeted quality of service. The purpose of this book is to survey the analytical design methods available to the practitioner. Table 1.1 lists the network design topics covered in this book. Because topological and tariff aspects of network design normally depend directly on the technology, the communication service, and age (as new tariffs are filed), they are not covered here. For a technological foundation, the reader is referred to two recent companion texts [1] and [5].

This treatment of the field elects not use the narrow definition of network design used by some academicians, which completely equates network design with abstract algorithmic topological problems that place points on a plane usually using artificial edge weights as key, or sole drivers. This restrictive definition misrepresents the daily functions undertaken by network managers, who represent the intended audience of this text. A broader definition is preferred that includes financial, queueing, traffic engineering, topological, and tradeoff analyses. *Even if the design task is restricted to strictly topological issues, many available algorithms oversimplify the real problem*, because of all the non-linearities and discontinuities of the underlying tariffs, traffic rates, actual geography, and service availability. For example, the topological optimum might be to place a node in a location in which the user does not have and does not want to rent property. Many services are available only at selected COs or cities (e.g., frame relay, cell relay, and switched T1). A related service discontinuity may be connected to the user's selection of the carrier; although a service may be available in a city, it may not be available from the carrier that the user has selected to be the major provider of the enterpisewide network services. Topological design per se, therefore, is not a very practical topic and should not dominate the more inclusive discussion in this book.

1.2.1 Useful for Narrowband Designs

The cost implications of network design are more critical at broadband than at narrowband and this book thus focuses on broadband networks. Of course, all techniques, models, formulas, and approaches described in this text are equally applicable to narrowband

Table 1.1
Network Design Topics Covered in Text

Chapter	Topic
2	Financial techniques
3	Optimization techniques
4	Queueing and teletraffic modeling
5	Queueing and teletraffic techniques
6	Performance analysis guide for lower layer protocols
7	The impact of source-dependent traffic
8	Relaxation theory
9	An example of quality-of-service management

services. For example a 1,000-mile dedicated voice-grade line costs approximately $900 per month; the cost of a same-distance T1 line is about $9,000 per month. If a manager miscalculates the required number of voice-grade private lines and installs 11 lines instead of 10 lines, it amounts to a $10,000-a-year mistake. However, if the manager installs 11 T1 lines instead of the needed 10 lines, it becomes a $100,000-a-year mistake.

1.3 DESIGN APPROACHES

There are five facets of network design activity: (1) source/sink locations and bandwidth requirements for each source-sink pair, (2) inventory of services to be considered, (3) tariff information for the services, (4) service availability for the specific geography, (5) tools that use the other four facets to automatically generate specified solutions and their costs. This section focuses on service selection from a procedural perspective.

1.3.1 Design Objectives

Recently, there have been instances in which the quality of the corporate information and its transmission have been given secondary priority in a desire to deploy the *least expensive network*. Fortunately, many network managers now realize that such information has become so fundamental to modern business and society that both its quality and the accuracy, effectiveness and timeliness of its distribution should be given prominent consideration in any network design.

The specific corporate objective in the optimization process should be stated explicitly and employed throughout the design process. In some cases, there may be a hierarchy of objectives. Some possible objectives in designing a corporate networks are to [5]:

- Minimize cost (i.e., build the cheapest network);
- Maximize the cost-performance ratio (i.e., get the most network for the investment);
- Maximize the quality of service
- Maximize profit (e.g., build a network that allows the firm to aggressively reach new regional, national and global markets);
- Maximize the profit rate (e.g., a utility);
- Minimize the risk of loss (e.g., a military network);
- Maximize safety (e.g., a network designed for a police department);
- Maximize the growth opportunity for the firm (i.e., build a network that can easily grow in the future);
- Maximize the prestige of the firm (e.g., buy state-of-the-art equipment to impress investors, competitors, and the public);
- Maximize workforce productivity.

These criteria are not all compatible with each other; however, a well-designed network can support a reasonable subset or cross-section of factors. Before any network design effort is undertaken, the network manager must decide which of these (or other) criteria are applicable to the company or a specific network. The issue of the optimization objective is revisited in Chapter 3.

Now that this author has a 17 Mips "Scintilla" workstation with 12 MB of random access memory, he realizes that the network/system designers of the early and mid 1980s were unsung heroes. These designers used a 2- to 4-Mips host to support up to 100 users through a wide area network (WAN) operating at 9.6 kbps, through a database management system, back over the WAN, with a total response time of 2–3 seconds. In contrast, this author can click on a mail tool menu on his workstation, which is connected to the local server via a 10-Mbps Ethernet network, and wait 10–20 seconds before the list of a few queued mail messages appears on the screen. A simple calculation reveals the flaws of the argument that the earlier approach was expensive: $15,000 × 100 = $1,500,000; thus, 100 workstations cost as much as a midrange mainframe.

1.3.2 Evaluation Over an Entire Enterprise

When evaluating alternative designs from a cost perspective, the network manager must consider the entire network as an ensemble rather than simply performing a basic tariff analysis based on one or two links (as is sometimes the case, particularly in trade press comparisons). For example, one might simply compare Service A and Service B and determine that the crossover point is x miles; in other words, Service A is better for links less than x miles in length and Service B is better for links of more than x miles. By itself, this information is inconclusive and may lead to an incorrect, overly simplistic service solution, unless the actual topology (or a reasonable surrogate thereof) is examined. To illustrate this point, consider Service A to be tariffed at $116 + $52/mile per month, and Service B to be tariffed at $179 + $42/mile per month. Which service should the manager select if, for network management reasons, the manager only wants one service? It all depends on the total topology. As illustrated in Table 1.2, a simple analysis would seem to imply that Service A is better for up to 6.3 miles while Service B is better beyond 6.30 miles.

Unfortunately, it's not that simple. Table 1.3 depicts three cases that illustrate the need to examine the overall topology. For simplicity, assume that the company in question has two groups of links, with 50 links in total. One group consists of shorter links that are all the same length. The other group consists of longer links that, again, are all the same length. (In reality, each of the 50 links might be a different, unique length.) In the first case, the only change in the overall topology is the length of the 40 longer links, which vary from 10 miles to 4 miles; the 10 shorter links are 3 miles each. The best overall service when the longer links are 10, 9, 8, and 7 miles is Service B; when the longer links are 6, 5 and 4 miles, Service A is best. In the second case of overall topologies, the lengths of both the shorter and longer links are constant (3 miles and 10 miles, respectively) but the percentage of longer links varies. The best overall service varies

Table 1.2
A Simple Comparison of Two Services

Mileage	Cost of Service A ($)	Cost of Service B ($)
1.00	168.00	221.00
2.00	220.00	263.00
3.00	272.00	305.00
4.00	324.00	347.00
5.00	376.00	389.00
6.00	428.00	431.00
6.30	443.60	443.60
7.00	480.00	473.00
8.00	532.00	515.00
9.00	584.00	557.00
10.00	636.00	599.00

from A at 22 instances of long links to B for any situation at or below 24 instances. In the third case, the lengths of both the shorter links and of the longer links vary as well as the percentage of longer links. Except in one instance, Service A is the best overall.

The critical importance of considering the total topology should be clear from this example. Examining the total network topology provides a more accurate appraisal of which service is best in a given situation and is likely to be the method that the customer would employ since it reflects the actual disbursement that the customer must be prepared to make.

If an actual topology is not available and/or the actual topology requires too much detail, then one should construct a surrogate topology that at least includes the correct number of sinks and sources with a reasonable dispersion over a geographic area. This dispersion should then be translated into usable mileages. For example, one can assume that the sources are uniformly distributed over a LATA (*local access and transport areas*), and that the distance from the source to the CO is a uniform 3 miles. (Alternatively, the distance might be 3 miles in 80% of the cases and 6 miles in 20% of the cases). Utilizing a fixed underlying surrogate topology (i.e., a topology model) to study a set of possible communication services, the services can be compared equitably. Comparative results usually will be strong and trustworthy.

1.3.3 Cost-Benefit Space

Figure 1.1 depicts the cost-benefit space that can be applied to various communication services. Different vendor and/or a vendor's product lines can be mapped to different quadrants of this space. This partition can be used from the provider's point-of-view as well as the user's. The communication manager should identify both the posture of the vendor in question as well as his/her own posture in regard to the network in question.

Table 1.3
Considering the Inventory of Links of a Network

Case 1

Length of shorter links (miles)	3	3	3	3	3	3	3
Length of longer links (miles)	10	9	8	7	7	5	4
Number of shorter links	10	10	10	10	10	10	10
Number of longer links	40	40	40	40	40	40	40
Network cost with Service A ($)	28,160	26,080	24,000	21,920	21,920	17,760	15,680
Network cost with Service B ($)	27,010	25,330	23,650	21,970	21,970	18,610	16,930
Best overall service	B	B	B	B	A	A	A

Case 2

Length of shorter links (miles)	3	3	3	3	3	3	3
Length of longer links (miles)	10	10	10	10	10	10	10
Number of shorter links	28	26	24	22	20	18	16
Number of longer links	22	24	26	28	30	32	34
Network cost with Service A ($)	21,608	22,336	23,064	23,792	24,520	25,248	25,976
Network cost with Service B ($)	21,718	22,306	22,894	23,482	24,070	24,658	25,246
Best overall service	A	B	B	B	B	B	B

Case 3

Length of shorter links (miles)	5	5.25	5.5	5.75	6	6.25	6.5
Length of longer links (miles)	6.5	6.5	6.5	6.5	6.5	6.5	6.5
Number of shorter links	30	32	34	36	38	40	42
Number of longer links	20	18	16	14	12	10	8
Network cost with Service A ($)	20,360	20,620	20,932	21,296	21,712	22,180	22,700
Network cost with Service B ($)	20,710	20,920	21,172	21,466	21,802	22,180	22,600
Best overall service	A	A	A	A	A	A	B

Some services can be considered "premium." Even though they may be expensive, they are very reliable and support many "bells and whistles." Such services may be deemed necessary for certain mission-critical components of the overall corporate network. Other networks may be based on "budget" services; if they fail or do not maintain constant end-to-end delay or block error rate (BLER—an old term that has been redefined here to encompass frame loss in a frame relay network and cell loss in a cell relay network), no harm will be done. An example of such a network could be an e-mail system.

Sometimes the message appears to be ambivalent. On the one hand, one is told that bandwidth is expensive, and hence it must be shared among users via multiplexing techniques (i.e., packetization, framing, or cellularization), rather than applied in a dedicated point-to-point fashion. At the same time, one is told that the 30% bandwidth

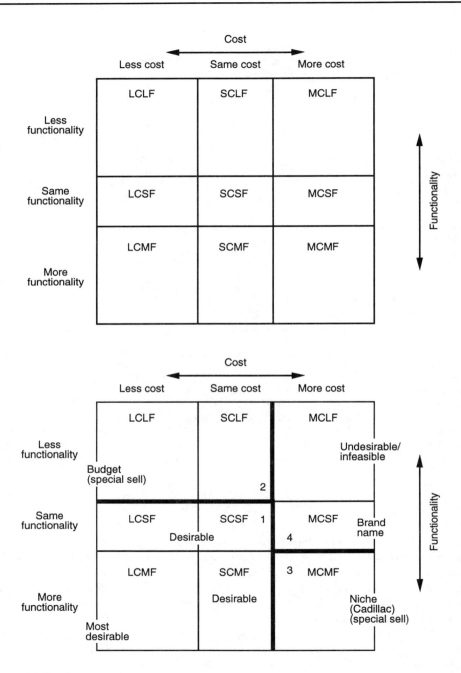

Figure 1.1 Partition of service space.

overhead to accomplish multiplexing (i.e., in packet, frames, and cell structures) is acceptable, supposedly because bandwidth is inexpensive and thus can be used inefficiently.

1.3.4 Cost Factors To Be Considered in Decisionmaking

When the key objective of a design is to minimize cost, as is often the case, the methods for comparing alternate strategies (Chapter 2) call for the exact identification of the annual cash flow afforded by a given alternative. This, in turn, calls for the exact quantification of the expenses associated with that alternative. Often, managers use the equipment costs in models to make a case. There are, however, many additional cost-generating factors that need to be considered in the process. Table 1.4 identifies some of these additional "hidden" costs, which are not always considered significant during the project assessment at startup but which can substantially alter the bottom line.

A large portion of the telecommunications expense results from managing the network, as identified in Table 1.4. Several studies have indicated that the management portion can be as high as 40% of the total cost, with transmission and amortized equipment each representing 30% [6]. Yet many technology-introduction cases ignore such costs.

Table 1.4
Cost Factors to Consider (partial list)†

Equipment costs
    Actual equipment
    Cables
    Software/licenses
    Documentation
Communication costs
    Initial
    Recurring
Rental costs for housing equipment
    (e.g., towers, remote concentrators, and switches)
    Real estate
    Floor space
    Air conditioning
    Lighting
    Sensors
    Security
    Planning and Administration
Electrical power
    Principal
    Backup
    Planning and Administration

(continued)

Table 1.4 (continued)
Cost Factors to Consider (partial list)†

Project feasibility study (staff time)
Project pilot
Pilot evaluation
Management review
Project implementation time/cost
        Construction
        Delivery costs
        Testing and validating
        Integration
        Delays and overruns
        Cost of service overlap
        Specialized installation staff
Fees
        Rights-of-way
        Licenses
Taxes
System/network operation and management
        Staff
        Benefits
        Management of staff
        Facilities
        Test equipment
        Training
        Turnover
        Ad hoc maintenance
        Maintenance (monthly fees)
        Insurance
        Cost of documentation
        Capacity planning
        Planning and administration
        Cost of network/system security (including appropriate tools)
Cost to backup system (including disaster recovery)
Lost productivity
Business risk
Financial management (i.e., bookkeeping and accounting)
Cost of capital
Technological obsolescence
Cost of eventual replacement
Decommission costs

†Partially based on [7–13]

    One example of a "hidden" network management cost is the staff needed to run a network control center. This staff potentially needs specialized and expensive skills (e.g., digital jitter testing, optical testing, satellite background, frame relay knowledge, and cell relay knowledge). After all, it is easy for a manager to decide that of the dozens of alternatives available, an obscure technology is desirable from the comptrollers' bottom line point of view; it is another matter to find competent technicians that not only are familiar with the technology, but know it well. The pool of technicians from which to hire someone with such skills will also be small or even nonexistent. "But we will train..." the manager says; therein lies the "hidden" cost. A two-shift operation plus backup for vacations and illnesses, would require three technicians. Given a turnover rate of 33% (which is not unusual for technicians), a manager will need to retrain one person per year; assuming three cumulative weeks of training per person and the total cost of compensation (pay + benefits at $60K/yr), the specialized staff training cost would be about $4,000 each year. This incremental cost needs to be considered as part of the overall system cost. This example assumes that the technicians do other jobs in addition to attending to the obscure technology; the $4,000 is for incidental training with new technology. If, on the other hand, the introduction of new technology necessitates additional staff that are dedicated to this new system, the entire payroll and benefit costs must be taken into account. (Another alternative would be to outsource the network, but this would entails an entirely different set of cost/benefit considerations.)

Carriers also must undertake network control on behalf of their customers, but they are able to take advantages of economies of scale in this realm. For example, they might have a staff of three or four to address a certain technology citywide. Presumably, not all users would have problems with the particular technology on the same day, thus allowing the service provider to spread the cost over many customers, which results in lower costs to the end-users.

Two additional observations are in order. First, data processing managers realized long ago that they can best serve their users within the corporate organization by keeping the number of programming languages to a minimum. They might have a COBOL shop and one or two database languages (e.g., IMS and FOCUS). They do not routinely develop production systems in languages such as Ada, Pascal, Cobol, Fortran, C, IDMS, IMS, RAMIS, FOCUS, SAS, and NOMAD 2. If they did, they would need to retain a staff that is familiar with all of these languages, which would require either superprogrammers that know five or six languages well or one to two people skilled in each language. The the data communication manager should consider this principle: Why bring in one instance of every possible technology available? Simply select a few technologies and "go with them." (Both software development and communications can be labor-intensive activities).

There will be numerous communication options available in the 1990s, which will make choosing the technology more challenging for the corporate network planner [1]. The availability of many services can be advantageous to the user who is willing to use multiple technologies to optimize various portions of the network. This approach can result into more cost-effective transmission and optimized response time. The downside of this approach is the need to acquire expertise in many new technologies, to deal with many network and equipment vendors, and to track the wave of technological progress, which now appears to a have a lifecycle of two years or less. The user will be traveling unchartered waters when testing newly available equipment and network services;

integrating new services into the existing network management system; and exploring new, unconventional, or not fully-tested migration paths. Fortunately, once some equipment is brought on board, companies tend to "lock in" to that technology in an effort to secure a payback, which ensures some stability.

Other users may prefer to choose a more conservative approach. These users may select a single technology across the corporate network, even though they realize that it may not be totally optimal for every facet of that network. Such an approach has the advantages of minimizing the required level of multitechnology expertise, involves dealing with fewer and more well-established vendors, and uses tested equipment as well as tested unit integration and migration paths. By not selecting the latest technology (i.e., technology that was announced during the previous year or so), these users let other corporations (which may have deep pockets) work out the "bugs," pitfalls, and downsides of the new technologies. Since the human aspect of running a network can entail up to 40% of the total expenditures, as noted earlier, one can wonder what business advantages there are in deploying a new technology that supposedly saves, for example, 10% of the transmission cost, if it requires a total or partial replacement of equipment and staff retraining (or hiring) that may require an expense equal to 20% to 30% of the total system cost [1].

Second, it is clear a priori that it is "cheaper to do things yourself," rather than let someone else do it, if one is willing to take the onus and has the necessary tools to do the job. It is less expensive to buy ingredients and cook a meal than to go to a restaurant to eat the same meal; it is cheaper to buy materials and build a house than to have it built on a turnkey basis. These comparisons do not take into account the person's time, the burden of the task, or the need for appropriate tools (e.g., pans or electrical drills). However, even a true cost comparison that includes all factors may corroborate this conclusion, because when we let someone else do something for us we must give the other person some profit for the service. It may indeed be cheaper to buy the components and setup a private network, but management must decide if it is willing to then maintain the network for the next 10 years, do the engineering and deployment with the ensuing risk, and acquire the appropriate tools (e.g., people and machines)?

Letting a service provider handle the network means:

- The provider has the onus, not the user. If the provider fails to deliver the system as contracted, it can be sued (one cannot sue one's own staff) and/or replaced.
- The user has less engineering and deployment risk, particularly if its staff has deployed only a few systems or none at all. The user also faces less challenge in terms of project management. The service provider, on the other hand, may have a professional staff dedicated to these functions that may have deployed hundreds of similar systems.
- Acquisition of appropriate tools that are not available in-house, and will be used only once, will not be necessary. (For example, a high-end PBX may appear superior to Centrex, but to install it may require the addition of highly-payed professionals to the staff for the duration of the installation. Once the installation is complete, what does the user do with these professionals?)

1.3.5 Service Selection Process

In the financial modeling portion of this book, it is assumed 1
services to compare has already been made through some ext
of-service modeling portion, the assumption is made that a s
selected and that the user is interested in obtaining some metrics on certain observation
variables (e.g., end-to-end delay, cell loss rate, and interfame delay variation).

The designer can select a set of communication services (e.g., switched virtual
circuit frame relay, SMDS, cell relay, dedicated DS1 lines, or dedicated DS3 lines) and
then perform a traditional minimum cost analysis. In fact, this process could generate a
table listing the best solution, the next-best solution, and the next-best solution after that,
and so on.

As suggested earlier, minimizing the cost is one standard design objective. But there
are other important factors. It is one thing to save a few dollars here and there; it is an
altogether different matter to design a network that is reliable, integrated, interoperable,
and enhanceable, and is considered a strategic resource by senior management, rather
than an overhead cost or corporate drain (i.e., fair game for outsourcing).

It should be noted that a decision based on cost can be completely analytical (i.e.,
reproducible, deterministic, and objective), if all the cost elements are appropriately
accounted for, as identified in the previous section. The factor analysis that is described
below, which aims at including additional factors, is not completely objective in that
different people may weight the factors differently and arrive at a different set of results.
In effect, the factor analysis tries to "get into the head" of the decisionmaker and capture
the nonquantifiable sense of the decision process. All of us are aware that decisions are
not always made in a completely rational manner. For example, the manager may play
golf with a VIP from a specific vendor and thus be favorably inclined toward that
equipment. Another manager may have been treated poorly when employed at Company
X, and therefore not look favorably at equipment from this company even though it may
be the best equipment.

The author has used this factor analysis in a number of large designs, typically in
conjunction with a cost-based approach. The results generated by the factor analysis tend
to give rise to a lot of debate and thus help the final decisionmaker determine the true
importance of certain presumed preferences.

There is, in fact, a discipline of statistics known as *factor analysis*. Factor analysis
is used when there are many factors (e.g., 100 or 200) that affect the end result, but with
which the cause-and-effect relationships are not clearly visible, cannot be easily
established, or simply cost too much to establish through measurements. This analysis is
used, for example, to determine the effectiveness of a TV advertisement. Such effectiveness
depends on many things such as: notoriety of actors in the ad, quality of production,
"raciness", volume of ad, number of words spoken, number of messages contained, age
of the people in the ad, appeal of the people in the ad, time-of-day when played, and the

on running the ad. Factor analysis provides a mechanism to narrow or cluster these various factors into a meaningful and manageable subset.

While the approach identified below does not apply the machinery of factor analysis proper, it provides a sense of the "soft" elements driving some network design decisions that may or may not be completely quantifiable in analytical form.

The first step of the suggested analysis is the identification of the important factors to be addressed. There could be hundreds of such factors. Table 1.5 depicts a set of factors used by the author for a number of studies in addition to transmission/equipment cost, which is always a factor. Some practitioners may find that they prefer a different set; perhaps the company in question has a set of factors that are critical to that particular organization.

These factors may have arisen out of a more fundamental grouping, shown in Table 1.6.

The second step entails applying weights to these factors for the particular network, application, and company in question. Then one sorts the factors in order of importance. Since high-granularity is often difficult to justify, it may be better simply to use four weights such as

1 = mandatory;
2 = desirable;
3 = nice to have;
4 = unimportant.

Table 1.5
A Set of Factors in Addition to Transmission/Equipment Cost

Ability to replace technology
Accounting and reporting capabilities
Bandwidth (bps per device)
BER/BLER
Consistency with international standards
Fault reconfiguration time
Initial connectivity cost
Installation time
Integration/compatibility with existing base
Migration cost (undepreciated capital)
Network management cost
Network management ease
Network management richness
Network nontransmission delays
Normal growth capabilities (expansion)
Reliability/availability
Security
Session setup time
Vendor product support

Table 1.6
Design Considerations at the Macro Level

Connectivity considerations
    Adequate bandwidth
    Reliability/availability
    Security
    Network nontransmission delays
    Session setup time
    Installation time
    BER/BLER
Network management considerations
    Network management ease
    Network management richness
    Fault reconfiguration time
    Accounting and reporting capabilities
Migratory considerations
    Integration/compatibility with existing base
    Normal growth capabilities (expansion)
    Ability to replace technology
    Vendor product support
    Consistency with international standards
Cost considerations
    Initial connectivity cost
    Recurring bandwidth cost
    Network management cost
    Migration cost (undepreciated capital)

At the same time, it may be useful to attempt to put some metric on values associated with these factors. For example, nontransmission delays could be limited to 500 ms; vendor support could be high (H), medium (M), or low (L); and security could be H, M, or L. Table 1.7 depicts an example of these factors for Automatic Teller Machines (ATM)[1] based on a sample of requirements for about one dozen banks. Observe that in each of the four categories, all the factors have *equal weight* (since we limited granularity to four values). Notice that there are several levels of variability (this is precisely the environment where factor analysis is applicable), including the factors, the company/industry, the application, and the weight of each factor. Different users or applications (e.g. a network supporting backoffice platform applications) may use different factors with different weights.

Both the assignment of the weight and the metric should be determined in cooperation with the users of the network, not arbitrarily set by the network designer.

The next step in the process is to determine how each of the communication services that the designer has in mind does or does not support the application requirement identified in the previous step. It would be nice to be able to say "yes" or "no;" however, the

---

[1]Outside this section, the acronym "ATM" means "Asynchronous Transfer Mode."

Table 1.7
Prioritized Factors with Requirement Metrics

Rank	Factors in Banking ATM Application	Requirement
1	Session setup time	0.5–1.5 sec
1	Reliability/availability	99.70%
1	Security	M to H
1	Fault reconfiguration time	2–6 hr
1	Network management cost	L
1	Initial connectivity cost	L
2	Network nontransmission delays	1–3 sec
2	Network management ease	M
2	Installation time	5–10 days
2	BER/BLER	1×10^{-5}
2	Integration/compatibility with existing base	M–H
2	Ability to replace technology	M
2	Vendor product support	H
2	Migration cost (undepreciated capital)	L
3	Bandwidth (bps per device)	30
3	Network management richness	M
3	Accounting and reporting capabilities	M
3	Normal growth capabilities (expansion)	M
4	Consistency with international standards	L

real answer often is "perhaps" or "most of the time." To that end, it is suggested that the manager use determinants such as very likely (VL), likely (L), and unlikely (UL), and construct a table similar to Table 1.8 (shown as example only).

The selection model is then applied as follows: if the least expensive solution (i.e., a network based in its entirety on the service in question) meets all of the factors in tier 1 (i.e., it has L or VL entries), then it is selected. If it fails to meet a factor in tier 1, then one examines the next best solution from the cost perspective and repeats the process. The process continues until a solution is found. If, at any point, a tie is found, one determines which solution has more VLs in the tier 1 group of factors. If a tie still exists, then proceed to examine the next tier of factors.

Table 1.9 provides the ranking in costs, based on the use of the services shown in Table 1.8, for a design of a 100-branch bank in a large metropolitan area and adjoining suburbs, with a centralized computer in one of the suburbs. The costs take into account the topology of the bank's locations, the amortized cost of the equipment, and the tariffs in place in early 1991. Each design is optimized; in other words, it is the best possible topology using the selected service.

Table 1.10 provides the new ranking when the factor analysis of Table 1.8 and the algorithm just described are applied. As it can be seen, the application of the factor analysis appreciably changes the rank order. The analog solution moves to the top since it is the only service to meet all the essential service attributes specified in Table 1.7.

Table 1.8

Illustrative Example of Factor Weights

Rank	Factors in ATM Application	Requirement	Packet Switching	Hubless DDS	DDS	Analog	User's T1 Multiplexers
1	Session setup time	0.5 to 1.5 sec	VL	VL	VL	VL	VL
1	Reliability/availability	99.70%	L	L	VL	L	L
1	Security	M to H	L	VL	VL	VL	L
1	Fault reconfiguration time	2–6 hr	L	UL	UL	L	VL
1	Network management cost	L	VL	L	L	L	L
1	Initial connectivity cost	L	UL†	L†	L†	VL	UL†
2	Network nontransmission delays	1–3 sec	UL	VL	VL	VL	VL
2	Network management ease	M	L	L	L	L	VL
2	Installation time	5–10 days	UL	L	UL	L	UL
2	BER/BLER	1×10^{-5}	L	L	VL	L	L
2	Integration/ compatibility with existing base	M to H	L	L	L	VL	L
2	Ability to replace technology	M	L	L	L	VL	L
2	Vendor product support	H	L	L	L	VL	L
2	Migration cost (undepreciated capital)	L	UL	L	L	L	L
3	Bandwidth (bps per device)	30	L	L	L	VL	L
3	Network management richness	M	L	L	L	L	L
3	Accounting and reporting capabilities	M	L	UL	UL	UL	L
3	Normal growth capabilities (expansion)	M	L	L	L	L	L
4	Consistency with international standards	L	VL	L	L	UL	L

† Requires installation of synchronous packet assembler/dissembler, channel service units, or T1 multiplexer—modems are assumed to be present in the existing network.

Table 1.9

Example of a 100-Branch Bank, Best Design by Cost

Rank	Service	Monthly Cost ($)
1	Hubless multidrop DDS, 5 yr contract	26K
2	DDS multidrop	30K
3	Hubless DDS multidrop	32K
4	Analog multidrop lines	34K
5	CPE T1 mux	48K
6	DDS	48K
7	Packet switching	55K
8	Hubless DDS, 5 yr contract	60K
9	Hubless DDS	75K

Table 1.10

Example of a 100-Branch Bank, Best Design by Factors Important to this Application

Rank	Service	Monthly Cost ($)
1	Analog multidrop lines	34K
2	DDS multidrop	30K
3	DDS	48K
4	Hubless multidrop DDS, 5 yr contract	26K
5	Hubless DDS multidrop	32K
6	CPE T1 mux	48K
7	Packet switching	55K
8	Hubless DDS, 5 yr contract	60K
9	Hubless DDS	75K

The requirement for low initial connectivity cost drives the re-sorting of the services, as shown in Table 1.10. The DDS solutions would require new channel service units in lieu of existing modems, a packet switching solution would require the deployment of a synchronous packet assembler/dissembler, and the T1 backbone approach would require new T1 multiplexers and channel service units.

1.3.6 Why Communication Quality Should Come First in Any Design

Companies have come to rely on their ability to communicate via voice, video, and, even more importantly, data. An interruption in communication, whether caused by a disaster or some systemic flaw, can have serious business implications. Table 1.11 depicts the revenue loss reported for a number of industries due to communication outages [1, 14].

As a motivation to master all the existing and evolving design techniques, consider any one of the following scenarios of what happens when a network is not properly

Table 1.11
Average Percent of Daily Revenue Lost, by Industry

Industry	Daily Loss for a 3-Day Outage	Daily Loss for a 2-Week Outage
Finance/banking	30%	45%
Public utilities	25%	50%
Insurance	15%	40%
Manufacturing	12%	30%
Services	10%	25%

designed. (These real stories of two Fortune 500 companies are primarily from a private PBX network pespective—poor traffic engineering—but can easily be cast in a data or video context.)

- The president of your company has finally been able to reach the CEO of another company, after a couple of weeks of playing "telephone tag." A minute into the conversation carried over the corporate PBX system, the two VIPs suddenly are disconnected. Each CEO is hesitant to re-initiate the call, unsure if the other will do so. Eventually, apologies will be flowing. Worse yet, an important business deal may get off on the wrong foot, or even go awry.
- The transmission is so poor (e.g, using marginal tariffed or private facilities or excessive compression and experimental voice coding techniques) that the voice is shifted one or two octaves higher. The authoritative, deep voice of a seasoned CEO ends up sounding like a soprano.
- The transmission is so poor that the levels are very low. The authoritative voice of the executive ends up sounding low and devoid of confidence.
- You are following the teleconferencing bandwagon, but when you try to connect two sites—not to mention more than two sites—you invariably get poor quality, dropout, fadeouts, and other productivity-reducing impairments.
- While the VP of Finance and a banker are talking, a sudden background pattern of tones, typical of some signaling gone awry, is heard. "What's that?" says one party. "What is what? I didn't hear anything," says the other. "Oh, it must have been at my end," says the first one.
- The organization is split over the two remotely-located buildings, with a private PBX network between the two locations. A customer who calls the organization (or employees themselves) are unable to transfer calls between the two buildings. (The ability to transfer calls is one of the most basic services, yet many state-of-the-art systems are not able to provide this function, because of the way they were engineered.) The customer is asked to redial another number; from the customer's point-of-view, this may be irritating, particularly if it necessitates a second long-distance phone call. (There is even an overhead monetary cost associated with

having to redial a second 800 number because the call will occupy two WATS systems.)
- The members of a reasonably large telemarketing group must go through the common corporate PBX. Because they are on the phone all day and the calls may be long, their traffic skews the performance of the system, lowering the grade-of-service to the rest of the population.
- A poorly designed disaster recovery plan (whose primary design goal was to save money) calls for putting all dedicated-line data traffic between terminals and a colocated host on dialup facilities to an alternate site. When a disaster occurs, the plan is found to be totally inadequate since the massive dialup traffic through the PBX swamps its capability to function effectively, and practically takes it down.
- A large number of PC users are given access to a modem pool, without properly assessing the potential impact of long sessions and engineering the system accordingly. Users experience high blocking.
- A client-server model that supports 15 users is poorly or underdesigned so that every time there is a server or network problem, the 15 workers are idle for hours in spite of their expensive workstations.
- A corporate videoconferencing system based on highly compressed video (128 kbps) is designed in such a manner that the head of the CEO looks like it has been blown up to three times its normal size every time the CEO moves his/her head.
- A mission-critical network is designed to use frame relay service in such a manner that frequently occuring network congestion results in a frame loss on the order of 30%. Response time, which used to be 3 seconds, with a variance of 2 seconds, now becomes 10 seconds with a variance of 9 seconds.

1.3.7 Some Pragmatic Conclusions

Several points about network design are immediately evident.
- A practitioner should not subscribe to a technology or solution based on the amount of media coverage that it receives at a given time. Old technologies like multiplexing and circuit switching are still very useful and cost-effective.
- What may be optimal for one firm, may actually be a poor solution for another. A clear message from linear programming (Chapter 3) is that the optimal solution is totally dependent on the objective (cost) function that is employed. In other words, no solution can be called efficient, until a specific efficiency measure is defined—what is efficient using one measure may be inefficient using another.
- A risk analysis that takes into account the stochastic nature of the business environment is always required, but rarely if ever done. This implies that the selected solution will, at best, "optimize the expected value," be "probabilistically optimal" or be the "maximum likelihood." This means that, given a specific case, even a solution that is optimal may lead to an undesirable result. More will be discussed in Chapters 2 and 3 on this issue.

- When analyzing a problem, all cost and risk factors must be explicitly taken into account, not only the most ostensible or convenient ones.

REFERENCES

[1] Minoli, D., *Enterprise Networking: Fractional T1 to SONET, Frame Relay to BISDN*, Norwood, MA: Artech House, 1993.

[2] "Enterprise Design: Big Bucks Can Be Saved with Network Design Tools," Mainframe Communications Report, June 25, 1991.

[3] Minoli, D., *First, Second, and Next Generation LANs*, McGraw-Hill, 1993.

[4] *Network Design Markets: Tools and Services*, New York: Network Management Report Inc., May 1991.

[5] Minoli, D., *Telecommunications Technology Handbook*, Norwood, MA: Artech House, 1991.

[6] "1991 Network Spending and Budgets on the Chopping Block—7th Annual Budget and Spending Survey," Networking Management, March 1991.

[7] Minoli, D., "Evaluating Communication Alternatives—Part 1: Cost Analysis Methods," Datapro Report, CA09-101–401, June 1986.

[8] Minoli, D., "Evaluating Communication Alternatives—Part 2: Pragmatic Network Design Issues," Datapro Report, CA09-101–451, June 1986.

[9] Minoli, D., "Numbers Add to Net Hassles," *ComputerWorld*, June 3, 1985, pp. 53ff.

[10] Minoli, D., " Higher Initial Costs Pay Off," *ComputerWorld*, June 6, 1985, pp. 93ff.

[11] Minoli, D., "The Path to Good Network Design," *ComputerWorld*, July 8, 1985, pp. 45ff.

[12] Minoli, D., "Planning Cuts Net Setup Costs," *ComputerWorld*, July 29, 1985, pp. 57ff.

[13] Minoli, D., "Network Documentation High Priority," *ComputerWorld*, August 5, 1985.

[14] Katz, M., "Online Ready Site Helps Ensure Survival of OLTP Applications," *Disaster Recovery Journal*, Jan/Feb/Mar 1991.

Chapter 2
Financial Techniques

2.1 BACKGROUND

The search for the most cost-effective solution to a given problem is an imperative fundamental not only of modern business life, but also of ancient cultures, and of nature. Geometry and simple algebra were born in Babylonian and Greek times for efficient management of land holdings (in addition to astronomy/astrology). In the 16th and 17th centuries, calculus was devised to find the optimal solution for physical equations governing movement; these theories eventually resulted in the Industrial Revolution. The 19th century saw the development of formal economic modeling, various optimization disciplines, and the fields of probability and statistics. World War II saw the creation of two of the more powerful tools available to the modern businessperson: computers and mathematical programming (particularly linear programming). Mathematical programming is a field of optimization and is unrelated to computer programming; it was developed to maximize the efficiency of the wartime machine (e.g., how to carry out the best bombing or how to best manage logistics and inventories).

Nature is the ultimate example of an optimal system at equilibrium. The concept of the shortest path between any two points is intrinsic and endogenous to the physical world. The need to find optimal solutions (i.e., solutions that consume the minimum amount of resources, regardless of what those resources are) to problems, is an obligation and responsibility at large of the human race, if we are to face the future confidently.

2.1.1 Financial Planning Needs in Networking

The data networking practitioner finds himself/herself in a microcosmos of the optimization continuum; he/she has the responsibility and priviledge to find the best solution to the company's data, video, and voice communications needs. Approximately 4% of the gross national product (GNP) is spent on communications in the United States. (GNP = $5,200B, telecommunications expenditures = $200B). This chapter provides some fundamental financial principles to guide networking planners and practitioners [1–2]. The aspect of the method is emphasized. A few examples are included; however, actual comparisons between and the cost factors of specific technologies are left to the reader.

The following observation from [3] was true when it was made, and is true all the more so now: "A great deal has been published on the scientific and technical aspects of telecommunications; very little on the engineering economics of the subject. The development of a [data communications network] is continuous, and long-term planning extending far into the future is essential; always the best use must be made of presently available capital and always in complex relationship with operating and maintenance costs, interest, depreciation and revenues."

The communications manager faces at least three daily challenges, as alluded to in Chapter 1. The first is the fast pace of the technology. The practitioner must constantly keep in touch with the latest developments to see how these affect the network in place. These currently include ATM,[1] third-generation LANs [4], multimedia, image communication, and SONET, among others [5]. The second challenge is from the aftermath of the new industry alignments, mergers, acquisitions, and joint ventures made possible by the liberalized and deregulated business environment. More responsibilities now fall on the end-user. The third challenge is the increased need for sophisticated and complex financial decisions that must be made with regard to new communications equipment and services, particularly concerning high-speed data and video. In addition, there is a clear need to understand "local needs," or the needs of one's organization, not the needs created by the trade press, the needs of some other company, or, least of all, the needs of the company where the manager last worked.

A few years back, a typical data processing/data communications installation might have consisted of a centralized multimillion dollar computer, plus a few thousands of dollars for remote communications equipment. Today, the scale has tilted in favor of the communications side. A typical installation may consist of a less-expensive computer complex (particularly from a cost per Mips perspective), and a multimillion dollar communications network. In the future, the scale is expected to continue to tilt all the way to the communications side. When the total expense was only a few thousands of dollars, the data communications manager could "get away" with simple and intuitive financial decisions. At this time, due to the figures involved, the communications manager must become increasingly more knowledgeable of financial and decision theory.

This analysis is even more important if one is considering establishing private networks that require major monetary outlays, rather than using carrier facilities (although there are advantages in the latter approach as discussed in Chapter 1). Carriers' services can always be discontinued; expensive feasibility studies and expenditures for hardware to support a private network cannot generally be recovered. Of course, carriers do major

---

[1]Beginning with this chapter, the acronym for ATM refers to Asynchronous Transfer Mode.

economic studies to insure resource efficiency; they also track technology to employ the latest and the best. Just because a network is private, rather than carrier-based, does not mean that one can do away with the sophisticated economic modeling and risk analysis that is required. In fact, when a manager is committing company money, he/she must be even more aware of the risk impact: a carrier's miscalculation with a new technology will not cost the company; a manager's miscalculation with a new technology will cost "hard dollars."

Sophisticated decision models have existed for several decades. Their need, however, was somewhat less important when the face value of the equipment was small, or when the useful life was in the 8-to-10-year range. At this time, equipment may well be technologically obsolete by the time it reaches the market, not to mention by the time it is finally deployed. Thus the importance of making the right decisions is much more critical. A key issue to be recognized, which already has been highlighted, is that a communications-related decision should not be made based on the elegance and novelty of the latest technological breakthroughs, but on the economic soundness of the decision, which compares all of the technologies available, including mature ones.

A collection of disciplines, generally referred to as decision theory, has evolved that can aid the practitioner in making sound decisions. Decision theory draws on the following areas [3, 6–11]:

- Financial analysis (including forecasting);
- Probability (Markov theory) and statistics;
- Risk analysis;
- Optimization theory (linear programming, in particular);
- Game theory.

A term that has also been used to describe this field is *engineering economy*.

Engineering economy in general, and linear programming in particular, are powerful tools that can be used for data communications resource management. Yet, such tools have been used mostly by common carriers and sophisticated institutions rather than by the general community because of the lack of familiary by a number of practitioners.

In this chapter, a basic and readable coverage of financial techniques is provided to familiarize the decisionmaker of the analytical machinery to use to make decisions that are defensible, successful, and beneficial to the establishment with which he or she is affiliated. Chapter 3 covers linear programming and other decision theory techniques. The emphasis is on concepts. Although a number of these calculations are now done using packaged software, it is critical that the decisionmaker understand what principles are at work. An example reinforces this point: A manager may place a response time analyzer (RTA) on a traditional data circuit, collect data, and then quotes results. At face value the manager may not realize that certain approximations and assumptions are made by the RTA, and hence the results are partly factual. Being familiar with the principles involved enhances understanding.

2.1.2 Analytical Process

Although interrelated and not always distinct, there are steps in the logical approach to a problem solution. A methodological approach to achieving a solution to a problem is to proceed along the following lines [12]:

1. Obtain an overview of the problem environment;
2. Determine what the goals and objectives are insofar as this decision situation is concerned;
3. Isolate the variables relevant to achievement of the objective;
4. Develop the functional relationships that will relate the variables to the goal;
5. Manipulate the model to obtain numerical results.

2.2 FINANCIAL BASICS

It is almost certain that, regardless of the network design objective selected, finances will be one of the underlying parameters. Communications managers increasingly are being confronted with financial decisions regarding the capital equipment needed to run an efficient and up-to-date network. Even when managers restrict themselves to technical issues and delegate financial questions to experts, they still need to understand why a particular choice was recommended over another.

Some of the basic concepts of financial analysis that are likely to apply to data communications and capital equipment (asset) aquisition, are discussed in this section. A more analytical approach for the interested practitioner follows in Section 2.3. First, a definition and explanation of the basic financial terminology is provided. Four decision methods for environments without uncertainty and risk are presented [13–15].

To guide this development, two examples are posed:

1. Should the manager buy some piece of equipment, such as a small ATM switch, for $20,000, or lease it for $800 per month ($9,600 per year)? In other words, should the manager buy service from a carrier at $800 a month, or build a private system that costs $20,000?
2. Should the manager buy a piece of equipment, such as a SMDS CSU, for $20,000 with a maintenance fee of $1,000 per month, or buy another model that costs $30,000 and has a maintenance fee of only $500 per month?

2.2.1 Financial Terminology

Basic vocabulary and terms that a communications manager should be familiar are identified in this section.

System Lifecycle. While most people in management give heavy weight to the initial cost of a given system, true financial analysis may corroborate the conclusion that what may initially cost more may turn out to be the cheapest solution in the long run. Apparent savings in components, modules, planning, or R&D for a system may be eliminated altogether by future high operating and maintenance costs. Conversely, what may seem like expensive "bells and whistles" during system deployment, may prove valuable over time, by reducing operating and maintenance costs or minimizing revenue loss due to system outage or unavailability.

In evaluating alternatives, one must consider not only the initial costs, but all the expenditures and income derivable over the system's lifecycle. Viewed from another perspective, the capital expenditures for a particular system may come at various time intervals. These observations imply that:

1. The financial measures must be assessed over the entire lifecycle of the investment;
2. Money has time value, which must be explicitly considered in the decision process.

Capital Assets. A physical asset used by a firm in producing goods or services.

Capital Budget. A statement of the firm's planned investments, generally based upon estimates of future sales, production needs, and availability of capital.

Depreciation. A deduction of part of the cost of an asset from the company's income in each year of the asset's life. Some typical minimal depreciation intervals are: 5 years for modems, PCs, and other small equipment, and 7 years for front-end processors, PBX, and other large equipment. In the recent past, an accelerated depreciation schedule has been approved that allows firms to fully depreciate a piece of equipment well before the end of its useful life. The motivation for this law was to permit some segments of the manufacturing industry to retire older (but still functioning) equipment and replace it with newer, more-efficient equipment, to fend off foregin competition.

Cash Flow. The dollars coming to the firm or paid out by the firm as a result of making a new investment. It is the difference between the income generated by the project (e.g., new sales, products, and benefits) and the necessary expenses (e.g., equipment costs and labor).

The decision models discussed below call for the net after-tax cash flows (CF1, CF2, CF3, and so on) to be used in the appropriate formulas; if these flows are incorrectly assessed, the models will not provide accurate results. This is the so-called garbage in, garbage out, or GIGO, principle. It is thus very important that the decisionmaker undertake a real effort to quantify as precisely as possible the associated costs and revenues. In particular, costs go well beyond equipment, as discussed in Chapter 1.

Amortization. A sinking fund established for settling debt financed assets. Writing off expenditures by prorating over a fixed period of time.

Cost of Capital. The interest rate being charged to secure a loan to finance a given project. For example, the prime rate, or the average rate on the securities (i.e., bonds and stocks) issued by the company. This figure represents the minimum acceptable rate of return on an investment or project undertaken by the company. Also called the *cost-of-money*, the cost of capital represents the obligation paid by a borrower to the lender for usage of the capital in the form of loan. Interest has been charged since antiquity. Invested capital will yield a gain or benefit for the original owner; interest is a measure of that financial benefit.

Measuring the amount of gain achievable from invested capital is crucial to any economic decision analysis. If a firm needs to borrow the money to construct a privately owned communications system, and the interest rate charged by the lender (e.g., bank) is 10% per year, then the benefit derivable from that communications system must be at least the equivalent of 10% or else there was no advantage in the undertaking. For example, no one would invest $1,000 in equipment to achieve a reduction of $1/month for a communications link, because the users must pay $100 a year to the lender.

What about the case where the user has the money and does not need to borrow it? Would the user then undertake the above project? The answer is still no because the user could now lend that money out (e.g., to a bank) and realize a nice return (such as $100 a year on a 10% interest deal).

Principal. The amount of money on which interest is paid by the borrower. It decreases according to the amortization schedule.

Interest. The same as the cost of capital. Interest can be demanded as simple interest or compounded interest. With the former, the borrowing charge is a linear function of the initial loan; with the latter, the charge is an exponential function of the original loan. Compounding always makes the amount due much larger than with simple interest. In business, compounding is the norm.

There are a number of ways in which a loan is repayed. Three common ways are:

1. Pay the interest due at the end of each period, and repay the entire loan at expiration. For example, $10,000 borrowed at 9% for 3 years would result in payments of $900 in the first year, $900 in the second year, and $10,900 in the third year.
2. Do not pay interest and principal until the expiration. In the above example, the first year disbursement is $0; the second year disbursement is $0; the third year it would be $12,950.30. ($900 of interest due in the first year but not paid, plus $981 of interest due in the second year but not paid, plus $1,069.30 of interest due in the third year.)
3. Interest and principal recovered via a number of equal installment payments. This is the familiar home mortgage type of loan. For the above example, the installment payments due at the end of each year are $3,950.60.

It should be noted that all three methods yield the same equivalent compensation to the lender. The amount of cash flowing into the hand of the lender is different with each approach, yet, financially, all three are identical. The formulas employed to calculate these payments assure the lender of this internal consistency. This is done via the *present value* concept.

Present Value. The value of money at the present time, even if the money is due at some future point. Money today is more valuable than that same sum a year down the road because of (1) inflation, (2) opportunity to invest the money and earn interest, and (3) the uncertainty of the future. For example, the present value of a pension is very small. A participant in a pension plan does not know if (1) he or she will live long enough to collect it or will quit before it is vested or (2) the company will go out of business before he or she is vested. Thus money in hand today would be more valuable and sure. The same concept applies to business cash flows. Money is normally discounted at the cost of capital. Therefore, given the same financial climate (i.e., prime rate, inflation rate, and so on), a network enhancement that promises to return $1 million in one year is better than an alternative that promises to return $1.05 million in two years.

Future Value. The value of money at some future point. For example, $1 dollar invested at a compound rate of 10% would be worth $2.15 in 10 years. (However, its purchasing power will be the same as at the present time, except if the rate of investment exceeds the rate of inflation.)

Lease. A contract between a lessor and a lessee, whereby the lessee pays a fee for the usage of a resource owned by the lessor. The fee is usually paid monthly and involves a fixed pre-negotiated charge.

Net Lease. A lease under which the lessee pays all maintenance and upkeep costs of the asset.

Third Party Lease. Also called leveraged lease, this is an arrangement under which the lessor borrows funds to cover part or all of the purchase price or the asset. The third party owns the equipment. Sometimes a firm buys the equipment, sells it to the third party, and then leases it back.

Sale and Leaseback. An arrangement under which the user of the asset sells the asset and then leases it back from the new purchaser (the same as a third party lease).

Salvage Value. Also called residual value, the price that the firm can receive for an asset after it has used it for an extended period of time, normally the "useful life" of the equipment.

Payback Period. The interval required for an asset to generate enough cash flow to cover the initial outlay for that asset. For example, an asset that costs $15,000 and generates an aftertax cash flow of $5,000 has a payback period of three years.

Breakeven Point. The level of cash inflow at which the firm is just breaking even; in other words, the point at which the company is earning a zero profit on a given project or investment.

Capital Gain (Loss). The difference between the original cost of an asset and its selling price. A capital gain or loss is realized when the asset is sold, and not before.

2.2.2 Decision Models

This section identifies four key decision making methods.

Net Present Value Method. The net present value (NPV) method is generally considered to be the best of the four methods listed. The first step involves calculating the net cash flow generated by the project; expenses (other than depreciation), capital expenditures, and taxes are subtracted from project revenues. (Taxes are calculated by applying the tax rate to revenues minus all project expenses, including depreciation). More information on this can be found in Section 2.3.

NPV is the sum of present value of all future cash flow minus the initial cost. It is the benefit that acrues to the firm from buying the specific equipmint (e.g., a private ATM switch or a diagnostic system). A positive NPV means that the project yields a rate of return exceeding the cost of capital; a negative NPV means that the project earns less than the firm could make by keeping the money in the bank. The method is thus summarized as follows:

- In an accept-reject decision, the project is selected if the NPV is positive; the project would not be undertaken if the NPV is negative.
- In comparing mutually exclusive alternatives (e.g., buy modem A vs. modem B, or deploy a private network vs. use a carrier), determine the alternative that has greatest NPV and select it, as long as the NPV is positive.

Internal Rate of Return Method. The internal rate of return (IRR) method gives the rate of return on a project. If the rate of return is high (i.e., exceeds the cost of capital or some higher value), then the project or alternative is selected. If the IRR is small, then the project is not selected.

IRR can be explained two ways. The technical explanation is that IRR is that rate that makes the NPV exactly zero. A more intuitive explanation is as follows: A manager has $I. If put into the intended project, this money will produce cash flow CF1 at time 1, CF2 at time 2, and so on. At what interest rate would the manager have to invest I in a bank to obtain the same cash flows? If this rate is small, do not proceed with the project because the bank could easly match that rate; if the rate is high, then undertake the project because you will not find a bank giving that high rate of return.

Thus, if the IRR exceeds the cost of capital, one would opt for the project.

The IRR method is not as good as the NPV method. In particular, in comparing alternatives, it is not correct to simply pick the alternative with the highest IRR. Consider a project that has in internal rate of return of 20% and one that has a rate of 50%; which is better? The 20% project actually may be better. For example, compare a project that costs $1,000 and has a 50% IRR to a project that costs $1 million and has a 20% IRR. The former will return only $500, the latter will return $200,000; the second project is better though the IRR is lower. A quick verification by way of the NPV will support this conclusion. In the second case, the manager is effectively investing $1 million that he/ she may have at his/her disposal as follows: $1,000 at 50%; or $999,000 at 10% (e.g., in a bank account).

After a year he/she would have

$$\$(1,000 + 500) + (999,000 + 99,900) = \$1,100,400$$

In the 20% IRR case, the entire million is invested at 20%, so that he/she would have $1,200,000, which is better.

Also it may be algebraically impossible to find the IRR; there are projects that do not yield a meaningful IRR (because of the "imaginary roots" of a polynomial).

The Payback Period Method. The payback period is the length of time it takes to recover the initial investment. The payback period method (PPM) postulates acceptance of a project or equipment only if the payback period is less than some specified value, for example, 36 months. When comparing two options, the one with the shortest payback period would be selected.

This method is not as good as the NPV method because it does not include cash flows beyond the payback period. These cash flows are still relevant to the issue, and should be considered.

Accounting Rate of Return Method. The accounting rate of return, also called the return on investment (ROI), method is defined as the average annual aftertax accounting profit generated by the investment or equipment, divided by the initial expense. This method is also inferior to the NPV because it does not evaluate cash flows or take into account the cost of money.

While these last two methods may have been used prior to the general availability of computing power since they are arithmetically simpler, the better method should now be used. In particular, with PC and mainframe spreadsheet packages now in wide use, it is much simpler to apply the correct methodology.

Solution to the initial examples. Consider the example of either buying some equipment for $20,000, or leasing it for $800 for 36 months. Assuming a revenue benefit from having installed the new equipment of $18,000 for each of three years, a cost of capital of 10%, an amortization of 36 months, a salvage value of $1,000, a tax rate of 50%, and an initial vendor discount of 8%, one finds with the NPV method that the *buy option is better*.[2] The NPV in the purchase case is $12,610; the NPV in the lease case is $10,440. Only when the equipment cost exceeds $24,280 does the lease option become the better choice. The lessor needs to make a profit and must charge accordingly; this drives the decision to the buy option. Tables 2.1, 2.2, and 2.3 depict, in a methodological way, the calculation steps that went into the decision.

In the case $20,000 plus $1,000/month versus $30,000 plus $500/month, the $30,000 option is better (the NPVs $2,310 and $90, respectively). Only when maintenance on the $20,000 item decreases to $840/month does this option become cost-effective.

2.3 ANALYTICAL MACHINERY

Some additional financial machinery is presented in this section to provide a skeletal foundation of financial mathematics for the interested reader. Readers that are already

---

[2]This consideration does not take into account risk—for example, that the configuration was wrong and had to be replaced later, in which case the rent option might have been better in the end. The issue of dealing with risk is discussed in Section 2.4.

Table 2.1
Economic Study for Lease Option

Cost of capital		10%
Initial purchase cost	$	0
Company's tax rate		50%
Salvage value	$	0
Fixed yearly revenue without project	$	0
Depreciation without project	$	0
Expense without project	$	0
Fixed yearly revenue with project		$18,000
Depreciation with project	$	0
Expense with project		$ 9,600

	Without Project	With Project	Difference
Revenues	$0	$18,000	
Expenses other than depreciation	$0	$ 9,600	
Taxes			
Revenues minus expenses	$0	$ 8,400	
Less depreciation	$0	$ 0	
Taxable I	$0	$ 8,400	
Tax	$0	$ 4,200	
Net cash flow for a generic year	$0	$ 4,200	$ 4,200

	Year 1	Year 2	Year 3
Net cash flow	$4,200	$4,200	$4,200
Present values	$3,820	$3,470	$3,160

NPV	$10,440		

satisfied with the discussion given above, or who do not possess sufficient analytical background can skip this section.

2.3.1 Cash Flows, Single Payments

Money has a time value as was already indicated. $2,000 now is more valuable than $2,000 a year from now. At 10% interest, $2,000 now is equivalent to $2,200 a year from now. A way to grasp the equivalence is to plot cash flows on a timeline. Figures 2.1a and 2.1b depict two simple monetary transactions: borrowing $2,000 for one year at 10%, and lending $2,000 for one year at 10%.

Table 2.2
Economic Study for Buy Option

Cost of capital	10%
Initial purchase cost	$20,000
Company's tax rate	50%
Salvage value	$ 1,000
Fixed yearly revenue without project	$ 0
Depreciation without project	$ 0
Expense without project	$ 0
Fixed yearly revenue with project	$18,000
Depreciation with project	$ 0
Expense with project	$ 0

	Without Project	With Project	Difference
Revenues	$0	$18,000	
Expenses other than depreciation	$0	$ 0	
Taxes			
Revenues minus expenses	$0	$18,000	
Less depreciation	$0	$ 6,333	
Taxable I	$0	$11,667	
Tax	$0	$ 5,833	
Net cash flow for a generic year	$0	$12,167	$12,167

	Year 1	Year 2	Year 3
Net Cash flow	$12,167	$12,167	$13,167
Present values	$11,060	$10,060	$9,890

NPV	$12,610		

The timeline is a good way to graphically depict monetary transactions. Given a single repayment F in the future, n years (or interest intervals) away for an initial loan P at interest rate i, such repayment must be

$$F = P \times (1 + i)^n$$

At $i = 10\%$ and $P = 1$: for $n = 10$, $F = 2.15$; for $n = 20$, $F = 6.72$; for $n = 50$, $F = 117.4$; and for $n = 100$, $F = 13,780$. This means, for example, that an IRA deposit of $1,000 at age 20 will be worth $117,400 at age 70.

The so-called "rule of 72" can be used to approximate future, single payment transactions: loan P at interest i will have to be repaid with the amount $2 \times P$ in $72/i$ years (for relativey low values of i, say $i \leq 10\%$).

Table 2.3
Equivalence of the Two Options at the New Calculated Price

Cost of capital	10%
Initial purchase cost	$24,280
Company's tax rate	50%
Salvage value	$ 1,000
Fixed yearly revenue without project	$ 0
Depreciation without project	$ 0
Expense without project	$ 0
Fixed yearly revenue with project	$18,000
Depreciation with project	$ 0
Expense with project	$ 0

	Without project	With Project	Difference
Revenues	$0	$18,000	
Expenses other than depreciation	$ 0	$0	
Taxes			
Revenues minus expenses	$0	$18,000	
Less depreciation	$0	$ 7,760	
Taxable I	$ 0	$10,240	
Tax	$0	$ 5,120	
Net cash flow for a generic year	$0	$12,880	$12,880

	Year 1	Year 2	Year 3
Net cash flow	$12,880	$12,880	$13,880
Present values	$11,710	$10,640	$10,430
NPV	$10,440		

The present value concept is key to financial decisionmaking. Turning the above formula around, the present value P of a future, single payment/repayment sum is

$$P = F \times [1/(1 + i)^n]$$

For example, $117,000 in 50 years from now is worth $1,000 right now; the two figures are financially equal. The present value can be viewed as the amount of money to put in the bank now to be able to face a future expense F, a number of years from now.

The two basic terms involved in future value/present value calculations are found in tables or can trivially be obtained with a PC (until 15 years ago, tables were the easiest route). However, to use these terms in formulas and analytical expressions, two symbols are employed to name these quantities:

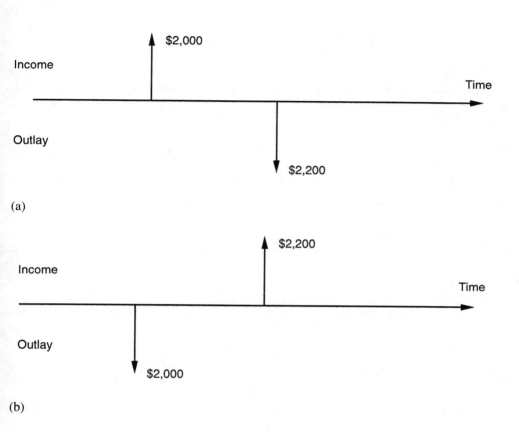

Figure 2.1 (a) Monetary equivalence, borrowing funds. (b) Monetary equivalence, lending funds.

$$(F/P, i, n) = (1 + i)^n$$

$$(P/F, i, n) = 1/(1 + i)^n$$

2.3.2 Cash Flows, Annuity (Several Equal Payments)

Financial terms normally involve making several payments over a number of years. This is the so-called annuity or mortgage plan. Payments resulting from an annuity are financially equivalent to a single payment (either upfront or at the end of some period), as shown in Figure 2.2.

For example, depositing $1,000 at 10% for three consecutive years will yield a future value (at the end of three years) of $3,152.50.

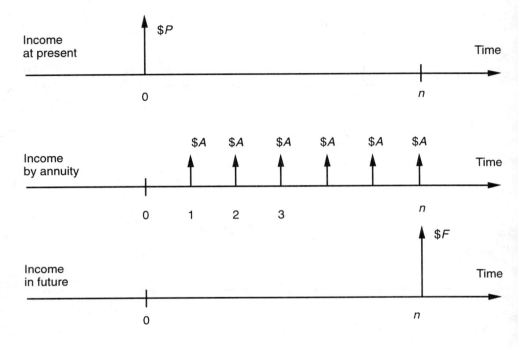

Figure 2.2 Equivalence of annuity payments.

The future value of these multiple payments (deposits) is obtained from the formula:

$$F = A(1 + i)^n + A(1 + i)^{n-1} + A(1 + i)^{n-2} + \dots + A(1 + i)^1 + A$$

where A is the annual deposit. This is written in abbreviated notational form as

$$F = A \times (F/A, i, n)$$

with

$$(F/A, i, n) = (1 + i)^n + (1 + i)^{n-1} + (1 + i)^{n-2} + \dots + (1 + i)^1 + 1$$

Again, this term can be obtained from a standard financial table.

The sinking term factor is the reciprocal of this annuity fund. It represents the required annual savings to meet a future obligation of F. Reversing the annuity equation listed above, the amount to be deposited is:

$$A = F/(F/A, i, n)$$

This is conveniently rewritten as

$$A = F \times (A/F, i, n)$$

clearly with

$$(A/F, i, n) = 1/(F/A, i, n)$$

Another typical question is: How much must one put in the bank right now to be able to then receive an annuity of value A for n years? This is the present value of the annuity. See Figure 2.3.

It can be shown that the present value P is

$$P = A \{[1/(1 + i)^1] + [1/(1 + i)^2 + 1/(1 + i)^3 + \ldots + 1/(1 + i)^n]\}$$

or rewritten as

$$P = A \times (P/A, i, n)$$

For example, installing a private facilities system will provide a net income of exactly $20,000 for each of three years. What is the present value of these cash flows? How much is this worth to the manager right now at 5% prevaling rates?

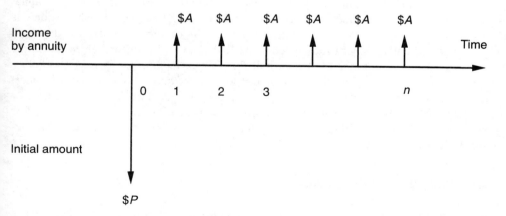

Figure 2.3 Present value of the annuity.

$$P = 20,000 \times (P/A, 5, 3)$$

Consulting a table (or programming the first three terms of the $(P/A, i, n)$ equation above), one obtains

$$P = 20,000 \times 2.7232 = 54,464$$

Note that this calculation resembles the NPV method described earlier, except that all cash flow incomes are assumed to be equal.

One last concept is the capital recovery factor, also called the loan repayment factor. This is the amount of money that can be withdrawn every year for n years, given an initial deposit of P. Reverting the above equation for the annuity net present value, one obtains

$$A = P/(P/A, i, n)$$

which can be rewritten as

$$A = P \times (A/P, i, n)$$

For example, depositing $5,446.40 right now at 5% would allow one to withdraw $2,000 for three years since

$$A = 5446.40 \times 0.367 = 2000$$

with $(A/P, 5, 3)$ obtained from a table, or directly by division of $(P/A, 5, 3)$, into 1 (the equation for this last term was given above). The reason for the terminology capital recovery stems from the fact that this formula can be used to determine what income is necessary to recover a capital investment given the rate of interest on the investment.

Until recently, the terms discussed above had to be obtained from tables. When the specific values could not be located on the table (for example, if the interest was 8.35% and one only had an integer-valued table), interpolation methods were used. Today, almost any PC can be programmed (or software is available) to calculate these terms. The only concern would be one of roundoff for large values of the horizon n. In reality, very few people need to calculate values for n exceeding 20; hence, standard calculation techniques should be adequate.

2.3.3 Cash Flows, Variable Quantities

So far, we have obtained present values (and future values) of cash flows that were of the same value. In a real life datacom problem, cash flows will most likely be different each year. For example, installation of a 20-switch private ATM network may cost $10 million with a *net* cash flow of −$8 million in the first year (namely, the expense in year 1 was $10 million, but $2 million that otherwise went to a long distance carrier is now saved); −$1.5 million in the second year (tuning and refinements); $35,000 in the third year; $3 million in the fourth year; $5 million in the fifth year; and −$1 million in the sixth year (technological obsolescence necessitates that numerous network components have to be upgraded at that time). See Figure 2.4.

Let $CF1$, $CF2$, $CF3$, and so on be the cash flows for years 1, 2, and 3, respectively. Then NPV is now calculated as follows:

$$P = CF1 \times (P/F, i, 1) + CF2 \times (P/F, i, 2) + CF3 \times (P/F, i, 3) + ...$$

where the $(P/F, i, j)$ terms for any year j were defined above.

Additional information, refinements, and applications can be found in any financial textbook, or [6] in particular.

2.3.4 Computing Net Cash Flows for Capital Budgeting

For the purpose of capital budgeting and selection of alternatives, the net cash flow of a project is

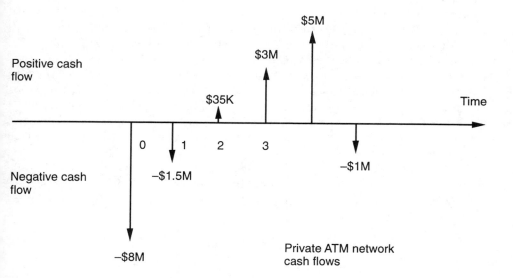

Figure 2.4 Variable cash flows.

net cash flow from project = cash inflows − cash outflows

$$= \text{project revenues} - \text{expenses other than depreciation}$$
$$- \text{capital expenditures}$$
$$- \text{income taxes}$$

with

income taxes = tax rate × (project revenues − project expenses other than depreciation
− depreciation)

Notes (based on [6]):

1. All revenues and expenses must be appropriately identified (see Chapter 1).
2. Depreciation affects the cash flow only through its impact on income taxes. Depreciation is not a cash expense; it is a way to spread the cost of an asset over the asset's life.
3. Taxes are computed as though the project were financed entirely with equity funds. Interest on debt is not included as an expense in determining taxable income.
4. Tax rates depend on current tax law and on the company revenues.
5. The method to determine the cash flow from a given datacom project is to compare the firm's cash flow *with* and *without* the implementation of the proposed project. The difference between the two is the additional cash flow due to the project.

Consider a private frame relay system that costs $1.2 million for 10 fully-configured switches, has a life of 10 years, a salvage value of $200,000 at the end of 10 years, and is depreciated on a straight-line basis at $100,000 per year (the difference of the initial cost and the salvage cost, divided by the project lifetime). The corporate tax is taken at 50%. At acquisition time, the cash flow is the initial project expense: −$1.2 million. The computation of the cash flow for subsequent years follows the layout of Table 2.1. Note that one must compare the various measures (i.e., revenues, expenses, and so on) for the status quo (no investment), as well as for the investment case. *What one is after is the net cash flow due to the new decision as compared to a no-change case* or to another alternative that could also be pursued. Note that the no-change case has its own intrinsic revenues and expenses (in this situation, the no-change case could be a carrier-based nationwide network).

For the example at hand, the net cash flow as compared to the status quo is $175,000 for years 1 through 9, and $375,000 on the 10th year (because of the salvage value).

These cash flows can now be employed in the variable cash flow formula described earlier to determine the NPV:

$$NPV = CF1 \times [P/(F, i, 1)] + CF2 \times [P/(F, i, 2)] + \ldots$$

$$+ CFn - 1 \times [P/(F, i, n - 1)] + CFn \times [P/(F, i, n)] - I$$

where I is the initial outlay.

2.4 FINANCIAL MODELS UNDER UNCERTAINTY

The economic analysis and models discussed so far were based on the assumption that complete information was available, and that no variability existed. Thus, a cash flow of $1,000 for year 3 associated with a selected telecom project was postulated to occur without fail, salvage values for equipment at the end of 10 years was postulated to be exactly as estimated 10 years earlier, and interest did not fluctuate. Clearly, the real world is not as predictable and stable as this scenerio. Variability in no way invalidates the modeling process outlined above; the manager must start somewhere, and if nothing else, he/she should at least perform the analysis discussed in the previous two sections.

Variability is a factor that is accepted and dealt with in engineering and management. Risk analysis recognizes the existence of variability and provides ways to select the best alternative under the circumstances.

Probability theory is the tool that is used to handle and manage variability. The basics of probability and probabilistic economic models are presented herewith; more information can be found in any good financial textbook, in particular [9].

2.4.1 Examples of Uncertainty

In a business environment, just like in real life, there are many examples of uncertainty. Uncertainty can be of the *smooth* type, or of the *singular* (discontinuous) type.

Smooth-type uncertainty refers to a relatively small swing in some of the underlying parameters on which the model is based. For example, the prime rate could go from 13% to 10%. This would mean that a firm might commit to a high finance charge to build a private-facilities network, just to see his competitor secure the same loan a few weeks later, at a much lower rate.

The singular or catastrophic type of uncertainty refers to a major alteration in operating parameters. Every so often, one hears of some major, unexpected explosion of an industrial district where all businesses are destroyed within a large radius. If one of these businesses had bought $250,000 of bypass equipment several weeks earlier, this loss would certainly be more significant financially than if it had simply leased a carrier's channel.

Smooth-uncertainty factors include

- Change in the interest rate;
- Change in a firm's data communications requirements;
- Unexpected delays in delivering vendor products.

Singular-uncertainty factors include:

- Nonrenewal of a lease, requiring relocation;
- Acquisition by another firm, and the ensuing streamlining;
- Sudden drop in the tariffed cost of carrier facilities;

- Vendor providing private communications facilities goes out of business;
- Vendor drops a product line;
- Equipment is found to be intrinsically flawed and is withdrawn (this happens at times with software packages).

Incorporating Risk in Financial Analysis of Telecom Projects

Every decision involves an element of risk. Sometimes the risk is so small that it can be disregarded as a factor to worry about. However, the user should never disregard the risk of a catastrophy, such as a fire, a flood, or vandalism, that can affect a computer center and related communications networks. The press provides ample examples of such occurrences and the consequences to the corporations that did not do any contingency planning. Even when the risk is recognized, it may have to be ignored because of insufficient data to quantitatively assess the impact of the risk [9].

Each alternative may involve several ensuing risk-states. Assesment of these liability outcomes includes: (a) identification of future states or conditions, (b) prediction of the probability of each state, (c) determination of returns associated with each state, and (d) identification of remedial action to be taken if the undesired state materializes and the associated cost. Future states can be anticipated, but not always controlled. Some of the risks to be considered by datacom managers were listed earlier; other risks include weather, economic or technological developments, legislation, and world affairs.

When pertinent data are unavailable, one approach is to at least follow a conservative regimen. For example, one can assume a pessimistic cash flow, rather than an overly optimistic one (unfortunately the latter is the norm, in an effort to "sell" the given projects to senior management). One may boost the internal rate of return required by a project before it is adopted above the basic accepted value.

Probability theory (discussed below) can be used in either environment: the probabilities can be used as precise measures of expected outcomes in the long run, or can be used to represent the degree of uncertainty about the true condition of a system. The first is an example of a priori probabilities: a fair coin will give a tail when tossed, with a probability of 1/2. In practice, prior knowledge of the probabilities is not likely; it is necessary in this case to rely on historical and empirical knowledge, and use this knowledge to estimate current probabilities.

2.4.2 Basics of Probability (Uncertainty)

Probability theory has been around for over a century (statistics somewhat longer), but it was only put on a sound basis in the early 1900s. The problem is one of precise definition. For the purpose of this discussion (and most undergraduate and graduate courses), an intuitive approach is followed.

The probability of an event is a number between 0 and 1 (inclusive at both ends) that represents the fraction of the number of times that this event occurs, given that a very large number of (re)tries of the very same experiment is observed. Consider throwing a fair die. The probability that the number 1 appears is 1/6 = 0.166666.... This means that if one threw the die 1000 times (i.e., the event is repeated over and over again), one can be fairly sure that 167 times out of the 1000 times the number 1 would materialize. The probability says nothing about any individual set of circumstances. For example, throwing the die 20 times may mean that 3 times one obtained the number 1; on the other hand, for a particular set of 20 throws, one may obtain 0 occurances of the number 1. (One can be "sure," however, that if the exercise was repeated 100,000 times, the number 1 would occur 16,666 times—conceivably the first 1 could occur on the 83,334th throw.)

Sample Space

In this context, the sample space is a listing of all possible outcomes to a decision and the associated probabilities. In idealized problems the sample space is small and well-defined; in problems faced by datacom managers, the sample space may be large and somewhat ill-defined.

For the dice problem above, the sample space is

- Face shows a 1: probability = 1/6;
- Face shows a 2: probability = 1/6;
- Face shows a 3: probability = 1/6;
- Face shows a 4: probability = 1/6;
- Face shows a 5: probability = 1/6;
- Face shows a 6: probability = 1/6.

When installing a microwave (tower) bypass, the sample space may look like this:

- No problem whatsoever (works on 1st day): probability = 0.01;
- Works after 2 days of fixing things: probability = 0.2;
- Works after 5 days of fixing things: probability = 0.6;
- Equipment must be returned: probability = 0.1;
- Tower falls down onto the street: probability = 0.01;
- Wiring found not adequate (job postponed): probability = 0.05;
- BER found unbearable after system is in operation: probability = 0.01;
- Nearby microwave system found to create unexpected interference: probability = 0.01;
- A million other things: probability = 0.01.

Independent Events

Events can either be statistically independent or dependent. Dependence means that the outcome of one event is influenced by or related to another event. For example, in a privately owned system comprised of a T1 multiplexer followed by two microwave radios, followed by another T1 multiplexer, the event E = "End-to-end link is OK" is dependent on the following four events (among others): A = "T1 mux number 1 is OK," B = Radio 1 is OK," C = "Radio 2 is OK," and D = "T1 mux number 2 is OK." In other words, if any one of the four elements fail (corresponding to the "complements" of events A, B, C, and D), then the end-to-end link fails.

Independence means that two events do not influence each other. For example, in the above case, events A and B are most likely independent, since one would not expect the T1 mux to influence the microwave radio. In the real world, most events are generally dependent either on each other or on some underlying factor. Often this dependence is mistakenly ignored, and independent models are used.

Independence affords an elegant theory, in the sense that the joint probability that both events occur is simply the product of the individual event probabilities (this is not true in a dependent case).

For example, if the probability that the T1 mux fails is 0.01 (namely, the probability of event A is 0.01; the same for event D), and the probability that the microwave radio fails is 0.05, then the probability that *both* a radio and a T1 mux fail is $0.01 \times 0.05 = 0.0005$.

Formally:

$$\text{Prob}(A) = 0.01, \text{ Prob } (B) = 0.05$$

$$\text{Prob } (A \text{ \& } B) = \text{Prob}(A) \times \text{Prob}(B) = 0.01 \times 0.05 = 0.0005$$

The meaning of probabilities is not always appreciated by the practitioner. Exactly what does the expression "the probability that the T1 mux fails is 0.01" mean? (Stated equivalently, "the probability of event A equals 0.01.") It does not mean that a given piece of hardware will fail once in 100 times (the equipment either fails or it does not); it means that if 100,000 companies (or some large number like that) purchased the equipment on March 1st and all turned it on on March 2nd, then 1,000 companies would find the equipment not working. This probability says nothing about a specific piece of equipment; only about a large ensemble of equipment.

Some other examples of probabilities in dealing with acquisition of communications equipment could be:

What is the probability that the equipment will not be fully installed by the date planned, and that double service charges have to be incurred (old service plus new service)?

What is the probability that the interest on the needed capital will drop two points if we postpone the project for three months?

What is the probability that the price of equipment scheduled to be deployed at regular intervals over a period of three years, will increase beyond the budgeted amount?

What is the probability that the system traffic will triple over the next two years, making this equipment unusable at that time?

Key Probability Facts

1. If two events are independent then Prob(A & B) = Prob(A) × Prob(B).
2. Prob(A or B) = Prob(A) + Prob(B) − Prob(A & B); if two events are mutually exclusive, then the last term is 0 and the probabilities are additive.
3. Practical problems are usually tackled by way of discrete probabilities. Namely, the number of all possible outcomes considered is finite and small. Theoretical problems (e.g., reliability and queueing) are generally approached as continuous—infinitely many outcomes—which requires calculus; it yields nice analytical results that may approximate a problem very well; however, all known physical problems are at some juncture discrete (quantum physics attests to that).
4. The sum of the probabilities of all possible outcomes must add up to 1.
5. Conditional probabilities represent a statement of additional information about the outcome of some event, given the known occurence of another event. Consider the events:

    a. $I1$ = Interest rate is at 10%;
    b. $I2$ = Interest rate is at 15%;
    c. $I3$ = Interest rate is at 20%;
    d. $J1$ = Inflation is at 3%;
    e. $J2$ = Inflation is at 15%.

    Knowing something about the events $J1$ and $J2$ will give us some useful information about events $I1$, $I2$, and $I3$. If we know that Prob($J1$) = 0.2 and Prob($J2$) = 0.8, then Prob($I3$) should be fairly high. These relationships are expressed as Prob($I3$ | $J2$), where | means "given." It turns out that

    $$P(A|B) = P(A \text{ \& } B)/P(B)$$

    (Note that, if A and B are independent, this relationship degenerates to a useless fomula; this is because the occurence of A has no bearing on the occurence of B in the case of independence).
6. The expected value is a standard measure for economic comparisons involving risk. It incorporates the effect of risk on potential outcomes by means of a weighted average; outcomes are weighted based on the probability of their occurence, and the sum of the products of all outcomes multiplied by their respective probability is the expected value.

    Thus, if outcome x_1 occurs with probability p_1, and outcome x_2 with probability p_2, and outcome x_3 with probability p_3, and so forth, the expected value is

$$E(X) = x_1p_1 + x_2p_2 + x_3p_3$$

$$+ \ldots \text{(the sum extending to however many outcomes there are)}$$

The term "expected value" only means that, in the long term, the average of the outcomes is very close to the value $E(X)$. Consider the outcomes of throwing a die: 1 with probability 1/6, 2 with probability 1/6, and so forth all the way up to 6 with probability 1/6. Then

$$E(X) = (1) \times (0.166) + (2) \times (0.166) + (3) \times (0.166) + (4) \times (0.166)$$

$$+ (5) \times (0.166) + (6) \times (0.166) = 3.5$$

In this case, 3.5 in not an expected event (3.5 will never occur), nor an assurance that given one throw the outcome is close to 3.5; what it means is that if the die is thrown 100,000 times and the outcome of the face is averaged out, the outcome will be pretty close to 3.5.

In fact, another statistical measure, called *standard deviation*, will allow the planner to determine what type of deviation he may in fact incur from the expected value. For the interested party,

$$sd(X) = sqrt[E(X^2) - (E(X))^2]$$

Chebyshev's Result

A very useful result of probability, known as Chebyshev's inequality, allows the datacom manager to *bound the risk* of any undertaking governed by a random process by knowing just a few things about that process. Let $\mu = E(X)$; then the probability that an event that deviates from the expected value (on either side) by more than k standard deviations, is less than $1/k^2$. By formula,

$$\text{Prob}[|X - \mu| > k \times sd] < 1/k^2$$

This gives a measure of how tight the possible events scatter away from the desired expected value. Some thought on this equation will show that the smaller the standard deviation, the tighter (more predictable) the outcome will be. This relationship holds for any random process. (To be more precise, for "any random process that has an expectation and a variance;" in practical terms, for all processes.)

Consider, for example, a private frame relay network that has a risk in term of the final cost. Assume that the possible costs are identified, and the risk assessed by way of probabilities. Assume that the expected cost will be $500,000, with a standard deviation of $150,000. Then

$$\text{Prob}[|X - 500,000| > 150,000 \times k] < 1/k^2$$

Thus, the probability that the project will cost more than \$800,000 will be less that 0.25 (\$500,000 + 2 × \$150,000); similarly the probability that the project will turn out to cost less than \$200,000, will be less than 0.25 (\$500,000 − 2 × \$150,000). Here, k was equal to 2. The probability that the project will cost more than \$950,000 will be less than 0.11 (\$500,000 + 3 × \$150,000); here $k = 3$. This is telling the datacom manager that if he/she implemented 100 of these projects (100,000 would be better), then only 11 of them, or fewer, will end up costing in the \$950,000 range.

If the standard deviation was \$50,000 instead of \$150,000, then the probability that the project will end up costing more than \$950,000 would be less than $1/11^2$, or less than 0.0082; this is fewer than 1 project in 100 overruning the budget. (Note that we used $k = 11$ in the above equation.) Hence, the tighter the standard deviation the less the risk.

Many situations follow a Gaussian process. Without explaining further what this means, the datacom practitioner can make note of the fact that, in this case, the probability that a given project overruns the budget by more than 3 standard deviation is 0.001 (1 in 1,000). This result is obtained by a more refined argument than the Chebyshev equation above (which only guaranteed that that probability had to be less than 0.11). The Chebyshev equation is a general tool, thus it is not as "surgical" as one would find with more complete knowledge about the actual underlying risk mechanism).

Financial Model

A profit-seeking individual or organization would opt for a project that has a *positive expected net present value, and a small standard deviation.* All other things being equal, the project with the highest expected net present value is selected.

Example

Consider two possible private-facilities options that have the following anticipated NPV payoffs, depending upon the achievable site penetration for a nationwide network based on line-of-sight and satellite footprint considerations:

	Management Does Not Approve	*Management Approves, 30% Penetration Achievable*	*Management Approves, 80% Penetration Achievable*
Microwave	−\$ 50,000	\$200,000	\$ 500,000
Satellite	−\$200,000	\$100,000	\$1,000,000

The initial development, research, feasibility, and pilot costs are shown under the no approval column. Note that the satellite option costs four times as much, but if good penetration can be achieved it would double the payoff; because of higher setup costs (satellite hub station) in the moderate penetration situation the payback is smaller than the microwave option. Some conclusions can be drawn even without additional probabilistic data: (1) a loss of $200,000 could be considered disastrous for a small company, while a loss of $50,000 may be an acceptable risk; (2) for a large company both levels of risk may be acceptable. Thus, the second alternative would have to be eliminated for the small company, no matter what the eventual payoff would be.

Before starting the project, the datacom manager is able evaluate the various risks and he/she came up with the following risk matrix:

	Management Does Not Approve	Management Approves, 30% Penetration Achievable	Management Approves, 80% Penetration Achievable
Microwave	0.1	0.6	0.3
Satellite	0.2	0.4	0.4

Now, the expected value of the microwave solution is

$$(0.1) \times (-50,000) + (0.6) \times (200,000) + (0.3) \times (500,000) = \$265,000$$

The expected value of the satellite solution is

$$(0.2) \times (-200,000) + (0.4) \times (100,000) + (0.4) \times (1,000,000) = \$400,000$$

The satellite solution has a better expected return; this assumes however that the risk can be borne by the user. What is that risk? The standard deviation for the two alternatives is

- Alternative 1: $173,000;
- Alternative 2: $502,000.

Now, in the first case, one expects $265,000 on the average. If things do not go very well, one may end up with $E(X) - sd(X)$ payback (for that matter $E(X) - 2sd(X)$, but that is more unlikely); in that case one would end up with $265,000 - $173,000 = $92,000 as payback. In the second case, if things do not go very well, one may end up with $400,000 - $502,000 = -$102,000, namely a loss. Therefore, while the second project may have a larger potential payout, it also involves more risk.

Generally, one is able to proceed with the net present value method described earlier, but instead of the static values, one would use expected values. Consider the following example:

A datacom manager in a company that has a fully-implemented end-user chargeback system is considering implementing a private-facilities frame-relay network and charging the various departments $1 per kiloframe. The cost of the original outlay is $2.5 million. The system is expected to survive six years after which it will have to be replaced because of technological obselescence so the system has zero salvage value. The datacom manager cannot precisely assess the revenue that can be collected from the internal users in future years but, based on past experience, he/she is able to quantify the risk according to the following schedule:

- $400,000 will probably be collected once in six years;
- $600,000 will probably be collected four times in six years;
- $800,000 will probably be collected once in six years.

Should the manager undertake the project?
The expected yearly cash flow for each of the six years will be:

$$(1/6) \times 400,000 + (4/6) \times 600,000 + (1/6) \times 800,000 = 600,000$$

Assuming a cost of capital of 10%, the expected NPV of the project is

$$600,000(P/A, 10\%, 6) - 2,500,000 = 600,000(4.355) - 2,500,000 = 113,000$$

Since the expected NPV is positive, it would be advantageous to initiate the project. Note, however, that the margin of profit is fairly small (only $113,000), so that this project is not outstanding. In fact the internal rate of return is 11.5%—one could put the $2.5 million into a six-year bank term account and achieve the same rate of return, without all the headaches of engineering, installing, and managing a complex project for six years.

Conclusion

Our treatment of the subject is very brief and limited. References [6] and [9] provide numerous refinements and examples of decisionmaking under risk. These readable references should be consulted by the interested practitioner.

2.4.3 Basics of Forecasting

The telecommunications practitioner must be able to take network-related data on past requirements, and look into the future with confidence. Capacity data may involve the number of users as a function of time, number of transactions, number of terminals, number of trunks between sites, number of files transfered, and so on. Forecasting is even more important to the manager thinking of setting up a private-facilities network. Carrier services can easily be added or deleted without major financial penalties; this is not generally the case with private facilities.

This type of capacity planning is required if the network is to continue to provide the desired grade of service, at any given time. Procurement may take months, or even years, if the budget must be approved and allocated by senior management. The manager must be able to extrapolate data into the future on which to base decisions, whether via carrier facilities or privately owned networks and facilities. This should be one of the first activities undertaken by anyone who is thinking of a privately owned network and is the reason for providing this section.

An extensive theory called sequential smoothing and prediction is available to assist the datacom manager in this task. References [16], [17], and [18] are three textbooks on this topic. Reference [16] is the most theoretical and complete of the three.

Several techniques exist. See [19] for more details.

Simple Techniques

The first group of forecasting techniques is based on averaging methods that take into account historical data regarding the variable of interest. The techniques most commonly used are: simple average, moving average, weighted average, and exponential smoothing.

In the average method, one simply divides the sum of past values by the number of available data points, and employs the resulting number as the forecast. This is very crude.

Data become perishable very quickly. In the moving average method, only a fixed number of recent data values are used, for example the past six months or year. The average is then postulated to represent the forecast.

The weighted average method gives appropriate, but arbitrarily assigned, importance to selected data terms. For example, very recent data may be more valuable than older data; conversely, older, more refined and filtered data may be more reliable than new, relatively unprocessed data. The average obtained this way is then postulated to represent the forecast.

Exponential smoothing is a technique similar to the moving average. The advantage of this technique, however, is that the raw data need not be stored and re-used every time an updated forecast is required. The new forecast is calculated from the old forecast itself plus a fraction of the amount from which the old forecast deviated from the actual value.

The fractional value to use is based on empirical experience. Exponential smoothing, though computationally elegant, essentially produces the same forecast obtained from the moving average (given the right value of the fraction).

Better Techniques

More sophisticated types of forecasting involve correlation, regression analysis (multiple regression, in the case of many variables), and—the most sophisticated method—time series analysis.

Correlation is a statistical technique to measure how closely two or more variables are related. Once that is established, one can get a feel for the value of the secondary variable, given observation of the first variable. Correlation expresses linkage, but does so in terms of a single parameter (the correlation coefficient). For example, the datacom manager is well aware that network delay is correlated to the number of active users: as the number of users increases, so does the delay.

Regression, though related to correlation, goes a step further and actually defines the functional relationship between variables. This is the best known technique, and is described here in some detail. The technique is also called least squares estimate. With this model, the underlying trend is assumed to be of the form

$$P = b_0 + b_1 t_1 + b_2 t_2 + b_3 t_3 + b_4 t_4 + \dots$$

where P is the value to be predicted, and t_1, t_2, t_3, t_4, and so on, are factors influencing the outcome. For example, in forecasting revenues P, a firm may find that advertisment dollars, t_1, quantity of goods manufactured, t_2, products quality, t_3, and so on, all have an effect. This is called the general linear model.

Many times, the variable of interest is a function of time, namely,

$$P(t) = b_0 + b_1 t$$

The goal here is to find a line that fits through a data scatter in a way that minimizes a statistical measure of risk ($\sum (y_i - y_b)^2$). See Figure 2.5.

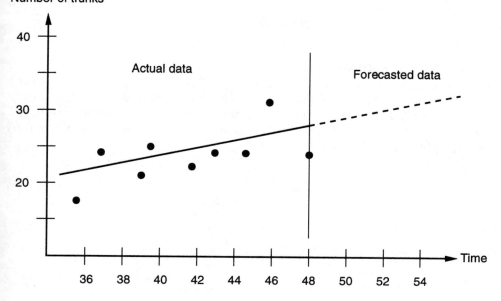

Figure 2.5 Forecasting with the least squares method.

To forecast P beyond a known time t_0 only requires the values of the coefficients b_0 and b_1. The formulas required to carry out this forecast are as follows:

$$b_1 = S_{ty}/S_{tt}$$

$$b_0 = y_b - b_1 t_b$$

with

$$S_{tt} = (\Sigma\ t_i^2) - (\Sigma\ t_i)^2/n$$

Σ meaning "the sum of" and n meaning the number of past intervals for which data are available; and

$$S_{ty} = (\Sigma\ t_i y_i) - [(\Sigma\ t_i)(\Sigma y_i)/n]$$

$$t_b = (\Sigma\ t_i)/n$$

$$y_b = (\Sigma\ y_i)/n$$

where y_i are the known past values.

A numerical example will show how simple these formulas really are. Consider a decision that needs to be made in the 47th month after the initial deployment of a given private network. Let y_i represent the number of trunks in month i between two pieces of equipment (e.g., two private ATM switches) that have been required in the past to meet the grade of service. The available data are

Month (t_i)	Number of Trunks Required (y_i)
34	21
37	24
38	25
39	25
42	28
43	26
45	29
46	28
48	31

Here

$$n = 9$$

$$\sum t_i = 34 + 37 + 38 + \ldots + 48 = 372$$

$$t_b = \sum t_i/n = 372/9 = 41.3$$

$$\sum y_i = 21 + 24 + 25 + \ldots + 31 = 237$$

$$y_b = \sum y_i/n = 237/9 = 26.3$$

$$\sum t_2^i = 34 \times 34 + 37 \times 37 + 38 \times 38 + \ldots + 48 \times 48 = 15{,}548$$

$$(\sum t_i)^2/n = [(372) \times (372)]/9 = 15{,}376 \ (372 \text{ was obtained just above})$$

$$\sum t_i y_i = 34 \times 21 + 37 \times 24 + 38 \times 25 + \ldots + 48 \times 31 = 9{,}902$$

We can now easily calculate the composite terms:

$$S_{tt} = [(\sum t_2^i) - (\sum t_i)^2]/n = 15{,}548 - 15{,}376 = 172$$

$$S_{ty} = (\sum t_i y_i) - [(\sum t_i)(\sum y_i)]/n = 9{,}902 - (372)(237)/9 = 106$$

$$b_1 = S_{ty}/S_{tt} = 106/172 = 0.616$$

$$b_0 = y_b - b_1 t_b = 26.3 - 0.616 \times 41.3 = 0.087$$

Thus, the forecasted number of trunks at any month t will be

$$P(t) = 0.087 + 0.616t$$

For example, at month $t = 55$, we would expect a need for $0.087 + 0.616 \times 55 = 34$ trunks; at month 60, we would expect 37 trunks. Of course, we can also backtrack to see how this linear approximation fits through the real data. For example, at month 39 we would have $0.087 + 0.616 \times 39 = 24.1$ or 24 trunks (compared to the actual 25); at 45 months, this equation gives 28 trunks (compared to the actual 29). It should be noted that this is the *best* straight line that can be plotted through this data. The data have been smoothed to fit a line. If a tighter fit is required, one may try to fit a quadratic or cubic through this set of points (this technique is not described here but can be found in the literature).

One should not try to use values of t that greatly exceed the last actual data point. For example, in the above example, forecasts for t up to 60 should be fairly accurate; one should not trust the predicted result at time 80. The exception would be if either a lot of historical data were available (i.e., n was large), or the process itself is very stable and predictable. One should recalculate the forecast at regular intervals, as fresh data become available.

Project lifecycles generally run into years. One should forecast expected future needs and determine if the equipment under consideration at project inception time will continue to be useful in the near future, or if it will need to be replaced soon. This least squares technique is well known to the statistical student and is very easy to use.

2.5 THE IMPACT OF TAX REFORM ON TELECOMMUNICATIONS

Although the U.S. income tax code has been modified a number of times during the past few decades, the changes are relatively minor and the basic features of the law essentially have been preserved. The 1986 tax reform, however, represented a dramatic change [20].

Tax Reform Act of 1986

Capital-intensive, regulated industries (such as the telecommunications industry) and users of large, customer-owned communications networks (such as banks and brokerage firms) were affected by a variety of provisions incorporated in the Tax Reform Act (TRA) of 1986. These new provisions range from reduced tax rates and a repeal of the Investment Tax Credit (ITC) to changes in rules governing amortization and the timing of income recognition. The business community felt the impact of the cost of tax reform, at an estimated level of $120 billion between 1986 and 1991 [20–23]. More tax changes are expected. For example, in 1993 there was talk of reactivating the ITC.

The accelerated cost recovery depreciation system (ACRS) was another incentive, along with the ITC, that had been used by companies and departments deploying company-owned facilities. Many observers believed that the reduction in marginal rates did not compensate for these two incentives. The phased-in reduction of corporate income tax rates went from 46% to 34%; other revenue-neutral tax base-broadening reforms also went into effect [21]). Because the lower marginal rates may in fact apply to a broader base, the tax burden of many companies appeared to increase in the recent past. Fewer privately owned telecom projects were initiated because of the decreased cash flow and the diminished tax value of these investments.

Most people have an intuitive understanding of the term depreciation, or a reduction in usefulness or value. For example, consumer goods (such as automobiles, stereo systems, and boats) diminish in value and utility with the passage of time. Traditionally, depreciation has been stated as a loss in service value due to wear and tear (depreciation from use) and obsolescence (depreciation of old technology).

For carriers, the FCC embodied a set of rules in the Uniform System of Accounts. Items with an expected useful life greater than one year must be treated as assets. Expenditures for durable goods are capitalized and are posted on a carrier's books as assets; the outlays for these assets (e.g., poles, switches, and computers) are not fully recovered during a single accounting period. Outlays for expenditures for short-lived items (such as pencils and paper) are accounted for like wages or rent and are recovered entirely in the current accounting period as an expense (chargeable in full to current ratepayers). The recovery of expenditures on durable goods is thus deferred to the ratepayers until future periods. In each subsequent accounting period, a portion of the current value of the plant and equipment is depreciated and treated like any other expense to be recovered [23]. The same general principles apply to a company acquiring telecommunications equipment, except that the depreciation is for taxation purposes rather that for rate-making purposes.

In the mid 1980s, it became fashionable (often without appropriate and/or complete financial justification) to deploy company-owned telecommunications facilities, rather than to rely on the services of carriers. Many of the institutions who followed that approach have now learned what the burdens imposed by such an approach really are. Superficially, based on incomplete financial calculations proposed by telecommunications managers (often without even consulting with the comptroller's department), it appeared that such solutions might be cost effective. However, these calculations often did not include hidden costs. In addition, the technology is now becoming obsolete so rapidly that these actions may have resulted in a company-owned infrastructure of aging and inefficient equipment. Reliance on carriers would have relieved the company from the burden of technological obsolescence. Starting in the early 1990s, large corporations have increasingly come to rely on carrier-provided services.

Impact on Telecommunications Users

While capital-intensive companies will feel a disproportionately heavy share of the tax burden, the telecommunications industry is expected to fare better that other capital-intensive industries. The U.S. Department of Treasury now has the authority to adjust class-lives of most assets based on actual experience. This points to a healthy environment for the carriers, enabling them to be the providers of choice in the majority of cases.

For example, computerized central office equipment is depreciated over 5 years, a 200 percent declining balance. This is in comparison to the tax code prior to 1986, which depreciated noncomputerized equipment over 10 years and computerized equipment over 5 years at 150 percent [21].

The outside plant is depreciated over 15 years, a 150 percent declining balance. Although the 15 years were also in effect prior to 1986, its depreciation life would have been extended to 20 years if its guideline life not been lowered from 35 years to 24 years.

The Alternative Minimum Tax and Leasing

The alternative minimum tax (AMT) contained in the Tax Reform Act of 1986 also affected the decisions made by telecom managers. Companies owning capital assets subject to the AMT found that often it was better to lease rather than purchase because of the reduced tax benefits enjoyed by purchased assets under the AMT provisions. The IRS requires that companies first compute their income tax under standard corporate tax regulations, and then again under the AMT. Companies must then pay the excess amount of minimum tax over the regular tax, in addition to the regular corporate income tax [22]. For many capital-intensive companies, the AMT is the tax that of concern.

In summary, the AMT rules provide

- A lower depreciation rate;
- A lower marginal tax rate;
- Addition of a book income preference item that substantially reduces the benefits realized by depreciation of purchased assets.

The AMT liability is computed at a 20 percent rate applied to the alternative minimum tax income, which is equal to the sum of the company's regular taxable income (or loss) plus tax preference items. This extended income has fewer deductions on a broader base of income categories than regular corporate taxable income.

Depreciation for computer and telecommunications equipment is computed under the AMT using the 150 percent declining balance method over five years (special rules apply for selected equipment). The end-effect of this method is to significantly decrease the tax depreciation deduction by reducing the depreciation rate from the previous 200 percent declining balance method. This approach is the ACRS method identified earlier. An equipment owner who pays regular corporate tax may calculate depreciation by using the 200 percent declining balance to straight-line allocation over the 5 years ACRS class-life. However, under the AMT rule, the same owner only realizes depreciation deductions of a 150 percent declining balance to straight-line allocate over the life of the equipment (and is also subject to further book depreciation adjustment). Application of these rules to actual computations will lead to the realization that, in an increasing number of situations, leasing will be more cost-effective than outright purchasing.

The interested reader should consult a tax specialist before making any decision based on tax considerations. The brief discussion above is meant only to sensitize the manager to some of the factors at play. This information tends to change over time, necessitating the assistance of a tax specialist.

REFERENCES

[1] Minoli, D., "Evaluating Communication Alternatives Part 1: Cost Analysis Methods," Datapro Report CA09-101-401, June 1986.

[2] Minoli, D., "Evaluating Communication Alternatives Part 2: Pragmatic Network Design Issues," Datapro Report CA09-101-451, June 1986.

[3] Morgan, T. J., *Telecommunications Economics*, 2d ed., England: Technicopy Limited, 1976.

[4] Minoli, D., *First, Second, and Next Generation LANs*, New York: McGraw-Hill, 1993.

[5] Minoli, D., *Enterprise Networking: Fractional T1 to SONET, Frame Relay to BISDN*, Norwood, MA,: Artech House, 1993.

[6] Schall, L. D. and C. W. Haley, *Introduction to Financial Management*, New York: McGraw-Hill, 1977.

[7] Bingham, J. E. and G. W. P. Davies, *Planning for Data Communications*, New York: John Wiley, 1977.

[8] White, J. et al., *Principles of Engineering Economic Analysis*, 2nd edition, New York: John Wiley, 1984.

[9] Riggs, J. L., *Engineering Economics*, New York: McGraw-Hill, 1977.

[10] Taylor, G. A., *Managerial and Engineering Economy*, 2d ed., New York: Van Nostrand, 1975.

[11] AT&T, *Engineering Economy—A Manager's Guide to Economic Decision Making*, 3d ed., New York: McGraw-Hill, 1977.

[12] Hughes, A. J. and D. E. Grawiog, *Linear Programming: An Emphasis on Decision Making*, Reading, MA: Addison-Wesley, 1973.

[13] Minoli, D., "Financial Analysis for the Communications Manager," *ComputerWorld*, August 26, 1985, p. 66ff.

[14] Minoli, D., "Defining Budget Terminology," *ComputerWorld*, September 2, 1985, p. 61ff.

[15] Minoli, D., "How to Choose the Proper Financial Model," *ComputerWorld*, September 9, 1985, p. 87ff.

[16] Morrison, N., *Introduction to Sequential Smoothing and Prediction*, New York: McGraw-Hill, 1969.

[17] Mayer, S., *Data Analysis for Scientists and Engineers*, New York: John Wiley, 1975.

[18] Ott, L., *An Introduction to Statistical Methods and Data Analysis*, North Scituate, MA: Duxbury Press, 1977.

[19] Verma, H. L. and C. W. Gross, *Introduction to Quantitative Methods: A Managerial Emphasis*, New York: John Wiley, 1978.

[20] Ben-Horin, M., et al., "The Impact of the 1986 Tax Reform Act on Corporate Financial Policy," *Financial Management*, Autumn 1987.

[21] Fisk, H. D., "The Impact of Tax Reform on the Telecommunications Industry," *Telematics*, February 1987.

[22] "Lease vs. Purchase," *Computer Economics*, September 1987.

[23] Darby, L. F., "The ABCs of Telecommunications Depreciation," *Telematics*, January 1987.

Chapter 3
Optimization Techniques

3.1 LINEAR PROGRAMMING AND APPLICATIONS

Linear programming is a powerful method often employed in operations research sciences to obtain optimal solutions to a wide variety of resource management problems. With the increased complexity of the financial and technological decisions faced by the telecommunications professional, it is appropriate to familiarize oneself with and utilize this tool for data and telecommunications decisions. A basic coverage is provided in this chapter [1–2].

3.1.1 Background

The linear programming approach provides an efficient mathematical method of determining an optimal strategy when there are numerous alternatives that might be pursued when seeking a certain objective and when the picture is clouded by the fact that the various courses of action are interrelated by numerous restrictions and constraints.

The essential elements of a linear programming situation are as follows:

1. There must be alternative courses of action.
2. The alternative courses of action, or the variables of the model, must be interrelated through some type of restriction.
3. There must an objective involved; this objective must be explicitly stated before the model can be built.
4. The variables in the problem must be *linearly* related, both in terms of resource usage and objective contribution.

These are, indeed, the typical factors at play in a telecommunications and data communications decision process.

Some usages of the methods involve industrial decisions, inventory, portfolio management, transportation, farming, construction, and scheduling. One reference [3] provides an excellent compilation of actual case studies from the business, which have been carried out in the recent past.

In the typical linear programming applications found in business, there are thousands (even tens of thousands) of variables and constraints. In the examples below, only problems with three or four variables are discussed; this is to keep the treatment at an elementary level. The small number of variables is not indicative of the power and applicability of the technique.

3.1.2 A Simple Example

Consider placing two transmission media of different characteristics in an existing conduit (for example, building wiring or interbuilding facilities). The first medium requires 8 mm^2 of cross-section area per cable, while the second requires only 4 mm^2 (such as twisted pair and fiber). However, the first medium costs $10 per kilofoot, while the second costs $70 per kilofoot. The total available area in the conduit is 4,800 mm^2. The total budget available for this project is fixed at $38,500. The bandwidth of the first medium is 3 DS1s, while the second is 5 DS1s (DS1 = 1.544 Mbps). The maximum number of pairs of the first medium that can be put in a conduit before electrical interference arises due to the skin effect is 500. (Skin effect is a physical process whereby the signal migrates to the outer surface of the conductor and around it in space.) Let

S = number of the small cross-section-area pairs;
D = number of the large cross-section-area pairs.

The goal of this particular decision is to maximize the throughput, C, while obeying the space and budget constraints. Expressed mathematically, one has a typical linear programming problem:

Maximize $C = 3S + 5D$

Subject to:
$$8S + 4D \leq 4{,}800 \quad \text{(conduit constraint)}$$
$$10S + 70D \leq 38{,}500 \quad \text{(budget constraint)}$$
$$S \geq 500 \quad \text{(interference constraint)}$$
$$S \geq 0 \quad \text{(logical constraint)}$$
$$D \geq 0 \quad \text{(logical constraint)}$$

The expression $3S + 5D$ is the objective function; it is the goal set by the person trying to solve this specific problem and it will lead to a particular solution, as we see below. If this same challenge was faced by a person whose goal was strictly to minimize the expense E, with the new objective function, then a different solution would be reached. Namely,

Minimize $E = 10S + 70D$

Subject to:
$$8S + 4D \leq 4,800 \quad \text{(conduit constraint)}$$
$$10S + 70D \leq 38,500 \quad \text{(budget constraint)}$$
$$S \leq 500 \quad \text{(interference constraint)}$$
$$S > 0 \quad \text{(logical constraint)}$$
$$D > 0 \quad \text{(logical constraint)}$$

is a totally different problem. (Note that $S = 0$ and $D = 0$ are omitted in the minimization process, because this is a trivial and useless minimum).

If this same challenge was faced by a person whose goal was to minimize the weight, W, of the resulting system (as would be the case for a submarine or aircraft system), then a different solution would be reached. If the first medium weights 400 kg per kilofoot and the second 20 kg per kilofoot, the problem would be:

Minimize $W = 400S + 20D$

Subject to:
$$8S + 4D \leq 4,800 \quad \text{(conduit constraint)}$$
$$10S + 70D \leq 38,500 \quad \text{(budget constraint)}$$
$$S \leq 500 \quad \text{(interference constraint)}$$
$$S > 0 \quad \text{(logical constraint)}$$
$$D > 0 \quad \text{logical constraint)}$$

Again, this is a totally different problem with different solution.

Going back to the original problem of maximizing bandwidth, one may attack the solution by way of the so-called graphical method. Because the problem is two-dimensional (namely, two media choices are involved), one is able to draw a graph and "search" for the optimal solution. This technique is only of pedagogical value; standard business problems may have hundreds of choices, so that the situation would be 100-, 1000-, or 10,000-dimensional. Two examples of this type of problem are: (1) how to select 100 stocks for a pension portfolio, and (2) how to setup cross-connections in real time through a telephone switch to support 4,000 simultaneous conversations. Several computerized programs exist to solve linear programming problems; all the user has to do is to plug in the numbers.

3.1.3 Graphical Solutions to the Simple Example

Three (arbitrarily selected) solutions that the planner may consider are:

P1: use 200 pairs of communications medium 1, and 200 pairs of medium 2;

P2: use 350 pairs of communications medium 1, and 500 pairs of medium 2;

P3: use 500 pairs of communications medium 1, and 450 pairs of medium 2.

These three possibilities are displayed graphically in Figure 3.1, which we may use because the problem is two-dimensional. Each of these plans results in a specific bandwidth in terms of DS1s. Plan P1 will result in $200 \times 3 + 200 \times 5 = 1{,}600$ DS1s, plan P2 in 3,550 DS1s, and plan P3 in 3,750 DS1s. Plan P3 would appear the best of these three choices; unfortunately, it violates the first constraint since this combination of media requires 5,800 mm^2 of conduit cross-section. The goal is to identify, from the infinite number of possible plans, the *feasible plan*, which generates the highest bandwidth without violating any constraint.

The first step in the graphical solution procedure is to identify those solutions that are potentially optimal. Since the optimal solution must satisfy all the constraints, the search can be restricted to the set of constraint-satisfying solutions. A pair (S, D) that satisfies all the constraints is called a feasible solution. The feasible solution with the highest objective function value (or the lowest in a minimization problem) is the optimal solution. In other words, the feasible pair (S, D) that, when plugged into the objective function $C = 3S + 5D$, gives the greatest value.

In Figure 3.2, the first constraint (cross-section area) is applied. A moment's thought will indicate that only the points at the left of or on the line (the shaded area in the diagram) satisfy the constraint. Plan P3 is not allowed, since it is infeasible because it violates the constraint. In Figures 3.3 and 3.4, the other two constraints are applied,

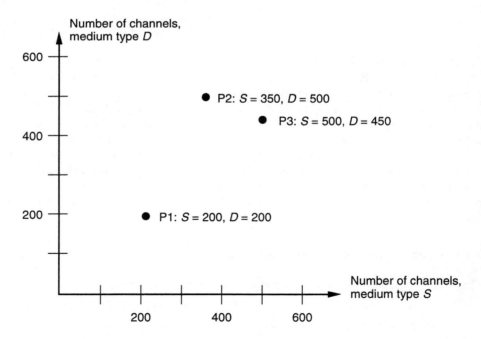

Figure 3.1 Graphic depiction of three proposed solutions.

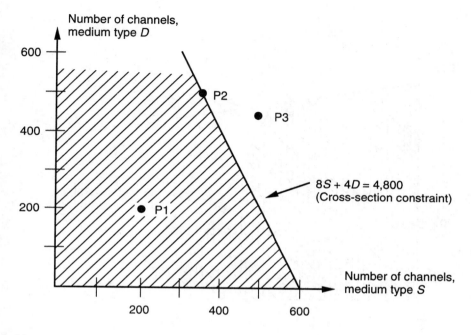

Figure 3.2 First constraint.

defining an ever smaller region of feasibility. The shaded area in Figure 3.4 represents all permissible solutions. But which of these solutions gives the best objective?

A fundamental result of linear programming, is that the *optimal solution will always be on a vertex of the feasible region*, not actually inside it (though all solutions inside the region are feasible). An entire edge may also be optimal (i.e., there may be more than one optimal solution), but at least one of the optimal solutions will be a vertex. In a multidimensional problem, the feasible region will be on the surface of the multidimensional hyperspace. It is impossible to visualize this geometrically, which is why multidimensional problems are always treated algebraically (numerically), not graphically.

An intuitive argument for the boundary optimality follows below for the example at hand. Armed with this result, we can now find the optimal solution by the graphical method, simply by evaluating the objective function at the few vertex points and selecting the best. Figure 3.5 shows that there are five vertices for this feasible region. These are:

Vertex 1: $S = 0$, $D = 550$;

Vertex 2: $S = 350$, $D = 500$;

Vertex 3: $S = 500$, $D = 200$;

Vertex 4: $S = 500$, $D = 0$;

Vertex 5: $S = 0$, $D = 0$.

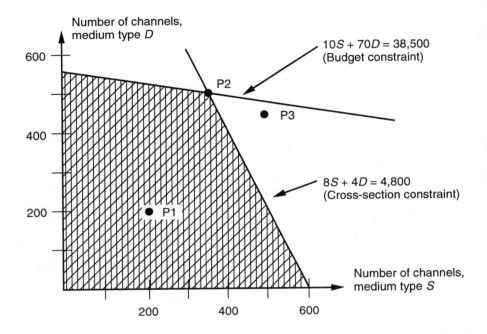

Figure 3.3 Second constraint added.

At Vertex 1 the objective function is $3 \times 0 + 5 \times 550 = 1{,}650$ DS1s; at Vertex 2, there are 3,550 DS1s; at Vertex 3, there are 3,500; at Vertex 4, there are 2,500; and at Vertex 5, there are none (nothing is being put into the conduit since D = 0, S = 0). The optimal strategy is at Vertex 2, to insert 350 pairs of the type 1 conductor, and 500 pairs of the type 2. See Figure 3.6.

To see that the optimal must be at a vertex, observe in Figure 3.4 that no interior point such as P1 can be optimal since we can increase the value of the objective function simply by moving upward or to the right until we encounter a constraint line [3]. Similarly, a boundary point on the constraint line can be improved by moving to a corner point. This sort of argument is formalized in linear programming to prove the result that the solution must always be a vertex.

Enumeration of all vertices, as we have just done, is one approach that works in a simple case like the one at hand. Another approach, that is the root of the well-known simplex method that provides solutions for lifesize problems, involves choosing a feasible point (such as $S = 0$, $D = 0$) and looking for a direction in which to move on the boundary of the feasible region to increase our objective. (In a real-life problem, there could be thousands of vertices in all dimensions. One is interested in finding a starting point that hopefully is fairly close to the eventual solution; hence the point 0, 0, ..., is not always

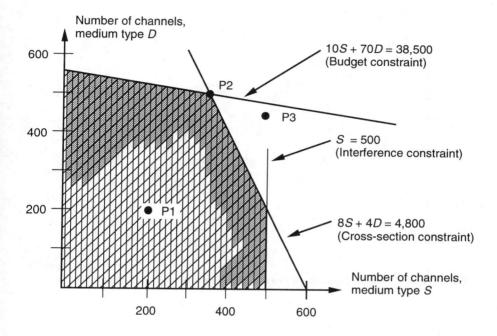

Figure 3.4 All constraints added.

a good choice. The simplex method contains a built-in procedure for accomplishing this). Refer to Figure 3.6 and note that increasing S will increase the objective function; thus we can move rightward along the S axis as far as possible, to the vertex. This will be the point $S = 500$, $D = 0$. At this point the value of the objective function is easily seen as 1,500. This is indeed greater than the value 0 with which we started at the point $S = 0$, $D = 0$.

At this juncture we can ask, "In what direction can we move so as to increase the objective again?" Clearly we do not want to go back to (0, 0) because that is where we came from. The only choice is to move upward along the line $S = 500$. It is now evident that when we increase D without decreasing S, the objective function will increase. Hence we move as much upward as possible, to $D = 200$. At this vertex, $S = 500$, $D = 200$, and the objective function will equal $500 \times 3 + 200 \times 5 = 2,500$. Again, this is indeed greater than the previous value of 1,500. Once more we look for a direction along the boundary for a feasible direction in which to move. We do not want to go back to where we came from so we must move northwest on the line $8S + 4D$. While moving in this direction will increase D, it will also decrease S, which is undesirable (for every two unit increment to D on this northwest course, S decreases by one unit). However, taking into account the coefficients of the objective function, we see that a unit increase in D will increase

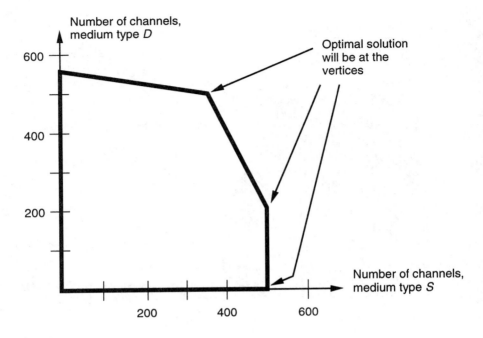

Figure 3.5 The theory shows that the optimum will be at the vertices.

the contribution to the bandwidth by 5, while a ¹/₂-unit decrease in S only causes a drop of 1.5 in the objective. Therefore, moving along this trajectory will actually be beneficial to us because we are picking up more than we àre giving up. We move northwest as much as possible, to the vertex $S = 350$, $D = 500$. At this point, if we try to move northwest to the next vertex, we note that for each unit of increase in D, S decreases by 7. The impact on the objective function would be an improvement of 5 (5×1), with a cost of 21 (7×3). This last movement is not worthwhile. Thus, the previous vertex ($S = 500$, $D = 200$) gave us the best solution; further movement in any direction from this point will only decrease the objective from the optimal value ($350 \times 3 + 500 \times 5 = 3,550$).

The simplex method, one of several methodical techniques to solve a linear programming problem on a computer (without the aid of geometry or intuition) works on this vertex hopping principle, traveling from one corner to the next until no direction exists for movement that will improve the objective. In more than two dimensions, choosing the direction in which to move can be quite difficult because there are more possibilities (at the vertex of a cube one can go in three directions; at the vertex of a 4-dimensional cube there are four directions; at the vertex of an nth dimensional cube there are n directions). Making the right decision is part of the elegance of the simplex method.

Using the earlier "brute force" technique of evaluating the objective function at each vertex point with an objective to minimize the cost ($E = 10S + 70D$), the optimum

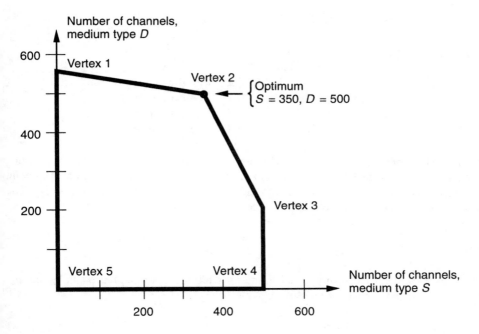

Figure 3.6 Optimal solution to the building-wiring problem.

would have been different. In this case, the optimum would be at $S = 500$, $D = 0$. If the objective had been to minimize the weight ($W = 400S + 20D$), the optimum would have been $S = 0$, $D = 550$. *This should reinforce the fact that the optimal condition depends strictly on what the objective is, and not on what another company may be doing or what the trade press may be trying to suggest.*

3.1.4 Other Issues Pertaining to the Optimal Solution

Three cases that are of interest arise in searching for an optimal solution, which we can illustrate graphically. These are:

- No feasible solution
- Alternative optima
- Unboundedness

No Feasible Solution

Assume, for example, that there are more than 900 customers in this building and that, for security reasons, each needs its own private pair of conductors, while at the same time one wants to maximize the number of derivable DS1s. The problem is now

Maximize $C = 3S + 5D$

Subject to:
$$8S + 4D \leq 4,800 \quad \text{(conduit constraint)}$$
$$10S + 70D \leq 38,500 \quad \text{(budget constraint)}$$
$$S \leq 500 \quad \text{(interference constraint)}$$
$$S > 0 \quad \text{(logical constraint)}$$
$$D > 0 \quad \text{(logical constraint)}$$
$$S + D \geq 900 \quad \text{(tenants constraint)}$$

where the last constraint is the new one. Figure 3.7 depicts graphically the set of constraints. We can see that the feasible region is empty, and that no solution exists to this problem. The formal solution algorithms would provide an indication, if this situation occurs. The problem is overconstrained, and no feasible solution exists.

Alternative Optima

In some cases, the number of optimal solutions is infinite. Assume, for example, that the objective function for the number of $DS1$s was

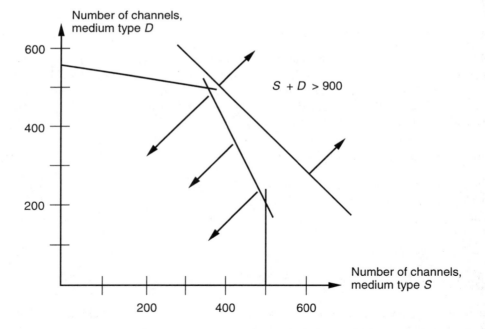

Figure 3.7 No feasible solution.

$$C = 3S + 1.5D$$

As we walk through the vertex-hopping technique discussed earlier and we come to the point $S = 500$, $D = 200$. As we move northwest along the constraint $8S + 4D = 4,800$, a one unit increase in D raises the contribution to the capacity by 1.5, but the associated $1/2$ unit decrease in S will decrease the capacity by exactly 1.5. Hence, by moving along the line $8S + 4D = 4,800$ leaves the value of the objective function unchanged. This means that any point on that polygonal edge gives the same optimal value. Any strategy (on that line) is an optimal strategy. Any one of the following decisions

$$S = 500, D = 200$$
$$S = 450, D = 300$$
$$S = 400, D = 400$$
$$S = 350, D = 500$$

will be a good one (in each case, $C = 1,800$). In practical terms, any of these strategies could be selected and implemented, or some other consideration (constraint) might be used for the final selection.

Unboundedness

It may turn out that the feasible region is unbounded; it extends infinitely into the plane. For example, the graphical method shows that no definitive optimum exists for the simple problem

$$\text{Maximize } C = 2S + 4D$$

$$\text{Subject to:} \quad 4S > 200$$
$$S - D > 0$$

The bigger that S and D are (such that $S > D$ and $S > 50$), the better the value of C is.

Other Issues

Other issues that may be of interest in the optimization process are: slack/surplus constraints, shadow prices, and reduced costs. These are defined and discussed in any linear programming text, in particular [3]. Additional aspects of the optimization process involve artificial variables, duality, sensitivity analysis, parametric programming, and postoptimality analysis [4].

Linear Programming Solution Software

The simplex method was the first technique to be widely employed. In addition, it is the cornerstone for other types of mathematical programming problems (including network problems, branch-and-bound methods for integer programming, and quadratic programs). It can be used to solve large problems with 5,000 to 10,000 constraints and 50,000 to 100,000 variables. This technique is implemented in many commercial packages.

The two most popular computer packages that have been used in the past are IBM's MPSX and CDC's APEX IV; other packages include MPS III (Ketron Inc.), and FMPS (Sperry).

3.1.5 Examples of Uses of Linear Programming

Below we explore some typical applications from the communications field.

Telephone Cable Plant Case

This example is based on reference [5] and deals with decisions that need to be made by a telephone company. A moment's thought will indicate that any user who might be contemplating a large private network faces similar challenges (though in different areas).

Carriers have to make many choices in facilities and related economics to provide service to its customers. By regulation, the company is allowed to earn some specific rate of return; the company is, however, obligated to keep control of both the costs of new plants and the operating costs. Regulated industries are thus very interested in minimizing the costs, which in turn simplifies the rate approval proceedings. Linear programming is an invaluable tool in this context.

One area in which linear programming is utilized involves the placement of a cable plant to serve subscribers. The goal is to determine what gauge or combination of gauges should make up the various sections of a plant to minimize cost, while meeting the signaling and transmission requirements. The issues to be considered are:

- There are four types of cable (26-, 24-, 22-, and 19-gauge), each with different costs and electrical characteristics.
- In order to signal a subscriber's set, the resistance of the circuit must be below a threshold (which depends on the gauge and on the circuit mileage).
- To achieve good speech communication, the transmission loss in decibels per kilofoot, must be below a threshold.
- The lower the resistance and the transmission loss of various ancillary facilities, the higher the cost.
- Any new addition to the plant must work with the existing plant.

All of these factors translate into a matrix of constraint equations that can be handled by linear programming. The solution to this actual problem is beyond the scope of this text.

Meeting Forecasted Growth

The Yankee Telephone Company (an independent in northern New England) used linear programming extensively in the 1970s to help plan their telephone system [3]. Initially serving a rural area, they anticipated a major migration of professionals from Boston to southern New Hampshire in the future. They predicted this migration based on a number of factors, including improved roads, higher Massachusetts taxes, and the industrialization of Route 128. The complex problem of delivering communications resources when and where needed, based on demographic forecasts and real estate developments, in a cost-effective manner, under the regulation of the state public utility commission, could not be tackled except by linear programming techniques.

Network Design Algorithms

The so-called budget network design problem (selecting a subset of point-to-point communications links subject to a budget constraint, so that the total weighted sum of the shortest paths in the network is minimized for delay and reliability considerations) is a fairly difficult optimization process. Recently, the problem has been addressed heuristically by way of a mixed integer programming problem [6]. A comprehensive description of this network problem can be found in [7].

Other Applications

Other applications of linear programming to telecommunications planning have been

- Flow control strategies in a network;
- Decentralized dynamic routing strategies, to minimize delay and avoid looping [8];
- Capacity allocation for networks carrying both voice and data;
- Maximizing throughput in communications switches and networks;
- Minimization of blocking in a network by adding communications equipment in a cost-effective fashion [9];
- Minimization of present worth of expenditures for expanding the capacity of a communications network in the face of increased demand for service; expense deferral is considered [10];
- VLSI chip design;
- Methods for forecasting traffic matrices [11];
- General management decisions regarding communications resources [12].

These are but some of the usages of linear programming in data and telecommunications planning. The interested reader is referred to reference [3] that contains over 30 actual examples of recent usage in the industry.

3.1.6 Other Mathematical Programming Techniques

Integer Programming

An assumption of the linear programming method is that the variables can be continuous, or fractional. In some cases, one must restrict the solution to an integer. The resulting linear programming problem with the added constraint is called an integer programming problem. Algorithms to solve integer programming problems are more complex and thus run much longer on a computer. One approach is simply to solve the corresponding linear programming problem, and roundoff the answer.

When the value of the optimized variables is large (for example $S = 500$ as discussed above), then the difference between the solution provided by the approximation and the real algorithm should be fairly small. When the expected answer is small in magnitude (such as 10), then the error can be large, and the true algorithm must be used. Integer programming is of interest mostly in solving theoretical-logical problems (for example, when a variable is allowed only the two values: $0 =$ false, $1 =$ true).

Nonlinear Programming

An assumption of the linear programming approach is that the constraints and the objective function are linear (i.e., there are no squared or cubed terms). Many of the nonlinear objective functions can, however, be approximated fairly well by a series of piecewise-linear segments. As long as one has concavity or convexity, one can solve the problem by using multiple variables. Reference [5] discusses this technique. Another approach involves simply replacing a curvilinear function by a linear function that approximates it, particularly when the index of curvature is small.

Quadratic function techniques are well-developed and fairly easy to employ. Reference [4] discusses the topic and the applicable algorithms in a readable fashion.

Other methods, particularly for non-monotonic functions, involves searching techniques. These are the so-called classical optimization techniques: the bisection method, the Fibonacci search, and the infinitesimal calculus [13].

Goal Programming

Goal programming is a special type of linear programming that is capable of handling decision situations that involve multiple goals [5].

Dynamic Programming

Dynamic programming techniques can be used to solve nonlinear problems; the technique involves treating a given problem as a sequence of smaller, easier-to-solve subproblems. The conversion of one larger problem into a sequence of smaller problems is the essence of dynamic programming. It can be used to solve problems that are not as rigidly structured as those tackled by the linear programming approach. This discipline was formalized between 1957 and 1962 by Bellman.

Consider the following example. A telecommunications manager has received proposals for five types of private data networking systems from bidders. The five projects have the following associated costs and net present value:

Project j Proposal	Cost in $1000s ($c_j$)	NPV in $1000s ($v_j$)
1	4	8
2	6	6
3	5	2
4	3	7
5	7	5

The total budget available is $15,000. Project 1 may involve buying a frame relay switch; Project 2 may involve buying a cell relay switch; Project 3 may involve buying a regular T1/T3 multiplexer; and so on. The manager must decide which of these projects to fund, in such a way as to maximize the total value that accrues due to this funding. Stated formally the problem is:

Maximize $8z_1 + 6z_2 + 2z_3 + 7z_4 + 5z_5$
Subject to: $4z_1 + 6z_2 + 5z_3 + 3z_4 + 7z_5 \leq 15$
$z_j = 1$ if project j is funded, $z_j = 0$ otherwise ($j = 1, 2, 3, 4, 5$)

In a small problem like this, one could list all possible solutions, eliminate the infeasible ones (those requiring more than $15,000), and select the optimal one. Complete enumeration in not useful for a large problem, since it grows exponentially in complexity (2^n with n = number of projects).

In abbreviated form, the list would look like this:

Projects Funded	Cost in $1000s	NPV in $1000s
None	0	0
1	4	8
...		
5	7	5
1, 2	10	14
1, 3	9	10
...		

Projects Funded	Cost in $1000s	NPV in $1000s
1, 5	11	13
2, 3	11	8
...		
4, 5	10	12
1, 2, 3	15	16
1, 2, 4	13	21
1, 2, 5	17 (infeasible)	
1, 3, 4	12	17
1, 3, 5	16 (infeasible)	
...		
1, 2, 3, 4, 5	25 (infeasible)	

It turns out that the choice of fund projects 1, 2, and 4 is the optimum, with a cash flow of $21,000 and an expense of $13,000 (not all the money is actually used up). Dynamic programming offers techniques (not discussed here) on how to make these sorts of decisions for large projects, without the burden of the "brute force" enumeration that would be impractical in a real problem. In encapsulated form the technique works as follows:

1. Decompose the original n-variable problem into a sequence of n sets of smaller problems such that each only has one variable and is related to the others via the constraints.
2. Solve the sequence of set of problems beginning with the last problem first.
3. Construct the optimal values of the variables working forward from the first problem to the last.

The interested reader may consult reference [13].

3.2 BASICS OF GAME THEORY

Until now we have assumed that a noncompetitive environment has existed in which the data/telecommunications manager can make decisions. In reality, this is hardly the case: the manager may be competing with another department for funds; the company may be competing with another company, trying do outdo each other in terms of service; the manager may be competing with a carrier in establishing an inhouse version of a service, while executives from the carrier are talking directly to the company's executives; and so on.

One interesting situation in which game theory is used in communications is by large users employing multiple interexchange carriers (IXCs). By and large, the top five carriers offer fairly similar services. Large companies normally subscribe to services from several of them (though one would do), and "reward or penalize" the carriers by the way in which they allocate traffic based on the carriers' recent reliability and customer support. The traffic level, however, is not allowed to drop below a certain threshold, since the customer knows that the carrier would drop the company from their priority customer list. Other examples of games involve typical user-vendor relationships, in which each tries to see how far the other one is willing to go. For example, the vendor tries to lower support on some equipment to a bare minimum, while the user tries to see how far the vendor is willing to go to obtain new business. This last situation may be of interest to a user contemplating setting up a privately owned network. Another application involves designing military or civilian data communications networks that are survivable to an "intelligent" attack by an inimical agent.

A brief survey of game-theory issues will be useful. This development is based on [14] and [15]. Use of sophisticated techniques such as game theory may appear farfetched to a data or telecommunications manager but, with the dynamic and fast-paced business climate of the late 80s and the 90s, all decisions are likely to involve gamble. This is particularly true when the end-user intends to invest millions of dollars to become, in some cases, a minicommunications carrier.

3.2.1 Background

In competitive decisionmaking, two or more decisionmakers are pitted against each other. Both are assumed to be equally intelligent and informed about the situation at hand. They are called *players*, their conflicts are called games, and alternative actions are called *strategies*. Von Neumann, the father of computers, laid the framework for what has become known as *game theory*.

Some treatment on games that involve two players is presented herewith.

3.2.2 Payoff Matrix

In a two-person game the payoffs associated with various strategies can be placed in a matrix (rows for one entity, columns for the other). Consider the example of data/telecommunications user A, and a long distance carrier B. Both A and B have strategies that they can employ in regard to each other. The user's strategies could be:

A1: Give all current traffic to B and let B know that all future growth in traffic will also go to the carrier.

A2: Give current traffic to B but let B know that unless B improves the quality of the service, future growth in traffic will go to another carrier.

A3: Let B know that, due to service problems, A is reducing the traffic given to B.

A4: Build a private network and give no traffic to B.

B's strategies could be:

B1: Provide minimal quality service to A.

B2: Give normal and reasonable service to A.

B3: Give outstanding service to A.

B4: Go out of the way to please A.

The payoffs of these strategies (according to some criteria) may be similiar to the following matrix:

	B1	B2	B3	B4
A1	−1	−2	+4	+5
A2	−1	+4	−3	−2
A3	0	+3	+1	+2
A4	−2	−3	+3	+1

If A selects alternative A1 and B selects alternative B1, the outcome is a loss of 1 unit (monetary or otherwise) for A, and a gain of 1 unit for B. If A employs A1 and B employs B4 the outcome is a gain of 5 for A and a loss of 5 for B. Because the sum of the payoff for any choice is 0 (when A wins, B loses), the game is called a *zero-sum game*.

Some standard factors of a zero-sum game are:

- The conflict is only between two parties.
- Each party has a finite number of alternatives.
- Both parties know all the alternatives available.
- Each gain or loss can be quantified by a single number.
- Both parties know all the payoff numbers.
- The sum of the payoffs for each outcome is zero.

3.2.3 A Reasoned Approach to a Solution for Small Games

The first step in the solution process is to *check for dominance*. Dominance means that an alternative is superior for one user all of the time. Both rows and columns must be checked. Looking at the columns that represent the alternatives available to B, one sees that no one alternative is better for every outcome of the other party's choice. For example, B3 is generally better than B4 (except in the case of A4). Looking at the alternatives available to A, we see that A1 is always preferred to A4 because of the large expense in building a private-facilities network (in this simple case). We can then eliminate the last row from the matrix. From B's point-of-view, B3 is always preferable to B4 (in this case, the vendor does not have to go out of his way to please the user to achieve a profit); no other dominance relationships exist. The reason behind these two-way dominance checks is that both parties are intelligent. Thus B would recognize that A would never actually use A4, which means in turn that B would not have to use B4. Look back what A4 and B4 mean: since A cannot afford to threaten B about building a private network, B's president need not take A's president to lunch and golf.

The end result of this preliminary analysis leads to the new situation:

	B1	B2	B3
A1	−1	−2	+4
A2	−1	+4	−3
A3	0	+3	+1

The second step is to ascertain the *existence of a saddle point*. A saddle point is defined as an outcome that is both the smallest number in its row and the largest number in its column. When both parties use the same alternative at every play (for example, the same data or telecommunications strategy when opening a branch office in Dallas, in Houston, and in Miami), then the party is said to be following a pure strategy. If a saddle point is present, it is advantageous to follow a pure strategy; otherwise, it is better to use a mixed strategy.

In the matrix above, the point A3, B1 is a saddle point. The saddle point is a minimax (the least of the maximum loss) and a maximin (the greatest of the minimum gain) at the same time. The meaning of the saddle point is further explained as follows: Alternatives A1 and A2 are attractive to the user because they allow a potential gain of four units (A can put the capital into a more profitable revenue-generating undertaking, rather than tie it up in the communications network). However, B can be assured that A will lose one unit (−1) by using B1 whenever A uses A1 or A2. A would also be attracted to A3 because no negative outcomes can occur from this alternative. Again B can thwart gains by A through its use of B1. Since A is astute and observes the advantageousness of B1 for B, A would select the alternative that minimizes B's gain from following the pure B1 strategy. This alternative is A3 (tell vendor that A's business may end up somewhere else). Because of the saddle point in this problem, both players can use a pure strategy, with A always employing alternative A3 (keep the vendor hanging), and B always using B1 (minimum acceptable service). The result is a standoff where neither side gains an advantage.

The underlying principle of choice is called maximin-minimax. B seeks the least of the maximum losses (minimax); A seeks the largest of the minimum gains (maximin).

When no saddle point exists, the players must turn to a mixed-strategy. This means that different alternatives are used for a certain fixed proportion of the plays. In theory, the alternative employed at each point is a random choice from the available alternatives, but the long term average is the fixed proportion just mentioned. In this case, one is interested in the expected value of the game: the average return that results from each player's following an optimal mixed strategy.

3.2.4 Solution Methods for Mixed-Strategy Zero-Sum Games

Every two-person game with a finite number of alternatives can be transformed into a linear programming problem, and solved accordingly. In addition there are special methods appropriate to certain conditions (for example a 2-by-2 game), which are less computationally complex than the general method.

3.2.5 2-by-2 Games by Way of a Data Communications Example

A game with two alternatives for each player is easily solved, and illuminates the need for a mixed strategy in a non-saddle point situation. This simple technique is discussed to point out the general approach. More extensive information can be found in references [14] and [15].

Consider the following situation:

LDC1: Long distance carrier (LDC) provides outstanding service.
LDC2: Long distance carrier provides minimally acceptable service.
USR1: User will set up own network.
USR2: User will give all traffic to the LDC.

with a payoff matrix:

	USR1	USR2
LDC1	1	5
LDC2	3	2

Note that all payoffs are positive. Therefore, LDC will be the winner. The user's goal is to limit his/her losses (LDC's gains) as much as possible. A mixed strategy is needed. Note that there is no dominance and there are no saddle points. Because there are no saddle points, sometimes LDC will use strategy LDC1, other times it will use LDC2. Similarly, B switches randomly between USR1 and USR2 (i.e., for some subportions of the network he will set up private facilities). The challenge for the user is to determine the proportion of times to use one strategy or the other.

The solution to this 2-by-2 problem is in four steps:

- Step 1: obtain the absolute value of the difference in payoff for each row and column.

	USR1	USR2	Difference in Payoff
LDC1	1	5	4
LDC2	3	2	1
Payoff Difference	2	3	

- Step 2: add the value obtained in Step 1 (both row and column totals will be identical). In this case, the result is 5.
- Step 3: Form a fraction associated with each row and column by using the values obtained in Step 1 as the numerator and the number from Step 2 as the denominator.

	USR1	USR2	Difference in Payoff
LDC1	1	5	4/5
LDC2	3	2	1/5
Payoff Difference	2/5	3/5	

- Step 4: Interchange vertically and horizontally each of the pairs obtained in Step 4. The fractions now represent the proportion that the various alternative should be used.

	USR1	USR2	Difference in Payoff
LDC1	1	5	1/5
LDC2	3	2	4/5
Payoff Difference	3/5	2/5	

Thus, the optimal strategy is for LDC to use LDC1 20% of the time and LDC2 80% of the times. The user should use USR1 60% of the time and USR2 40% of the times.

The long distance carrier would use LDC2 more often because of its higher minimum gain (two units instead of one). The user would rely on USR1 more than USR2 because of lower minimal and maximum losses in this example. The validity of these choices becomes apparent when one looks at the value of the game outcome.

The long-run return is the expected value of all the outcomes to one party. Given the mixed strategy, the probabilities of the outcomes are the following (see the previous matrix and note that we have independent events where the probabilities multiply):

LDC1, USR1 : 3/25 (= 3/5 × 1/5);
LDC1, USR2 : 2/25 (= 1/5 × 2/5);
LDC2, USR1 : 12/25 (= 4/5 × 3/5);
LDC2, USR2 : 8/25 (= 4/5 × 2/5).

The expected return for party LDC is then

$$3/25 \times 1 + 2/25 \times 5 + 12/25 \times 3 + 8/25 \times 2 = 65/25 = 2.6$$

This means that the carrier can expect a profit of 2.6 units in the long run. The user's gain is simply −2.6 units (a loss or an expense). If the user tried to improve his position by changing strategy to a pure USR1 strategy, LDC would soon recognize this and switch accordingly to a pure LDC2 strategy. The value of the game would then change to 3 (the outcome of the combination LDC2, USR1 in the original matrix). Thus, the user would end up losing more.

3.2.6 Practical Usage

Game theory is not a cure-all for decisionmakers, nor is it purely a theoretical science. It must be used in conjunction with the other methods listed in this chapter. Some practical industrial applications have been realized and the discipline is fairly new. Some of the difficulties of the theory are

- Assigning meaningful payoffs;
- Solving very large problems;
- Handling non-zero-sum and multiplayer games;
- Taking into account conditions that do not conform to the assumption of the theory (e.g., collusion, conciliation, or irrational players).

Despite the difficulties, there is much to be gained from an awareness of the reasoning behind game theory.

REFERENCES

[1] Minoli, D., "Evaluating Communication Alternatives—Part 1: Cost Analysis Methods," Datapro Report CA09-101–401, June 1986.

[2] Minoli, D., "Evaluating Communication Alternatives—Part 2: Pragmatic Network Design Issues," Datapro Report CA09-101–451, June 1986.

[3] Shapiro, R. D., *Optimization Models for Planning and Allocation: Text and Cases in Mathematical Programming*, New York: John Wiley, 1984.

[4] Van de Panne, C., *Methods for Linear and Quadratic Programming*, New York: American Elsevier, 1975.

[5] Hughes, A. J., and D.E. Grawiog, *Linear Programming: An Emphasis on Decision Making*, Reading, MA: Addison-Wesley, 1973.

[6] Wong, R. T., "Probabilistic Analysis of a Network Design Problem Heuristic," *Networks*, Vol. 15, 1985.

[7] Magnanti, T. L., and R. T. Wong, "Network Design and Transportation Planning: Models and Algorithms," *Trans. Sci.*, Vol. 18, 1984, pp. 15–55.

[8] Casalino, G., et al., "Decentralized Dynamic Routing in Data Communications Networks," *IEEE Proc. of Melecom '83*, Volume 1.

[9] Kortanek, K. O., et al., "A Linear Programming Model for Design of Communications Networks with Time-Varying Probabilistic Demands," *Nav. Res. Logist. Q.*, No. 1, March 1981, pp. 1–32.

[10] Smith, R. L., "Deferral Strategies for a Dynamic Communications Network," *Networks*, Vol. 9, No. 1, Spring 1979, pp. 61–87.

[11] Debiesse, J. L., "Comparison of Different Methods for the Calculation of Traffic Matrices," *Annals of Telecommunications*, Vol. 35, No. 3–4, April 1980, pp. 91–102.

[12] Mason, L. G., "Network Optimization with Capital Budget Constraints," Record of Second International Network Planning Symposium, 1983.

[13] Lev, B., and H. J. Weiss, *Introduction to Mathematical Programming—Quantitative Tools for Decision Making*, New York: North Holland, 1982.

[14] Fryer, M. J., *An Introduction to Linear Programming and Matrix Game Theory*, New York: John Wiley, 1978.

[15] Riggs, J. L., *Engineering Economics*, New York: McGraw-Hill, 1977.

Chapter 4
Queueing and Teletraffic Modeling

The next three chapters aim at providing tools and techniques to study the performance of a network. Performance typically involves one or more of the following aspects:

1. End-to-end delay;
2. End-to-end throughput;
3. Blocking (a measure of unavailability of required resources);
4. Data loss (particularly in a broadband environment), such as frame loss (frame relay), cell loss (cell relay), and protocol data unit loss (SMDS).

The design process can proceed iteratively by looking at the topology, assessing the performance measures (e.g., end-to-end delay) and then proceeding to either tune the topology (e.g., adding hubbing locations) and/or add communications resources (e.g., adding trunks, channels, or bandwidth).

4.1 GOALS OF THE CHAPTERS

Chapter 4 provides some of the theory pertaining to modeling techniques, including limitations and simplifications normally made. Chapter 5 provides more detailed queueing results. Chapter 6 includes an inventory of queueing formulas specifically tailored to common communications situations. Chapters 4 and 5 have a telecommunications perspective, while Chapter 6 has a data communications perspective.

In this chapter, the powerful tools of queuing theory, which are now commonly employed to optimize and fine-tune communications systems of all types (i.e., voice, data, and video), are brought within reach of the practitioner who is only equipped with a background in intermediate algebra. A number of examples from the telecommunications environment are discussed to provide a sense of how these models are applied and to highlight the methodology. Numerical evaluations are carried out to depict how the user can derive real results from the analytical formulas. Queueing is a somewhat esoteric discipline due to its intrinsic mathematical complexity. Yet, the basic models and resulting formulas should be well within reach of the practitioner, since these involve only algebraic expressions.

The information contained herewith will be useful for a network designer and/ or network administrator who seeks to optimize or fine-tune the telecommunications infrastructure to increase performance without necessarily increasing costs. Two major tables have been included: a glossary of queueing terms and a summary of key traffic distributions. In effect, these two tables form the synopsis of this chapter, and can be used as a brief overview or for reference.

Performance analysis in general, and queueing in particular, are not completely a cookbook subject where one can list telecommunications situations with juxtaposed ready-made solutions. Desired solutions often must be found on a per case basis, predicated on specific conditions related to one's own system and guided by explicit optimization objectives. Consequently, the goal of this chapter is to convey the *method* and illustrate the discipline, rather than provide a compilation of ready-made solutions. These methods can, in turn, be applied by the practitioner to the specific situation at hand in the organization. As indicated, Chapter 6 does provide some ready-made formulas.

4.2 INTRODUCTION

Queueing is the discipline that addresses congestion and ways to deal with it. The theory can be used to predict delay, minimize delay, estimate queue length, estimate required number of servers, and so on [1–2]. Typical queueing applications include vehicular traffic studies; consumer service studies (e.g., the number of bank tellers, fast food store sale positions, hospital beds, or city taxicabs); and, of major interest here, communications.

Queueing theory is a subdiscipline of the more general mathematical discipline of *Probability*. *Teletraffic* is a special application of queueing to a specific set of classical traffic communications problems, particularly in the telephone arena. See Table 4.1.

Table 4.1
Relationship Between Various Analytical Disciplines Available to the Network Designer

Discipline	*Area of Study*
Probability	Events in which the outcome is not certain
Queueing	Congestion and delay when service requests are probabilistic
Teletraffic	Queueing in a voice and data communications environment
Statistics	Data collection in any probabilistic environment

Telecommunications, data communications, and computer systems are all examples in which the number of resources made available by the carrier, selected equipment, or communications manager, is less than the maximum number of entities asking for usage of said facilities. In turn, this implies that either some users will have to wait until other users give up the facility, or they may be denied service. Queueing analysis has become fundamental to the design and management of systems in the aforementioned three fields.

The content of this chapter corresponds to a typical college course in queueing theory, without concentrating on the mathematical proofs for the results [3–9]. This material should also reinforce the fact that, while there are savings that can derive from applying queueing methods to telecommunications networks, the required expertise is not trivial; it may pay for an organization to hire a specialist for a few days rather than try to master a discipline that depends intrinsically on several advanced mathematical concepts.

4.3 QUEUEING FUNDAMENTALS

Consider the design of a trunk bundle between either two traditional telephone switches or two ATM switches. There may be a several thousand local loops (customers) terminating at each of the two switches. Certainly one would not provide thousands of trunks for this interoffice link. First, on the average, only about 5 percent of the customers terminating on the switch may be requesting service simultaneously; secondly, only 50 percent, on the average, may wish to communicate with customers homed on the second CO, and vice versa. In this example, if each CO had 5,000 loops, only 125 customers, on the average, need resources on the east-west bundle, and a different set of 125, on the average, need resources on the west-east bundle. The system would thus be designed to accommodate this average requirement, say E.

At some particular time, a certain number of customers exceeding the average by some increment may demand service; these extra customers will have to wait since the system was designed to accommodate only the average E. Equivalently, at some other point in time, a number of customers less than E will require service. Unfortunately this slack, or spare capacity when less than E customers need service, cannot be saved or stored up for a future time when more than E customers approach the system. To further appreciate this point consider a barber shop with three barbers. If at 10:00 a.m. only two customers show up and the third barber is idle, the resulting slack is useless sometime later when four customers show up (except that the third barber is perhaps not as tired—in queueing theory, however, servers are never tired).

Intuitively, one can see that the larger the variation in customer arrival, the more the delay. If the average E is 20 and the variation is 2, then at some point the number of customers will be 18 and at some other point it will be 22. Here, the overload is small and the delay in those instances also would be small. However, if the variation is 10, then at some point the number of customers will be 10, with lots of slack, and at some other point it will be 30. Here, the overload is large and the delay would be correspondingly large. The variation in customers approaching the system is controlled by what is called the *arrival distribution.*

In addition to the spread in customer arrivals, the delay is a function of the service time. Consider again the barber example above: if a typical haircut takes 10 minutes, in those cases in which a fourth customer walks in, he/she will have to wait at most 10 minutes (perhaps less because a cut was already underway). If a typical haircut takes 60 minutes, then the fourth customer may have to wait up to 60 minutes. The implications of the service aspects are controlled by what is called the *service distribution.*

In this chapter the term customer is employed to provide an intuitive grasp of the underlying concepts. However, a customer need not be a human requesting some obvious service; it could be an ATM cell requiring processing, a voice call requiring connection, a program requiring access to a hard disk, a user inquiry needing a record from a database, and so on.

4.3.1 Queueing Components

A *queueing environment* is a system in which congestion is encountered because the resources of the service administrator are less than the total instantaneous requirement. A *queueing model* is a mathematical abstraction of that real-world situation, whose goal is to provide analytical expressions that can be employed to assess the performance of a flow of customers (e.g., telephone calls, data packets, ATM cells, or LAN tokens) through the queue.

At least seven variables come into play when looking at congestion systems; these factors include:

- Composition of the different classes of arriving customers, if more than one class approaches the queue. For example: at a unisex barber shop, women and men would be two classes because presumably the service time for members of these two classes are intrinsically different;
- For each class, the customers' arrival distribution (the nature of the arrival process);
- For each class, the size of the population generating the traffic.
- The distribution of the queue server service time (the behavior of the servers). In many communications systems this is equivalent to the calls' length distribution;
- The way in which the queue that builds up is managed (i.e., first in first out, random order, or priorities);
- The maximum length of the queue (depending on buffer space);
- The behavior of the customers that are delayed (e.g., call retries, defections, jockeying, balking, bribing, or cheating).

4.3.2 Queue Notation

A convenient notation that is used to label queues is:

$$A/B/m/K/p$$

A is the code name of the arrival distribution to the queue (discussed in the next section); *B* is the code name of the service distribution of the queue; m is the number of servers available; K is the number of buffering positions available (maximum size of the waiting room—in the barber example, the shop may only permit 10 people to queue up, because of room size restrictions); and p is the ultimate population size that may possibly request the service (for a barber shop in New York City, p may be approximately 4 million). *When not needed (or clear from context), the last one or two symbols are not employed.* This universally used nomenclature was introduced by D. G. Kendall in 1951.

Figure 4.1 presents, in standard schematic form, various types of queues normally found in communications systems. The diagram shows customers arriving, at the left, to a resource for which they have to queue. The frequency with which customers join the queue is controlled by the arrival distribution A. In the first part of the diagram, only one

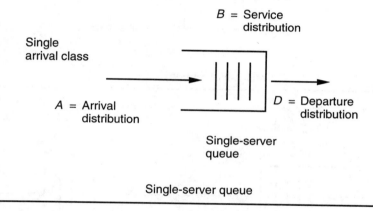

Single-server queue

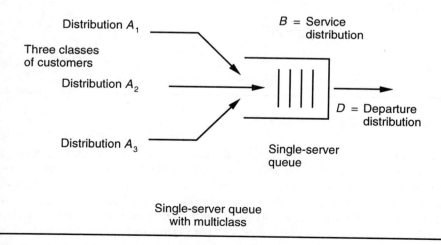

Single-server queue
with multiclass

Figure 4.1 Queues, shown schematically.

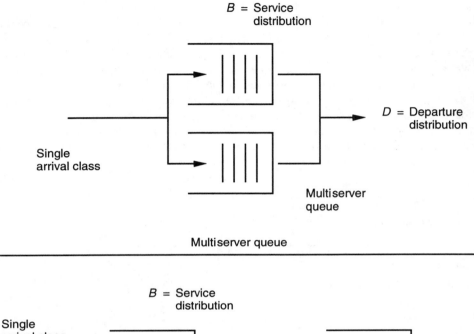

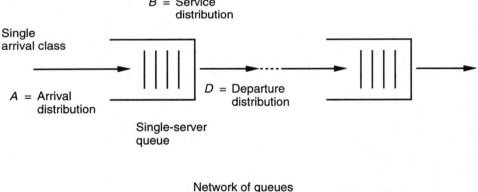

Figure 4.1 (continued) Queues, shown schematically.

type of customer approaches the system; in the second part of the diagram, three distinct classes of customers approach the system; in the third and fourth parts, a single class of customers arrive. The open rectangle with vertical lines is a representation of the queue, which provides service based on the service distribution B. In the first two parts of the diagram, only a single server is available; in the third part, two servers are available; in the fourth part, two queues in series are encountered. On the right of the standard schematic, one can see the departure distribution D, which represents a description of the departure behavior of the served customers.

Some of the more common distributions encountered in various telecommunications situations are: the memoryless, M (this is also known as the exponential distribution); the r-stage Erlangian, E_r; the r-stage hyperexponential, H_r; and the deterministic, D. A generic distribution is called G. The term memoryless is really a misnomer, but since it is a traditionally accepted name for the exponential distribution, it is employed here. (The reason for this term stems from the fact that under this distribution—and only under this distribution—the probability that a customer who has already waited T minutes will have to wait another Z minutes, is the same as the probability that a customer just joining the system will have to wait Z minutes. The distribution does not remember that the customer already waited for T minutes, thus the term memoryless arises.)

For example, the system M/D/3/20/1000 is a queueing system (barber shop) with an interarrival time controlled by the exponential distribution, a fixed service time (the time needed to cut hair, which is independent of hairstyle and the customer's physiognomy), a three-server system with room for up to 20 customers to wait, and a maximum clientele of 1000 people.

Some of more typical queueing models of relevance to telecommunications are as follows:

- M/M/1: memoryless (exponential) interarrival distribution; memoryless service distribution; and one server. This is typical of situations involving a communications server such as a voice-storage system connected to a PBX or a file server for electronic mail connected to a LAN.

- M/M/c: memoryless (exponential) interarrival distribution; memoryless service distribution; and c servers. This is typical of tie line bundles between switches or PBXs, with c trunks in the bundle, or dialup ports for modem pools or other resources.

- M/D/1: Memoryless interarrival distribution; fixed (deterministic) service time; and one server. This is representative of a trunk servicing a packet-switched network or cell relay stream.

Other models will be identified below.

4.3.3 Probability Distributions

The concept of probability distribution was already discussed in Section 2.4.2. More information is provided here.

In a probabilistic or random queueing system, arrivals and service time are not known a priori. The behavior of these quantities must therefore be specified by way of a *probability distribution*. In a probabilistic case, one does not expect a unique result, answer, or event; instead, a number of possible outcomes could materialize. The probability distribution lists each outcome and the likelihood that it will materialize.

There are two types of arrival and service distributions that control a queueing system: discrete and continuous. *Discrete distributions* are those in which the sample space is composed by of a denumerable number of events (in mathematics, denumerable means a finite number or an infinity equivalent to the number of integers); *continuous distributions* are those in which the sample space is composed of an infinite number of points (with an infinity exceeding the number of integers). Distributions and their properties are the purview of probability theory.

Of course, specifying the *type* of distribution is not sufficient; one also has to specify any and all parameters that describe that distribution. For example, one might have a memoryless system with an average of 5 arrivals per unit-time, or one with 15 arrivals per unit-time. Some distributions require specification of more than one parameter.

Two examples of distributions are provided to illustrate the concept of probability distribution.

Example 1 (Discrete Distribution): Delay in an Ethernet Local Area Network. The common bus of the LAN is time-slotted into intervals of equal length. The slot corresponds to the time required to transmit a fixed-size packet. Since there are many users on the bus trying to "grab" the same slot for transmission, a collision may result, and none of the data can be passed. When a user's communications controller detects that its own data have collided, it will reschedule transmission at a future slot (offset from the present slot by a random number of slots). Assume that at any slot the controller will transmit a backlogged packet with probability $p = 0.1$, and not transmit with probability 0.9. The distribution controlling the process is the geometric distribution. This distribution has as sample space of the integer set (list of possible outcomes); the probability of occurrence of integer i is $p(1 - p)^i$, with p being a given parameter between 0 and 1. Assuming that the slot length is 50 ms, it follows that:

Probability packet will be retransmitted in 0 slots $= (0.1)(0.9)^0 = 0.100$
Probability packet will be retransmitted in 1 slots $= (0.1)(0.9)^1 = 0.090$;
Probability packet will be retransmitted in 2 slots $= (0.1)(0.9)^2 = 0.081$;
Probability packet will be retransmitted in 3 slots $= (0.1)(0.9)^3 = 0.072$;
Probability packet will be retransmitted in 4 slots $= (0.1)(0.9)^4 = 0.065$; and so on.

Retransmission in 0 slots means immediately following the slot in which the collision was detected. The average number of slots before retransmission will be $(1 - p)/p = .9/.1 = 9$. Thus, the average total time for a transmission attempt would be $9 \times 50 = 450$ ms. This is the same technique used by the burst communications system (wireless LANs). It is also used in some very small aperture terminal (VSAT) systems transmitting voice or data.

Example 2 (Continuous Distribution): Mean Time Between Failures (MTBF) of a Private ATM Switch Line Card. Many failure phenomena have a temporal distribution following the exponential distribution. Assume that MTBF has distribution function: $0.001e^{-0.001h}$, then the probability that failure within h hours will be $1 - e^{-0.001h}$. (The change in formula is due to the integration process required for continuous distributions, in order to obtain nonzero probability values—this last expression is the cumulative distribution function.) One has:

Probability card will fail within 100 hours $= 1 - e^{-0.1} = 0.1$;
Probability card will fail within 1,000 hours $= 1 - e^{-1} = 0.63$
Probability card will fail within 10,000 hours $= 1 - e^{-10} = 0.99$; and so on.

The average time to failure is $1/0.001 = 1000$ hours; the variance is $1/0.000001 = 1,000,000$.
    Table 4.2 depicts some key distributions utilized in performance and congestion studies.

4.4 QUEUEING ANALYSIS METHODS

The underlying real-life mechanism of a queue can be *deterministic* or *probabilistic*. In a deterministic queueing system, arrivals and service time follow an established and unvarying pattern. While few phenomena are truly deterministic, two approximations to this situation exist.

Case 1. The large majority of the customers are predictable, with a small subset being unpredictable. For example, in regard to the arrival of mortgage payments to a bank, 95 percent of the customers may pay reliably every month and only 5 percent may default or delay payment.

Case 2. One is interested in the combined behavior of a large group of customers, not in the behavior of an individual customer. A powerful set of results from probability shows that the behavior of a large number of entities generally can be predicted with high accuracy.

    In terms of queueing models (mathematical abstractions of queueing environments), the almost universal approach is to employ the probabilistic analytical methodology, rather than the deterministic methodology (research literature on the latter is very limited).

4.4.1 Mean and Variance

As indicated, a distribution specifies all the events $(x_1, x_2, x_3, \dots, x_n)$ that could occur, and the probability $(p_1, p_2, p_3, \dots, p_n)$ that each of these events actually occurs. The mean of a distribution X is defined as $E(X)$, from the term expected value, and is calculated as follows:

$$E(X) = x_1 p_1 + x_2 p_2 + x_3 p_3 + \dots + x_n p_n = \sum x_i p_i$$

with the last expression being a convenient mathematical notation for that sum. The variance of a distribution is defined as

$$V(X) = (E(X^2) - E(X)^2)$$

wherein, from the above definition

Table 4.2

Common Probability Distributions Encountered in Queueing Environments

Part 1: Discrete Distributions

Name	Sample Space	Probabilities	Parameters	Mean	Variance
Bernoulli	0 1	p $1 - p$	Any decimal p between 0 and 1	p	$p(1 - p)$
Binomial	Any integer i between 0 and a fixed n	$\begin{bmatrix} n \\ i \end{bmatrix} p^i (1 - p)^{n-i}$	Any decimal p between 0 and 1	np	$np(1 - p)$
Poisson	Any integer i between 0 and ∞	$e^{-z} z^i / i!$	Any coefficient z greater than 0	z	z
Geometric	Any integer i between 0 and ∞	$p(1 - p)^i$	Any decimal p between 0 and 1	$(1 - p)/p$	$(1 - p)/p^2$
Negative binomial	Any integer i between 0 and ∞	$\begin{bmatrix} k + i - 1 \\ i \end{bmatrix} p^k (1 - p)^i$	k is greater than 0; p is between 0 and 1	$k(1 - p)/p$	$k(1 - p)/p^2$

Part 2: Continuous Distributions

Name	Sample Space	Probabilities	Parameters	Mean	Variance
Uniform	Any number x between a and b	$1/(b - a)$	Any number a and b with $a < b$	$(a + b)/2$	$(a - b)^2/12$
Normal	Any real number x between $-\infty$, and $+\infty$	fe^{-g} with $f = 1/s\sqrt{2\pi}$ and $g = 1/2[(x - \mu)/s]^2$	Any number μ; s is positive	μ	s^2
Exponential	Any positive number	he^{-hx}	Any number h greater than 0	$1/h$	$1/h^2$
Gamma	Any positive number	$rx^{a-1}e^{-x/b}$ with $r = 1/\Gamma(a)b^a$ and Γ being the Gamma function	Any numbers a and b greater than 0	ab	ab^2
Erlang-k	Any positive number	$(tk)^k x^{k-1} e^{-ktx}/(k - 1)!$	t is positive; k is an integer	$1/t$	$1/kt^2$

$$E(X^2) = x_1^2 p_1 + x_2^2 p_2 + x_3^2 p_3 + \dots + x_n^2 p_n = \sum x_i^2 p_i$$

Distributions can also be continuous. Here the sample space is "infinitely large" in the sense that any real number could be an outcome (e.g., with temperature readings, the temperature could be 85° F, 86.2° F, 87.43° F, or 88.367652° F). These situations are also described by establishing the probability of any such event using what is called the probability density function (PDF), which is similar in concept to the listing of probabilities illustrated above but in functional form (see Part 2 of Table 4.2). However, the PDF cannot be employed directly as can be discrete probabilities. One must first go through an integration process (similar to a summation) and obtain the cumulative distribution function (CDF). Traditionally, however, one finds descriptions stated more frequently in terms of PDFs rather than CDFs (this is why Table 4.2 depicts the PDF).

Before proceeding, an example of the probability concepts defined thus far is provided. Consider throwing a die. As already discussed in Section 2.4.2, the distribution of this event is

Event (Number on face)	Probability
1	$1/6$
2	$1/6$
3	$1/6$
4	$1/6$
5	$1/6$
6	$1/6$

The mean (expected value) of the number on the die face is

$$E(X) = 1 \times 1/6 + 2 \times 1/6 + 3 \times 1/6 + 4 \times 1/6$$
$$+ 5 \times 1/6 + 6 \times 1/6 = 3.5$$

The variance is calculated by first obtaining $E(X^2)$:

$$E(X^2) = 1 \times 1 \times 1/6 + 2 \times 2 \times 1/6 + 3 \times 3 \times 1/6 + 4 \times 4 \times 1/6$$
$$+ 5 \times 5 \times 1/6 + 6 \times 6 \times 1/6 = 15.16$$

from which

$$V(X) = 15.16 - (3.5)^2 = 2.91...$$

Instead of using the long expression $E(X)$, mathematicians often represent the mean of a random variable X as "x with a bar on top." The notation x_{bar} will be used herewith instead, as needed.

4.4.2 Measures of Queue Performance

The typical *measures of performance and effectiveness* for the study and assessment of a queueing system are: the waiting time for each customer, the number of the customers in the system, the length of the busy period (the continuous interval during which the server is busy), the length of an idle period, the work backlog, and the departure distribution. This last quantity is very crucial when the overall service to a customers involves queueing up in several steps for different resources. Series-of-queues are very typical of communications and computer systems.

Because of the probabilistic nature of the approach, one would like to obtain probability distributions for each of these performance measures; once one has the probability distribution, one has complete probabilistic knowledge of the situation. It turns out that this goal is generally too ambitious. Few queueing models allow a complete and explicit solution in terms of the distributions. In practice, one is (or must be) satisfied in obtaining only the first or second moment of the distribution; the first and second moment correspond to the *mean* and *variance* of the distribution. These two moments provides a fair amount of information about the phenomenon. To have more knowledge, one would need several dozen or, actually, an infinite number of moments of the distribution (the distribution and the infinite set of moments of that distribution are two equivalent ways to have complete knowledge of the phenomenon at hand).

4.4.3 Some General Queueing Terms

Some of the basic terms required to understand queues are defined herewith.

Utilization Factor

This is normally represented by the Greek letter ρ. It is the ratio of the rate at which work enters the system to the maximum rate (capacity) at which the system can perform this work; ρ always varies from zero to one. This is a key characterization of the queuing model: as ρ approaches one, the delay through the system becomes infinite. The work that an arriving customer brings into the system is equal to the number of time units of service that he/she requires. Thus, for a single-server queue,

$$\rho = \text{(the average arrival rate of customers)} \times \text{(the average service time)}$$

The arrival distribution A has an expected value of tbar, the average time between different customers arriving at the queue. The reciprocal of t_{bar}, ($1/t_{bar}$), which is normally denoted by the Greek letter λ, is the average arrival rate of the customer. Therefore, one has

$$\rho = \lambda \times \text{(the average service time)}$$

For convenience, define the expected value (average) of the service distribution as x_{bar}. One then has the key definition of the utilization ρ:

$$\rho = (\lambda) \times (x_{bar}).$$

A single-server queue has a maximum capacity for carrying out work that equals one second-per-second, and each arriving customer brings an amount of work equal to x_{bar} seconds. Since, on the average, λ customers arrive per second, λ multiplied by x_{bar} seconds of work, on the average, is brought in by customers each second. The reciprocal of x_{bar}, $1/x_{bar}$, is generally called by the Greek letter μ. Thus, it follows very simply that for a single-server queue

$$\rho = \lambda/(1/x_{bar}) = \lambda/\mu$$

For a multiserver queue one has

$$\rho = (\lambda) \times (x_{bar})/\mu$$

wherein μ is the number of servers.

Squared Coefficient Of Variation

This is another figure of merit to assess the performance of a queueing system. This coefficient is defined as follows:

$$C_x^2 = V(A)/(t_{bar})^2$$

wherein $V(A)$ is the variance of the arrival distribution. For deterministic arrival rate this coefficient is equal to zero. For the exponential distribution, the coefficient is one. For an Erlang-k distribution the coefficient is equal to $1/k$.

When the coefficient is small (i.e., between 0 and 0.7), then the arrival rate is fairly regular. The arrivals will tend to be evenly spaced; the distribution is said to be smooth. When the coefficient is around 1 (i.e., between 0.7 and 1.3), the arrival process is considered similar to the Poisson distribution and the arrivals tend to be random. When this coefficient exceeds 1 (i.e., greater than 1.3), then the arrivals tend to cluster and arrive in bursts. As the value of the squared coefficient increases, the congestion increases and the queue becomes longer.

Little's Result

In 1961, with some later extensions by other researchers, J. D. C. Little proved one of the key general results of queueing theory. This very useful theorem states that if L_q is the average number of customers in a queue and W_q is the average queueing time, then the following relationship holds:

$$L_q = (\lambda) \times W_q$$

This equation states that the average number of customers in a queueing environment is equal to the average arrival rate of customers to that queue, multiplied by the average time spent in that queue.

Also, if L is the average number of customers in the system (in the queue plus in service) and W is the average system time (queuing time plus service time), then the following relationship holds:

$$L = (\lambda) \times W$$

Note that $W = Wq + x_{bar}$ wherein x_{bar} is the average service time.

These relationships can be explained intuitively as follows. Consider a customer who just arrives. On the average he/she steps into service after W_q seconds. Suppose that when he/she steps into service, he/she looks over his shoulder and counts the number of customers who have lined-up in the back of him/her. On the average this number is L_q. It also took, on the average, $1/\lambda$ for each of the L_q to arrive, and the total time it took for the L_q arrivals to form behind him/her must be equal to his waiting time; thus $(L_q) \times (1/\lambda) = W_q$, from which the desired result follows. The argument is similar for L. This result is used frequently in analytical calculations to relate the queue length to the delay, and vice versa.

Consider the example of a M/M/1 model with an average interarrival time of 1 packet every 0.2 seconds to a packet assembler/disassembler (PAD), which is then output toward the user over a communications line operating at 9.6 kbps. The packet length is 1,440 bits. Here one has

$$\lambda = 1/t_{bar} = 1/0.2 = 5$$
$$x_{bar} = 1440/9600 = 0.15$$
$$\mu = 1/x_{bar} = 1/0.15 = 6.66$$
$$\rho = (\lambda) \times (x_{bar}) = \lambda/\mu = 5 \times 0.15 = 0.75$$

We shall see below that for an M/M/1 system with utilization ρ, the average queue delay is

$$W_q = \lambda/[(\mu) \times (\mu - \lambda)]$$

thus

$$W_q = 5/[(6.66) \times (6.66 - 5) = 0.45 \text{ sec}]$$

Applying Little's result, the average number of packets that need to be buffered is

$$L_q = (\lambda) \times W_q = 5 \times 0.45 = 2.2$$

Other Terms

Other key terms of a queueing system are defined in Table 4.3.

Table 4.3
Basic Glossary of Queueing Terms

Term	Definition
Algebraic equation	A formula, which may be long and complex, that involves only addition, subtraction, multiplication, division, exponentiation, and root taking. Such an equation is easily programmable on any PC. The final answer to all queueing models included herewith is an algebraic expression. (Equations that are *not* algebraic include: differential equations, difference equations, integral equations, and transform equations. These equations are often employed in the process of obtaining the final answer of a queueing model; sometimes the researcher is unable to complete the derivation and will provide only these types of equations as the solution to the model in question.)
Average customer arrival rate	Represents the number of entities (e.g., humans, packets, or calls) reaching the queueing system in a unit of time. This average is denoted by the Greek letter λ. More generally, one would prefer to know, if possible, the full distribution of the arrival process.
Average number of customers in the system	The average number of customers that are being served plus those that are in the actual queue; it is denoted by L.
Average queue length	The average number of customers actually in the queue (it omits those that are currently being served); it is denoted by L_q.
Average service rate	The average number of customers that can be served by a server per unit-time; it is denoted by the Greek letter μ.

Table 4.3 *(continued)*
Basic Glossary of Queueing Terms

Term	Definition
Average time required to complete service	The average total time spent waiting for service. It includes the time in the queue plus the time to be actually served; it is denoted by W.
Average time spent in the queue	The average time spent waiting to move through the queue, prior to stepping into service; it is denoted by W_q. It is one of the measures-of-effectiveness that one wants to derive.
Birth-death (BD) systems	Those queueing systems in which the change in state at any one moment is $+1$, 0, or -1. In other words, a single customer is serviced and leaves the system; no customer leaves or joins the system; or a new customer joins the system. The M/M/c-type queues are BD systems.
Chapman-Kolmogorov (C-K) equations	Fundamental equations that relate system states and provide transition probabilities, from which the behavior of the queue can be deduced. All Markovian systems (including birth-death systems) obey these equations. It is the job of a researcher to identify the C-K equations and to solve them to obtain a workable algebraic expression; the practitioner is generally only interested in the final solution, and not the process used to get there.
Customer	Any entity that requires some service dispensed by a server with limited resources (so that a queue would form). The customer could be a human being or some other entity (such as a computer program, a call, a packet, a cell, or a frame).
Exponential service distribution	The distribution of the service process wherein the PDF of the service time is he^{-hx}. This distribution is very common in queueing theory. In several communications problems, the service time is actually the length of the message or the duration of a call. Exponential interevent time and the Poisson number of events per unit-time are equivalent characterizations of the same process.
First in first out (first in first served)	The queue management discipline wherein customers are admitted into service by their order of arrival. Other typical methods are: priority scheme, last-in-first-out, and random order.
Infinite-server queueing system	A system that has infinitely many servers, such as the M/M/∞; this is typical of self-service applications in which the customer is serving himself/herself.

Table 4.3 *(continued)*
Basic Glossary of Queueing Terms

Term	Definition
Kendall's notation	The notation to categorize queue models. Queues are described by five letters: A, B, μ, K, and p. A is arrival distribution, B is service distribution, m is the number of servers available, K is the number of buffering positions, and p is the ultimate population size that may possibly request service. When not needed (or clear from the context), the last one or two symbols are not employed. This convenient nomenclature was introduced by D. G. Kendall in 1951.
Lambda (λ)	The average number of customers who arrive per second. It represents the mean of the arrival distribution.
Little's result	One of the key general results of queueing theory. This very useful relationship states that if L_q is the average number of customers in a queue and W_q is the average queueing time, then the following relationships hold: $L_q = (\lambda)W_q$ and $L = (\lambda)W$.
Markovian model	Those systems in which future behavior depends only on the present and not the past. A birth-death system is a special type of Markovian model.
Mu (μ)	The average number of customers served per second. It represents the mean of the service distribution.
Multiqueue multiserver queueing system	A queueing situation in which customers form several lines and the server mechanism is composed of several entities. For example the M/M/c model.
PDF	The probability density function is the mathematical formulation of a continuous distribution that provides a description of the probability that any event x in the sample space will actually occur.
Poisson arrival process	One of the most commonly-used distributions for the arrival of customers (e.g., calls or packets) to a telecommunications queue, which is named after the French mathematician who invented it. It describes the probability that a number of customers will arrive in a unit of time. It corresponds to an exponential distribution for the interarrival time and is used in such models as M/M/1, M/M/c/c, M/G/1, and so on.
Pollaczek-Kintchine (P-K) equation	A relationship that can be used in the M/G/1 model to obtain measures of queue performance given just the mean interarrival time and the mean service time with its variance.

Table 4.3 *(continued)*
Basic Glossary of Queueing Terms

Term	Definition
Probability of *n*-customers in the system	The probability at steady state that one will find n customers (e.g., calls or packets) waiting to go through the queue; this is denoted by p_n. This is a crucial piece of information that must be quantified by the researcher trying to solve a model since all other measures of queue performance depend on it.
Queue	Any system that experiences congestion. An environment in which the number of resources (e.g., trunks or buffers) made available by the system administrator is less than the number of customers who would like access to those resources.
Queue discipline	The method employed by the server mechanism to pick customers from the queue. The most common method is first-in-first-out (FIFO), but others are available, including customer selection based on a priority scheme.
Queue performance measures	A set of results that provides the typical quantities that are required to assess a queue. Standard measures are average queue length and average delay, though others are also of interest.
Server	The part of a queueing system that provides the service requested by the customer. For example, the PBX, a trunk bundle connected to a PBX, a LAN, or an ATM switch matrix.
Server utilization ratio	Generally represented by the Greek letter ρ, a measure of how busy the server will be. Normally, this ratio will have to be less than one or the delay will be infinite (when ρ is greater than one, the server is not able to keep up with the incoming work requests). It is defined as $\rho = \lambda/\mu$, wherein λ is the average number of customers who arrive per second, and μ is the average number of customers served per second.
Single-queue multiserver system	A queueing system in which all customers wait in a single pool, and then are served by a mechanism consisting of several servers (e.g., a bank with a single line and several tellers).
Source population	The ultimate population of users that request service. This is generally assumed to be infinite, though, in reality, it never is.
Traffic intensity ratio	This coefficient is defined as the ratio of the arrival distribution variance to the square of the mean interarrival time. When the coefficient is small (i.e., between 0 and 0.7), then the arrival rate is fairly

Table 4.3 *(continued)*
Basic Glossary of Queueing Terms

Term	Definition
Traffic intensity ratio (continued)	regular, arrivals will tend to be evenly spaced, and the distribution is said to be smooth. When the coefficient is around 1 (i.e., between 0.7 and 1.3), the arrival process is similar to the Poisson distribution, and arrivals tend to be random. When the coefficient exceeds 1 (i.e., greater than 1.3), then arrivals tend to cluster and arrive in bursts. As the value of the squared coefficient increases, congestion increases and the queue becomes longer.

4.5 MODELS AND THEIR LIMITATIONS: A NONDOGMATIC VIEW

In this section, we "demythologize" the machinery that is employed in traffic analysis. Theoreticians tend to take a dogmatic view of the models. In particular, they insist that the aggregate of any kind of electronic traffic—data, voice, video, image, and message traffic—leads to a Poissonian distribution, although the central limit theorem of probability states that the sum of independent random variables leads to a Gaussian distribution. It is of some comfort to note, though, that signal analysis engineers believe that the sum of random signals is a Gaussion distribution. There are two reasons to "demythologize" these models:

1. The practitioner, while using these models, should realize that there are highly constrictive limitations to their *exact utility* (i.e., they will always have an approximate utility).
2. Practitioners do not consider this subject forbidden territory, as the theoreticians would like it to remain. A nondogmatic view is preferred.

Consider the following "thought experiment." There are five people in a certain workgroup all connected with a LAN. Each produces eight business letters a day on their PC, which are sent to the LAN-resident printer. Now assume that five more people are hired into the workgroup and connected to the LAN. Would the original five people now send only four letters a day to the printer? Assume that 10 more people are hired into the workgroup and connected to the LAN. Would the original five people and the recently-hired five only send two letters a day to the printer now? Assume that 20 more people are hired into the workgroup and connected to the LAN. Would the original five people and the fifteen previously-hired now only send one letter a day to the printer? That is exactly what a Poisson model predicts (necessitates?). Experience tells us quite the opposite. Each person hired will tend to send a similar number of documents to the printer as each original member of the workgroup did. (For productivity reasons, the new hires are expected to produce approximately the same amount as the existing employees). Perhaps there is more competition now and each person may try to outdo the other by producing and printing 10 letters per day. There will also be the inevitable e-mail explosion—the more people in a workgroup, the greater the amount of (marginally useful?) e-mail. All of this is contrary to the requirements of the Poisson model.

In order to understand and effectively use the arsenal of available tools, one must first be familiar with what each model is and is not and its intrinsic limitations. This is crucial since indiscriminate use of a mathematical model, or a "cookbook formula," without detailed knowledge of the underlying assumptions, may result in corporate networks that do not operate as expected and which experience some of the performance problems listed in Chapter 1.

In this section we will learn the limitations of models, the additional limitations of probabilistic models, and, in particular, the limitations of the most popular probabilistic models [10–11].

4.5.1 Understanding Models

Models are *simplifications* of the real world that allow a parametric analysis of a problem, particularly when a large number of variables are involved. In this process, many variables and factors may be ignored, discounted, or simplified.

The purpose of a model is to interrelate variables functionally in such a way that one is able to obtain predictions with respect to one quantity as some or all of the other variables attain new values. Models are useful or desirable when one needs to obtain an equation or "law" that one requires to factor into a larger process. For example, one may have a model of how a certain type of substance behaves that one uses to predict how a mixture of this substance with another substance behaves. This, in turn, helps to understand how the resultant product of the chemical reaction works so that one is able to estimate the strength of the mechanical component molded from the material and, finally, one can predict the durability of the machinery built from this plastic. Because of this chain of calculations, it is desirable to have analytical relationships connecting the variables.

A model can be deterministic, probabilistic, or statistical.

A *deterministic* model provides a functional relationship (such as an algebraic equation, a differential equation, a difference equation, or an integro-differential equation) in which the behavior of the desired variable is exactly fixed by knowledge of the other variables. For example, if M represents the money (in dollars) in a person's pocket, then without doubt or ambiguity,

$$M = 0.01p + 0.05n + 0.10d + 0.25q + 1.0D + 5.0F + 10.0T$$
$$+ 20.00Tw + 50.00Fi + 100.00H$$

wherein p is the number of pennies in the person's pocket, n is the number of nickels, d is the number of dimes, D is the number of one dollar bills, F is the number of five dollar bills, and so on.

A *probabilistic* model is one where the behavior of the interested variable can be related to other desired variables only by a range (the technical term is probability distribution) of values or possibilities. The number of outcomes then becomes *multiplicatively large,* rather than unique as in the deterministic case. Given a single observation, one is not able to predict which of these possible outcomes will actually materialize; one can, however, establish a range, or even identify a bounded set of outcomes with some "confidence of certainty." The interesting and useful aspect of probability models is that if one conducts enough measurements and/or repetitions of the same underlying experiment, one is generally assured that certain aspects of those experiments are predictable. We illustrate these three points below and make some philosophical observations. Many real life problems, including communications in general and broadband design in particular, are treated as probabilistic problems. They require a probabilistic model to interrelate variables of interest, which often include cost, delay, blocking, and bit error rate, among others.

Before continuing the discussion on probabilistic models, a word on *statistical* models: statistical models do not claim a cause-effect relationship between the variables that the other models postulate, yet they provide certain empirical relationships that are corroborated or perhaps simply documented by observation (see below).

4.5.2 Multiplicative Issue of Probabilistic Models

Consider the following example involving two people. Each person has three coins in his/her possession. What is the total combined amount of money in their possession? The problem is not ostensibly deterministic; in other words, we are not able to come up with a specific, unique answer to the problem. We will be able to come up only with a range and, if we are lucky, with a subset of values.

The first person could have any one of the following fifteen possible combinations:

$3p$	($0.03)
$3n$	($0.15)
$3d$	($0.30)
$3q$	($0.75)
$2p,1n$	($0.07)
$2p,1d$	($0.12)
$2p,1q$	($0.27)
$1p,2n$	($0.11)
$1p,2d$	($0.21)
$1p,2q$	($0.51)

$1p,1n,1d$	($0.16)
$1p,1n,1q$	($0.31)
$1p,1d,1q$	($0.36)
$2n,1d$	($0.20)
$2n,1q$	($0.35)
$2d,1q$	($0.45)

Thus, the amount of money in the pocket of one person ranges from $0.03 to $0.75, along with thirteen other possibilities. In this case, all fifteen possibilities are distinct; in general, some outcomes could coincide, reducing slightly the number of outcomes. To appreciate the multiplicative effect, note that if we are interested in the total amount of money available to the two people, there are 15 times 15, or 225, possibilities ranging from $0.06 to $1.50. (Note that some values coincide and that in this particular case there could be at most $150 - 6 = 144$ distinct possibilities). To see what the 225 possibilities are, note that the first person could have the $3d$ combination, while the second could have $3n$; $3d$; $3q$; $2p,1n$; or any of the other combinations (15 cases). Or the first person could have the $3n$ combination and the second could have $3n$; $3d$; $3q$; $2p,1n$; or any of the other combinations (15 cases); and so on.

It is important to remember that, given a probabilistic situation, one is unable to predict correctly the desired amount—one can only predict a range. For example, one is not able to predict that between two ATM switches, one needs exactly six SONET trunks; one can only predict that one would need between four and nine (or perhaps "seven on the average," which is the figure of merit normally quoted).

As the number of variables grows, the number of possible outcomes grows accordingly in a multiplicative fashion.

4.5.3 Inability To Predict Given a Single Case

One intrinsic consequence of a probabilistic mechanism is that the observer is not able to predict the exact outcome of a *single situation*. For example, if one looks at the delay to provide dial tone, one may be able to say that it should be between 0.25 sec and 5 sec. However, one is not able to challenge the CEO by saying, "pick up the telephone and I guarantee right now that you will get a dial tone from the PBX in 1.3072328 seconds."

In fact, if improperly used, probability can lead to erroneous results. This issue bothered mathematicians for over a half a century, before they were able to put the discipline on a valid foundation in the early 1900s. (The implication was that, under the right framework, probability theory could be legitimized.)

4.5.4 Many Repetitions of the Same Experiment

If one conducts enough measurements and/or repetitions of the same underlying experiment (the technical term from probability theory), then one is generally assured that certain aspects of those experiments are predictable. For example, one might be able to say to the CEO, "I bet that if you pick up the phone 20 times, the dial tone delay will be less than 1 second at least 15 times." Similarly, one is not able to predict the specific outcome of a single throw of a die. On the other hand, one can confidently predict that if the die was thrown 600 times, 100 of these 600 trials should result into a "1."

4.5.5 Philosophical Observation

A truly probabilistic environment (technically known as random or stochasti) is one in which the outcome is intrinsically unpredictable, as, for example, in throwing a die. Indeed, the inability to predict the outcome of this die experiment is not due to some lack of knowledge; no matter what measurements one may conduct (e.g., wind velocity, light intensity, humidity, or altitude), one would still be unable to characterize the outcome.

Probability is often applied incorrectly as a substitute for knowledge. The result of many processes is not really an unpredictable event. It is just that we do not have sufficient data to solidify a conclusion, which indeed would be possible if we took the time to measure the appropriate parameters and collect and employ the data. The crucial difference is that the underlying mechanism is not unpredictable; the answer can be ascertained precisely if only we wish to do so. The above coin problem is an example of an experiment in which the underlying mechanism is not really random. We are able to determine the exact amount if we obtain the right measurement. In a truly random environment, one is unable to predict the result, no matter what measurements are taken. A measurement of interest above would be the coin weight (diameter would be another one): if one knew the weight of each of the coins in the pocket, then one would be able to predict the amount (which is how a vending machine determines amounts). This coin example, then, is a case in which probability is used to cover-up ignorance about the situation (or lack of desire and/or resources to make the appropriate measurements).

Pragmatically, it is acceptable to use probability to "get around" ignorance (as in the above coin example), but it should be remembered that if the problem is not truly random, then one could always obtain a measurement and secure the precise answer. Of course, it may be more economical to follows the probabilistic method. While using probability and the ensuing models for these reasons, however, one should not lose track of the fact that it is a substitute for a process that may be more accurate.

4.5.6 Statistical Models

Certain models are statistical in nature and involve with correlation, analysis of variance, and factor analysis. Though related to the probability models described above, the statistical model does not claim the cause-effect relationship that the other models postulate. In other words, the probabilistic model says that if you throw the die, a number will result; the model is unable to predict the exact number that will result. The statistical correlation may be strictly circumstantial. No causality is a standard term used to describe this interrelationship. For example, by comparing lots of data, one may observe that every time it rains in New York City, the stock market goes up one point. While this sort of statistical relationship may be true, there is no cause-effect interrelationship or rationality between the two phenomena. [12]. Statistical models are often used in advertisements and social science studies.

4.5.7 Modeling Traffic

We will now focus on the models employed to study traffic and to design networks. In some cases, traffic may indeed be random (i.e., it is unpredictable no matter what measurements one carries out); in other cases, traffic is deterministic and could be characterized if one only took the time to make the right measurements. For example, the output of a trunk carrying data of a fixed packet length (e.g., ATM cells) at medium-to-high channel utilization is deterministic, regardless of the nature (random or otherwise) of the arrival process. One packet every P/S seconds will appear at the output of the trunk (P = packet length in bits, S = speed of the trunk in bps).

Generally, one assumes that the traffic is random and employs one of the expressions from queueing theory to calculate performance, even though a strictly measurement-driven approach may be better and may be possible at times. Given this a priori choice of methodology, one is able to invoke the results of *teletraffic theory* to carry out design calculations. Teletraffic relates grade-of-service measures (such as blockage, delay, and buffer lengths) to parameters that probabilistically describe the traffic arrival profile.

Several classical teletraffic models are used over and over again by telecommunications professionals. These models, however, have two types of limitations: (1) they are probabilistic when a deterministic model (with a lot of ancillary data) may be appropriate; (2) they make certain assumptions that may not be consistent with real life (see the next section).

Of course, more complex models could be developed and used. To derive and solve even a relatively simple analytical model can take substantial effort (a half- to one-person-year or more is not unusual). Even when the model is constructed, it may be intractably complex to solve mathematically in closed form. And even if it can be solved in closed form, the equation may be so complex that the designer decides not to employ it. For example, a closed-form equation for the exact solution of a fourth-degree polynomial equation exists, but it is so complex that most people prefer an approximate method called Newton-Ramson.

In summary, common models have limitations. Models that are solved in closed form and thus more accurate could be formulated, and then programmed into computerized design tools for use in the engineering process. In reality, this approach is not often employed; the simpler models are used instead. For this reason, it is important to at least understand the limitations of the common models.

4.6. LIMITATIONS OF CLASSICAL MODELS

This section should be read as background material. One should not emerge from this discussion with a pessimistic assessment of the models so often employed, but simply with an appreciation of the limitations of these models and, hence, the sense that one should not rely entirely on a dogmatic answer but, whenever possible, on a more measurement-based methodology.

The pragmatist who routinely consults modeling tables (such as Erlang B tables) to determine the number of lines needed to support given traffic patterns may be overlooking some specific assumptions made by the models that could lead to suboptimal designs. Understanding these limitations is crucial to any design effort. Before moving on to the analytical models and refinements, we will identify some of the issues.

4.6.1 Assumptions That Rarely Hold

Following are descriptions of several assumptions that are intrinsic to many models and that tend to diverge from the conditions typical of network environments [1–2, 10–11].

Number of System Users

Many models assume, for mathematical reasons, that the number of users that need to access a certain resource is infinite. Even presuming that all other assumptions made by the common network models (such as Erlang B) are valid, this assumption alone can lead to drastically different results compared to the answers reached when the real population size is considered.

For example, with a PBX in New York that is interconnected with tie lines to a PBX in Miami, the number of corporate users who in any one day may wish to call Miami is not only not infinite and not equal to the entire corporate staff (e.g., 1,000 people), but may be as small as a dozen people or fewer. Any engineering done with a popular model that assumes an infinite population will sometimes lead to incorrect results. These models have been employed by large telephone companies, which may be the reason why they have acquired legitimacy in the eyes of practitioners trying to design small or medium private voice networks. While these models may be appropriate to use when designing a network for a central office that serves 20,000 customers or a transatlantic TAT-8 cable carrying 40,000 simultaneous conversations, they may be deficient when designing a corporate network to support those 10, 20, or 30 users per day who need to call a specific remote on-net location.

The Engset model, which is a more sophisticated model, uses most of the same assumptions as the Erlang B model but takes into account the finite character of the user population and therefore leads to a more realistic determination of the resources needed. Formulas that use infinite populations can, in some situations, suggest the use of twice as many lines or ports as models that take into account actual user populations. This coul represent a significant added expense.

Disappearing Calls/Users

Many network models also assume that blocked calls (or, more generally, service requests are not retried, when in fact these calls are rarely lost and may indeed be retried withi seconds, particularly with autodialers, computer-originated traffic, and the camp-o routines of smart message terminals or switches. In other words, the model will sugges the use of fewer communications facilities than may be actually needed because of th number and frequency of the retries. A user who is determined to make a phone call wil generally keep on trying until he/she is able to get through. Heavy system overloads wil stimulate repeated attempts; special events and promotions can cause major increases i call origination in selected areas; and catastrophic events (e.g., an earthquake, flood, c hurricane) often create overloads in limited areas.

For example, a problem analyzed by this author consisted of a computer in metropolitan area calling a sparse population of terminals in a smaller city to delive electronic mail. After receiving messages from the sender, the computer was programme to attempt to route the message within one minute for up to 50 tries, with the interva increasing slightly with the number of attempts, before rescheduling the call.

Time Invariance

Another assumption of popular classical optimization models is that traffic patterns ar consistent with respect to time, when in fact they intrinsically vary by the time of da and week and by the source of the traffic. There is no guarantee that a given populatio will behave with any certainty in an intrinsically stationary fashion. Monday and Frida morning business traffic may resemble shock waves—everybody tries to use the facilitie The clearest example of the failure of the Poissonian M/M/1 and similar models is th arrival rate at a fast-food restaurant located near an office complex: the distribution c arrival is practically zero between 10 a.m. and 11:30 a.m. and then an impulse, or shoc wave, begins at 11:30 a.m. when the large corporations in the vicinity let out all th employees at the same time for lunch. A similar scenario occurs with mass transit at rus hour. Fortunately, the designer of a private network need not worry about the Mother' day or Christmas day traffic abnormalities that affect the public telephone network However, he/she would have to worry if the company ran a big quarterly promotio involving many customers calling the firm using an 800 number.

Some industries (e.g., travel agencies and retail stores) are affected by seasona factors. If the seasonal effect is substantial and predictable, it may be incorporated int a design. For example, one might order additional WATS access lines in August i preparation for the November through January shopping season.

Computer-generated traffic may almost be deterministic at high load (such as when a buffer fed by bulk storage empties out to a circuit every 10 ms) and bursty at lighter loads. This limitation could be circumvented by using time-dependent queueing models; however, in practice, this generally is not done.

Mixed Types of Traffic

In most situations, the traffic may be mixed from several radically different sources, such as data and voice input to a PBX and incoming local telephone traffic versus incoming national toll traffic versus incoming international traffic. Popular models do not account for this traffic mix. Holding times may be a function of the time of day, message content, and other factors. Traffic patterns at business centers differ from those characteristic of rural and semi-rural areas. The classical models may have been fine until a few years ago when PBXs only carried voice. In regard to public and private ATM switch sizing—with traffic consisting of data from terminals, workstations, servers; LAN traffic; voice storage; file transfers from PCs; and video—the assumption of single type of traffic needs to be revisited.

User's Independence

Another assumption made in many optimization models is that all users are independent of each other (also called independently and identically distributed or IID) when, in fact, the opposite may be true. Consider the problem of determining the number of foreign exchange lines needed between a centralized customer service center and a node in a star-configured data communications network (a real problem once confronted by the author). All data customers go through a concentrator in the remote city. A failure in the concentrator or data communications line would prompt all customers in the given city to call the centralized customer service center. These calls would not be independent of each other; the traffic appearing at the tie-line, or FX bundle is correlated.

The large majority of published models that aim at deriving system performance (i.e., delay, throughput, and so forth) assume that the constituents of the community under study are totally independent of each other. There are two reasons for this assumption:

1. Mathematical simplicity for model solution;
2. Uniqueness of the independence condition. Dependence is not expressible in a unique formula; the world is very complex and dependency can take a large number of forms, depending on the underlying mechanism. Technically, mathematical independence is expressed as

$$\text{Probability } (A \text{ and } B) = \text{Probability } A \times \text{Probability } B$$

while dependence is expressed as

$$\text{Probability } (A \text{ and } B) = \text{any admissible function involving}$$
$$\text{Probability } A \text{ and Probability } B$$

Yet, many systems exhibit deep intrinsic dependencies. Even systems that could reasonably be classified as independent (such as toll traffic arriving at a toll switch), lose their independent status under certain circumstances. For example, on Mother's Day, toll traffic arrivals are not independent because the population is driven by societal mechanisms that dictate a certain behavior "across-the-board." Because the dependence condition is no uniquely expressible, one is not able to derive general and elegant results; this is why this subject is rarely if ever approached by the theoreticians and the literature on the subject is very limited. Nonetheless, since dependence is part of any feedback system, it must be considered whether or not elegant results are obtainable.

Surprisingly, once the dependence function is specified, the mathematical analysis is fairly simple. The challenge is to assess the nature of the dependence itself for a given system. Dependence of traffic typically affects ethernet LANs that employ random-access schemes, which are susceptible to instability. It also can adversely affect very small aperture terminal satellite (VSATS) networks using random-access techniques (see Chapter 7).

A system optimized with an independence formula may degrade or fail altogether under the strain of dependent traffic. Two examples of dependency are illustrated here.

First, consider a battleground scenario in which packet radios (digital radio employing the same random access techniques as used in LANs) are placed on soldiers backpacks. Traffic generated by a localized theater is highly dependent on external factors For example, if an artillery shell hits an area, many soldiers may react in a correlated fashion; if bombs are dropped from an enemy aircraft, the same coordinated reaction may be expected; if a formation of inimical hardware is sighted from a panoramic vantage point in the theater, dependent traffic would increase.

Another example of dependency is provided by the financial services industry. The concern for dependency in this environment is that all branches are connected by a broadcast voice channel called "hoot-n-holler." The same verbal message with buy/sell tips and information is simultaneously broadcast to all account executives (AEs). The AEs have several phone lines through the key or PBX system, and data terminals, which also may be through the PBX. As the AEs of any movement or rally in the market, the immediately start to make phone calls to their customers, and/or access the data system to make inquiries or place orders. This setup with the hoot-n-holler wire is a feedback system taken to the extreme. The tenacity of the reaction to a bit of market information may not be fully appreciated by individuals outside the industry; one may get a hint by considering the activity at a trading booth of a major stock exchange. Thus, a movement in the stock market would cause an arrival profile into a branch PBX that is highly correlated. It can be shown analytically that dependency and correlation require additional bandwidth (direct outward dial channels, direct inward dialing channels, or other PBX channels/resources) to avoid grade-of-service degradation.

These are but two of the many examples of dependency tha[t] design.

Dependency is the reason why one may be unable to obtai[n] public network, or is delayed for 10, 20, or 30 seconds during a localized disaster when people, in a dependent way, are trying to employ the system. The "all trunks busy" message is another familiar consequence of dependency (though this can also be caused by other factors). When a locality experiences a disaster, many people in distant places may try to call the city in question.

While some arrival profiles are independent, many are not. One can rationalize that the traffic arrival rate to a customer service bureau on an 800-number connected to a PBX, can be memoryless. In other words, the action of caller number 317 is totally unrelated to any action of caller 316, caller 315, caller 314, and so forth. Even this is not always true—has anyone tried to call a vendor of PC software two weeks after they put a new release of their existing software on the market? The new software may have an obvious bug and all the users may call to inquire or complain.

A particular type of dependence is autocorrelation, in which traffic is related to itself on the time axis. Autocorrelation contradicts the assumption made in standard models that all traffic is independent in relation to itself; this assumption is technically related to the memoryless condition. However, most events are dependent on something that happened prior to them, instead of existing in the vacuum as the models suggest. For example, it is reasonable to believe that outgoing traffic from a telephone station is autocorrelated with incoming traffic to the same station. If the person who designed the networking facilities assumed that all the calls put on the system would independent, he/she risked an incorrect design unless at least some effort was made to incorporate the autocorrelation. Imagine, for instance, that the boss comes in at 8:01 a.m. and asks, "Why haven't we installed that terminal in Miami on the LAN for the regional vice president?" One can be absolutely sure that the phone calls that follow are not random but highly correlated.

- The first call is to a subordinate in New York to get a status report on the installation; the subordinate has no definitive information.
- The second call is to the Miami communications/MIS administrator to get the local view; he/she says that the terminal vendor didn't deliver.
- The third call is to the terminal vendor in Miami; he/she promises to deliver today.
- The fourth call is to the Miami MIS administrator to relay this information.
- The fifth call is to the MIS director in New York to ascertain that the mainframe was GENed to accept the new terminal.
- The sixth call is to the Miami VP to assure him/her that the terminal will be in today.
- The seventh call is to the boss to tell him/her that everything is under control.
- The eighth call is be to the subordinate to tell him to make sure he/she keeps on top of the situation.

It is now 9:17 a.m.

Chapter 7 works out one example in closed form to show the impact of correlated traffic.

Memoryless Behavior

The above scenario crystallizes the deficiencies of all mathematical models that assume memoryless traffic arrival profiles: they simply imply that business is conducted in a vacuum without any consideration of priot events. Memoryless conditions suggest that what happens in the next few time intervals (e.g., minutes) is totally unrelated to what happened in the past few time intervals.

Other Assumptions

Other pathologies of standard networking models that a designer should be aware of when trying to optimize networks include the following:

Steady State

Standard optimization models assume that networks operate in a steady state. All available formulas make this assumption. Only the simplest model, the so-called M/M/1, offers a tractable (though highly complex) transient solution, as the true time-dependent behavior is called. Most communications systems operate in a transient mode, rather than in a steady state mode. Steady state basically means that users generate traffic that is stable with reference to time; in other words, if that traffic is stable, the system will eventually reach the steady state. It suggests that traffic reaching a an ATM switch or PBX has the same effect on the equipment as a stone dropped in a pond has on the water—the surface contour of the pond is temporarily in a turbulent state that calms down within a few seconds or minutes. What the practitioner has available to him through the conventional teletraffic formulas is an expression that describes the surface of the pond a long time after the stone is dropped. This formula would be valid if only a single stone is dropped and if the observer waits a certain (large) amount of time. However, if stones are constantly being thrown into the pond (at an interval that is shorter than the settling time), then the steady state equation is approximate, at best, and useless, at worst.

Because the traffic arrival rates are quite variable with respect to time, the communications systems (i.e., PBX, processor buffers, packet switches, frame relay switches, and ATM switches) never actually reach a steady state.

Filtering

Because both voice and data traffic are buffered, serviced, and manipulated at various stages within a communications system, one rarely has a "virgin" traffic input. This changes the original character of the traffic even if it happened to follow the theoretical Poissonian models implied by the above discussion in the beginning. This change could affect on the number of facilities needed.

For example, a voice message coming to a person's desk through a switching apparatus represents a different type of traffic than the same message routed to a voice storage unit after going unanswered. In the former case, the PBX is done once it routes the call to the destination station; in the latter case, the PBX also is responsible for handing-off the call to the voice storage system. The fact that the message was first posted to the destination station implies a smoothing-out of the arrival profile.

Single Call Per Interval

Another assumption intrinsic to Poissonian models is that a specific user is only able to generate one call into the system in a short interval. This assumption may also be weak. For example, the traditional vision of a stockbroker with several simultaneously-active phones through the same PBX is potentially accurate. With narrowband ISDN, a user has two or even three open sessions (2B + D). With BISDN, up to 4,096 simultaneous connections can be initiated over a single user-network interface. A computer may simultaneously initiate several dozen calls through the PBX or ATM switch, as in the case of an electronic message system that broadcasts the same message to many mail boxes.

4.6.2 Impact of Assumptions

The aggregation of all the constrictive assumptions described above results in the Poissonian models (i.e., Erlang B family, Erlang C family, M/M/1, and so on), which are the "bread and butter" of classical teletraffic engineering. Professional telecommunications managers may be nominally aware of these limitations, yet may continue to employ these models. Because of the criticality of a large enterprise-wide network to an organization, it may be advantageous to employ more sophisticated design techniques. The issues listed above are just a few of the simplifications imposed by standard models. In some cases, these simplifications may not have a significant impact; in other cases, they may have a substantial effect.

An empirical fact that generally can be counted on is: the simpler a model is, the easier it is to use but also the more approximate it is; the more sophisticated and accurate the model is, the more difficult it is to use but the more accurate it is. The extra effort involved in using a more complex model may be well worth it the end. More cost-effective designs that provide a better grade-of-service at the same time are the rewards for those who endure.

4.7 CONCLUDING COMMENTS ON MODELS

The points presented above are not meant to imply that analytical models are not useful, but rather to convey some of their limitations, particularly those of the more popular ones. Models play an important role in developing a sound network design. There are many models in the literature and some do attempt to be realistic by including some real-life factors. Often, though, these models either are not used by the practitioner (he/she may not be aware of them or has not realized the need to move away from standard models) or are too computationally complex to be employed.

In some cases, a corporation may need to hire professional teletraffic consultants and engineers to carry-out a complex design. This option is preferable to attempting to learn and apply a very complex discipline from scratch, and should pay for itself in a very short time in terms of better service and lower recurring costs. Unfortunately, in many organizations, teletraffic engineering is a fairly low-level function and sometimes is assigned to entry-level personnel.

When evaluating network models, it is important to maintain a focus on the improvement being sought. The percentage of improvement attained by using one model over another should always be explicitly established. That determination will be worth the time and expense. It would be wasteful, for example, to try to optimize a network using a more accurate model when an input traffic component may have an inherent error range of ± 20 %. Yet very few telecommunications managers have a "firm handle" on the traffic figures that represent facilities usage. Indeed, determining these figures is not a trivial task. If the traffic input is within an error range of ± 20 % (for example, one presumes that the network is going to handle 20,000 messages a day when it may actually handle anywhere from 16,000 to 24,000 messages), it would not pay to try optimize the network with an ultra-sophisticated model. In this case, an Erlang B or C model may suffice; any additional effort should first be directed at obtaining more accurate traffic figures, and later on the modeling itself.

Some users have been known to try to fine-tune one part of their network design to ± 5% of accuracy while other parts are left at ± 20% accuracy. The practitioner should keep a proper perspective of network models so that the confidence and reliability of the various assumptions and parameters are in the same approximate range. This awareness should be maintained without expending resources to refine a part of an equation and the corresponding data, only to find no valid marginal utility. This approach toward network models will actually save design and implementation money for a typical Fortune 500 firm. The error in a computation is always as large as the largest error in any one variable, regardless of the degree of accuracy of other variables.

Another important factor to remember in this regard is the validity of the available data. Some people feel that they can rest assured as long as they have, for example, three sources of the data. In reality this argument can be fallacious. Are the three sources of the data independent, or just three copies of the same data? For example, a telephone company bill, a comptroller's PC file, and a corporate communications file are not necessarily three independent (i.e., trustworthy) sources of data. The comptroller's data are most likely a database created from the telephone company bill, and is therefore a secondary source of little, if any, value. (It could even contain errors and corruptions from transcription.) The corporate communications' data, used to track expenses, are also probably based on the telephone bill. *Just because one has three sources does not mean that one has reliable data.*

Resist the temptation to feel confident based on the number of data sources, unless you can demonstrate that they are independent, up-to-date, and consistent. Of course, the PBX, ATM switch, file server, or router itself can unequivocally provide answers to some traffic questions. However, this is not generally the case when it comes transmission facilities management.

In conclusion, one must be aware of the following when designing networks:

1. The popular models are very approximate. One should appreciate a priori that a design based on these models is intrinsically a "first cut." The design process involves continual fine-tuing—one cannot walk away from it after the initial plan is made.
2. If possible, to use or derive a more accurate model. Some of these refinements are mentioned to in the next section; others may be found in the literature. This approach involves additional data and computer programs to solve numerical problems. Simulation may occasionally prove useful.
3. Make sure that all the variables used in a model have the same degree of precision, or confidence. If 99 pieces of data are known within a range of $\pm 5\%$ but 1 piece is known only within a range of $\pm 20\%$, it is likely that the final answer will only have a 20% level of precision.
4. Most important of all, routers, PBXs, switches, protocol monitors, and other such equipment provide excellent measurements. It may be well worth it to use the real scenario documented by the equipment (i.e., the actual arrival distribution, actual number of people requiring resources, actual blockage, and so on) rather than a hypothetical environment set up by an abstract model. A lot of the design strategies currently in use are leftover from the days when one had no access to a computer and was forced to work with a simple equation that could be tabulated or solved in closed form. With the advent of computers, many of the previous limitations of a data-driven approach have effectively vanished; teletraffic practitioners should weigh the advantages of employing real data instead of constrictive, stochastic assumptions made solely for the purpose of solving the integrodifferential/difference equations.

Practitioners who design networks must make dozens, if not hundreds, of assumptions and engineering judgments, many of which are ignored by optimization models. One does not always find these issues treated extensively in the thousands of theoretical queuing models available. In particular, modeling usually does not address adequately the issue of customer behavior, not only in terms of traffic but in market dynamics, vendor loyalty, tariff and pricing sensitivity, and reaction to improvement or degradation of service. In the end, one may very well wonder if the cumulative sum of all errors—a few of which were described above—will result in an incorrect number of facilities. Indeed, these issues may be in part responsible for the degraded service sometimes experienced by a number of private networks.

REFERENCES

[1] Minoli, D., "Queueing Fundamentals for Telecommunications," DataPro Report MT30-405-202, January 1987.
[2] Minoli, D., "Engineering PBX Networks: Part 1—Design Models," DataPro Report MT30-315-101, September 1986.
[3] Cooper, R. B., *Introduction to Queueing Theory,* 2d Ed.; New York: North Holland, 1981.
[4] Bear, D., *Principles of Telecommunication Traffic Engineering,* England: Peter Peregrinus, 1974.
[5] Kleinrock, L., *Queueing Systems,* Vol. I and II, New York: Wiley-Interscience, 1975.
[6] Cohen, J. W., *The Single Server Queue,* Amsterdam: North Holland, 1969.
[7] Jaiswal, N. K., *Priority Queues,* New York: Academic Press, 1968.
[8] Syski, R., *An Introduction to Congestion Theory in Telephone Systems,* London: Oliver and Boyd, 1960.
[9] Gross, D., and C. M. Harris, *Fundamentals of Queueing Theory,* New York: John Wiley, 1974.
[10] Minoli, D., "Net Optimization Takes Practical Insight," *ComputerWorld,* May 6, 1985.
[11] Minoli, D., "Network Models Inadequate?" *ComputerWorld,* May 13, 1985.
[12] Fisz, M., *Probability Theory and Mathematical Statistics,* New York: John Wiley, 1963.

Chapter 5
Queueing and Teletraffic Techniques

In this chapter, we review the popular and commonly-employed classical models [1–2]. The assumptions intrinsic to these models will not be further discussed. (As indicated in the previous chapter, these assumptions generally are: memoryless users, memoryless servers, infinite population, time invariance, steady state, user independence, single type of traffic, no filtered traffic, blocked calls not resubmitted, and so on.) Additional information can be found in References [3] through [25]. These references also contain some more sophisticated models, which are generally found in journals rather than in texts.

At least six model variables come into play when looking at congestion systems and queues in general. Assuming a single type of traffic reaches a switch, such as an ATM or frame relay switch, these factors are:

- The arrival rate distribution;
- The size of the population generating the traffic;
- The distribution of the calls' length;
- The way the queue that builds up is managed (i.e., first-in-first-out, random order, or priorities);
- The maximum length of the queue, depending on buffer space;
- The behavior of the customers that are delayed (i.e., call retries, defections, reneging, and balking).

In the discussion that follows, we will describe some of the basic combinations of these six factors. Observe that if each factor has three possible subcases—in reality, many more are likely—then one has 729 discrete models with which to contend. A repertoire of tools is thus needed in designing broadband networks.

Both queueing models (more applicable to data communications, as discussed in Sections 5.1 and 5.2) and teletraffic models (more applicable to voice and video communications, as discussed in Section 5.3) are examined. Chapter 6 particularizes some of these models to specific communications environments.

5.1 BASIC QUEUEING MODELS

5.1.1 M/M/1 Model

The M/M/1 model is an exponential interarrival system, with a single server obeying the exponential distribution. The queue management discipline is first-in-first-out. As defined earlier, let $\rho = (1/t_{bar})/(1/x_{bar}) = \lambda/\mu$. Then the probability that there will be n customers in the system is

$$p_n = (\rho)^n (1 - \rho)$$

The average number of customers in the system is

$$L = \rho/(1 - \rho)$$

This last expression can also be written as

$$L = \lambda/(\mu - \lambda)$$

The number of customers in the queue is

$$L_q = (\rho)^2/(1 - \rho)$$

The average time spent waiting in the queue is

$$W_q = (\lambda)/[\mu (\mu - \lambda)]$$

The total average time in the system is

$$W = 1/(\mu - \lambda)$$

Note that Little's formula states that

$$L = (\lambda) W$$

For example, consider a private ATM switch with a multimedia messaging server connected to it. The large ("infinite") number of users generate requests with an exponential interarrival time, at an average of one request every 500 ms. The database inquiry mechanism has been determined by observation to require exponential service time, with an average lookup time of 475 ms. What type of service will the users receive? Here $t_{bar} = 0.500$ and $x_{bar} = 0.475$, so that

$$\lambda = (1/t_{bar}) = 2.0$$
$$\mu = (1/x_{bar}) = 2.105$$
$$\rho = \lambda/\mu = 0.95$$

The probability that n customers will be trying to access the messaging system is

$$p_n = (\rho)^n (1 - \rho) = (0.95)^n (0.05)$$

so that

Probability 0 users $= p_0 = 0.05$
Probability 1 user $= p_1 = 0.0475$
Probability 2 users $= p_2 = 0.0451$ and so forth.

The average number of customers waiting in the system is

$$L = \rho/(1 - \rho) = 0.95/0.05 = 19$$

$$W = 1/(\mu - \lambda) = 1/(0.500 - 0.475) = 40 \text{ sec}$$

This may be too long; an end-user might become frustrated waiting 40 sec to hear or see the message after he/she presses the Enter key on the station pad or terminal.

The system administrator is considering the idea of purchasing a new disk drive and controller that would reduce the service time to 0.350 ms. The drive costs $15,000. Is the expense justified in terms of improved response time? The new calculations to answer the question are as follows:

$$\lambda = (1/t_{bar}) = 2.0$$
$$\mu = (1/x_{bar}) = 2.85$$
$$\rho = \lambda/\mu = 0.7$$

The average number of customers in the system is now

$$L = \rho/(1 - \rho) = 0.7/0.3 = 2.3$$

The total average time in the system is

$$W = 1/(\mu - \lambda) = 1/(0.500 - 0.350) = 6.6 \text{ sec}$$

The new drive would certainly improve the situation considerably for this messaging system. Note a key fact that is typical of queueing systems: the new drive is better than the old one, but although it is not even twice as fast (the old read time is 0.475 versus the new read time of 0.350), the delay is improved by a factor of six. Conversely, the traffic load might go up by only 1%, but the delay might increase by 100%. See Figure 5.1. This is why one must be familiar with the results of queueing theory when designing a telecommunications or data communication system.

The equations above provide the average waiting time. In the M/M/1 case, one can actually derive the full distribution of the waiting time. For more information, the interested reader can consult any of the reference books listed at the end of this chapter.

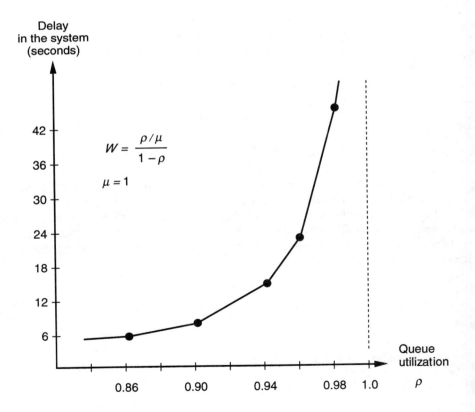

Figure 5.1 Sensitivity of delay to the queue utilization.

5.1.2 M/M/1/K Model, FIFO Queue Discipline

The M/M/1/K model is a system with a limited number of waiting positions: only K positions are available (by definition, K also includes the number of servers). This is typical of many real situations (e.g., a store, bank, or restaurant). It is also characteristic of communications systems, for example: trunks in a transmission system between two ATM switches, registers in a traditional telephone switch, dialup ports to a frame relay packet assembler/disassembler (PAD), and buffers in a front end system (FEP). Again, one sees the need for the results of queueing theory, since the grade-of-service in such a system is intimately related to the number of available queueing slots. In addition, many customers may be blocked in this situation; the designer needs to know how many customers are turned away (or as shown later, the number of servers that would be required to serve, for example, 99% of the customers).

The probability that there will be n customers in the system, with n clearly less or equal to K, is

$$p_n = (\rho)^n (1 - \rho)/[1 - (\rho)^{K+1}], \text{ when } \rho < 1$$
$$p_n = 1/(K + 1), \text{ when } \rho = 1$$

The average number of customers in the system is

$$L = (\rho)(g/h), \text{ with}$$
$$g = [1 - (K + 1)(\rho)^K + K(\rho)^{K+1}]$$
$$h = [1 - (\rho)^{K+1}](1 - \rho)$$

The average number of customers actually in queue is

$$L_q = L - [(\rho)(1 - \rho^K)]/[1 - (\rho)^{K+1}]$$

The average time spent waiting in the system is obtained from Little's formula:

$$W = L/[(\lambda)(1 - p_K)]$$
$$W_q = W - 1/\mu$$

For example, consider a teleshopping system that has five 800 toll-free numbers staffed by a single operator ($K = 5$). When the single operator is busy, the calls are held in a queue by way of an announcement. However, since there are only five lines in the rotary, at most only five customers can be in the system at any one time (one in service and four waiting). Data collected show that

$$\lambda = 5 \text{ per min (average customers arriving per minute)};$$
$$\mu = 6 \text{ per min (average customers served per minute)}.$$

Before deciding to get more WATS lines in the rotary (still with one operator), the owner of the shop wants to know the average system size, the average queue length, the average waiting time for service, and the average waiting time for those customers that are held by the announcement.

Using the above equations, the owner calculates that

$$\rho = 5/6 = 0.833$$
$$L = \{0.833\ [1 - 6(0.833)^5 + 5(0.833)^6]\}/[0.833(1 - 0.833^6)] = 1.97$$
$$L_q = \{1.97 - (0.833)[1 - (0.833)^5]\}/[1 - (0.833)^6] = 1.22$$
$$p_5 = [(0.833)^5(1 - 0.833)]/[1 - (0.833)^6] = 0.10$$
$$W = 1.97/[(5)(1 - 0.1)] = 0.438 \text{ min}$$
$$W_q = (0.438 - 0.167) = 0.271 \text{ min}$$

To determine how many customers are lost on the average, one must determine the probability of an arriving call finding four people waiting for the operator, and multiply this by the average arrival rate λ. The desired number is

$$(\lambda)(p_5) = (5)(0.10) = 0.5 \text{ customers per min}$$

or one customer every two minutes. Thus, it may pay for the owner to get a few more WATS lines, since this number is fairly high (10% of arriving customers are lost).

5.1.3 M/M/c Model

The M/M/c model is a multiserver queueing system with c servers. This system finds wide applicability. Examples include: a bridge toll plaza with many booths, a bank with many tellers, a trunk bundle with several trunks in the bundle, a fixed-head disk drive in which several records can be read/written simultaneously, a customer service bureau with several incoming 800-lines and several reps, and a PAD with several incoming ports.

The equations for the measures of effectiveness of the M/M/c appear to be complicated but, in reality, are straightforward algebraic expressions that can easily be programmed in BASIC or any other PC language. It was indicated that in a multiserver queue

$$\rho = \lambda/(c)(\mu)$$

Note $n! = n(n - 1)(n - 2)(n - 3) \ldots (3)(2)(1)$. For example, $5! = (5)(4)(3)(2)(1) = 120$. For convenience of notation, $r = \lambda/\mu$. Then the equations for FIFO queue management are:

$$p_n = [(\lambda)^n p_0]/[n!(\mu)^n], \text{ when } n \text{ is between 1 and } c$$
$$p_n = [(\lambda)^n p_0]/[(c)^{n-c} c!\ (\mu)^n], \text{ when } n \text{ exceeds } c$$

The p_0 term required in these two equation must be calculated first, and is

$$p_0 = 1/\left[\left(\sum_{n=0}^{c-1} r^n/n!\right) + cr^c/c!(c-r)\right]$$

The nomenclature $\Sigma r^n/n!$ is a mathematical short hand for the expression

$$(1 + r + r^2/2 + r^3/6 + r^4/24 + \dots + r^{c-1})/(c-1)!$$

One finds the average waiting time in the system to be

$$W = \{r^c(\mu)/(c-1)![c(\mu) - \lambda]^2\}p_0 + 1/\mu$$

whereas from Little's formula the average number of customers in the system is

$$L = (\lambda)W$$

An example will clarify how these expressions are really very simple. A printer server connected to a LAN actually has three printing devices that can be employed by the printer server manager as needed in order to meet requests from LAN users. Print requests average six per minute and each printer can print, on the average, three jobs per minute. The following two measures are of interest:

1. The average time a job must spend in the printer-server system;
2. How many print jobs, on the average, are waiting.

Here $c = 3$, $\mu = 3$, $\lambda = 6$. Thus $r = \lambda/\mu = 2$. Thus, one has

$$p_0 = 1/[(1 + 2 + 2^2/2!) + 3(2)^3/3!(3-2)] = 0.11$$
$$W = 1/3 + \{3(2)^3/2! \,[(3)(3) - 6]^2\}(0.11) = 0.48 \text{ min}$$
$$L = (6)(0.48) = 2.88$$

5.1.4 M/M/c/K

Consider now the case in which the arrival distribution and the service distribution are exponential. There are c servers, but there are only K waiting positions; customers reaching the system when the K positions are full are turned away (K inlcudes c servers, i.e., the total number of customers in the system). The equations for this model are a bit more algebraically complex than those of the previous model, but essentially similar. Again,

$$r = \lambda/\mu$$
$$s = \lambda/(c)(\mu) = \rho$$

One then has

$$p_n = [1/n!] \, (r)^n p_0, \text{ when } n \text{ is between } 1 \text{ and } c - 1$$

$$p_n = [1/(c)^{n-c} c!](r)^n p_0, \text{ when } n \text{ is between } c \text{ and } K$$

$$p_0 = 1/\left\{ \left[\sum_{n=0}^{c-1} (r)^n/n! \right] + [r^c/c!] \times [1 - s^{K-c+1}]/[1 - s] \right\}, \text{ when } s \text{ is not equal to } 1$$

$$p_0 = 1/\left\{ \left[\sum_{n=0}^{c-1} (r)^n/n! \right] + (r^c/c!)(K - c + 1) \right\} \text{ when } s \text{ is equal to } 1$$

$$L_q = \{p_0[(c)(\rho)]^c \rho\}\{1 - (\rho)^{K-c+1} - (1 - \rho)(K - c + 1)(\rho)^{K-c}\}/\{c!(1 - \rho)^2\}$$

$$W_q = L_q/[(\lambda)(1 - p_K)].$$

(The algebraic expression for L is too long to show here, but is approximately $L_q + c$.) Again, these expressions can easily be programmed on a PC. An example will clarify the application of these formulas. Consider the previous situation of the LAN printer-server, with the additional limitation that, because of storage considerations, only seven jobs total can be queued by the system. Assume here that $\lambda = 1$, $\mu = 0.166$, $c = 3$, and $K = 7$. Then, $r = 6$ and $\rho = s = 2$. Next, one must calculate p_0.

$$p_0 = 1/\left\{ \left[\sum_{n=0}^{2} (6)^n/n! \right] + [6^3/3!] \, [1 - 2^{7-3+1}]/[1 - 2] \right\}$$

$$= 1/\{[(6)^0/0! + (6)^1/1! + (6)^2/2!] + [6^3/3!] \, [1 - 2^5]/[-1]\}$$

$$= 1/\{[\, 1 + 6 + 18 \,] + [36] \, [31]\}$$

$$= 1/1141 = 0.00088$$

Then

$$L_q = \{0.00088[(3)(2)]^3 2\}\{1 - (2)^{7-3+1} - (1 - 2)(7 - 3+1)(2)^{7-3}\}/\{3!(1 - 2)^2\}$$

$$= \{0.00088[6]^3 2\}\{1 - (2)^5 + (5)(2)^4\}/\{3!\} = 3.08 \text{ jobs}$$

The delay is

$$W_q = L_q/[(1(1 - p_7)]$$

The p_7 term can be calculated from the expression above and is around 0.5, so that $W_q = 6$ min.

5.1.5 A Classic Result When Comparing the M/M/1 to the M/M/c Queue

Given the information provided thus far, one is now able to appreciate a classical result of queueing theory. This result says that it is always better to have a single server whose power is equal to the total power of c servers, than c servers with c queues. In other words, given three bank tellers, it is better to let them function as a single server and form a single line, than to form three separate lines.

The following example demonstrates this result (the general result can be demonstrated analytically based on the formulas). Assume that each teller can serve three customers per minute, that there are three tellers, and that the customer arrival rate is six per minute. In the M/M/3 case one has

$$\lambda = 6, \ \mu = 3, \ c = 3, \ r = 2$$

and, as calculated in the M/M/c example earlier, the delay is 0.48 min per customer. In the single line case, the combined teller pool can handle nine customers a minute; thus in the M/M/1 case, one has

$$\lambda = 6, \ \mu = 9$$
$$W = 1/(\mu - \lambda) = 1/(9 - 6) = 0.33$$

min per customer; which is considerably better than the 0.48 min calculated for the M/M/c. Intuitively, the result is justified based on the fact that if there are three lines, and one line empties out, the idle server is of no benefit to the other two lines (no queue switching is assumed in the model—queue switching may "automatically" occur with people, but it may not happen with computer resources). *Note that this result indicates that, with the same staffing, one can provide better service to the customers. This carries over to the telecommunications field: if a system is properly configured in regard to queueing, one can provide a better grade-of-service while keeping the cost constant.*

One example in which this finding this might apply is in designing a tie bundle between two PBXs. One might dedicate the first 12 channels of a DS1 link to hunting by PBX1 to communicate with PBX2, and dedicate the last 12 channels to hunting by PBX2 to communicate with PBX1. Effectively, one has segregated the service-providing resource into two servers. The above discussion shows that it would be better from a grade-of-service point of view not to segregate the T1 link, but to let each PBX hunt for the first available trunk.

5.1.6 M/M/c/c (Erlang B Formula)

A special case of the M/M/c/K model and the listed formulas is of great importance to the telecommunications field. When one lets $c = K$, one obtains the Erlang loss formula (also known as the Erlang B formula), which is probably known by every practitioner. This formula has been used to engineer the telephone plant since it was derived by A. K. Erlang in 1917. As users started to employ PBXs in the 1950s and 1960s, the formula was exported to that environment; when data communications started to emerge in the 1960s and 1970s, the formula was carried over.

In this model, the queueing positions are equal (in fact, they coincide with the servers). Each server is a trunk in a trunk bundle of c channels. A user requiring a trunk will either get one of the c channels or be turned away. Note that in this system there is only blocking not a delay, since there can be no more users than there are servers (i.e., $K = c$).

Specializing the formulas given above, one obtains the following expression for the probability that c servers (channels) are occupied:

$$p_c = \{[(c)(\rho)]^c/c!\}/\left\{\left[\sum_{n=0}^{c}[(c)(\rho)]^n/n!\right], \text{ with}\right.$$

$$\rho = (\lambda)/[(c)(\mu)]$$

This expression is simpler than the previous formula because p_0 works out to be straightforward. This equation is easily programmable on a PC, like all others given above, but, because of its importance, it has been tabulated in the well-known Erlang B table.

A small portion of an Erlang table is provided below. There are three variables shown in the table: the number of channels, the probability that all such channels are in use, and the amount of traffic offered to the entire queueing system. By knowing any two of these variables, one can derive the third. Let $A = (c)(\rho)$.

A Portion of an Erlang B Table

c	$p_c = 0.001$	$p_c = 0.01$	$p_c = 0.05$	$p_c = 0.1$
5	$A = 0.76$	$A = 1.36$	$A = 2.22$	$A = 2.88$
10	$A = 3.09$	$A = 4.46$	$A = 6.22$	$A = 7.51$
15	$A = 6.08$	$A = 8.11$	$A = 10.6$	$A = 12.5$
20	$A = 9.41$	$A = 12.0$	$A = 15.2$	$A = 17.6$

Usage Type 1. The arriving traffic and the number of channels are known; obtain the probability that an incoming call will find all channels busy (i.e., there is no room in the queue). For example, 12.5 units of traffic arrive at a PBX trunk bundle with 15 channels. What is the percentage of calls unable to get through? Using the above table, one finds that 10% of the calls will be blocked ($p_{15} = 0.1$).

Usage Type 2. The arriving traffic and the type of blockage are known; determine the number of channels required to achieve the desired grade of service. For example, 4.46 units of traffic arrive at a PBX trunk bundle; the designer wants to make sure that only 1% of the calls are turned away. How many channels are required? Using the above table, one finds that 10 channels are necessary to do the job.

Usage Type 3. The number of channels and the blockage (p_c) are known; determine the offered traffic that can be handled by the queueing system. For example, 20 channels on a T1 link are allocated as trunks. By design one keeps the blockage at 5%. How much offered traffic can such a system really carry? Using the above table, one finds that the system can carry 15.2 units of traffic.

The importance of this formula lies in the fact that not only does it hold for the M/M/c/c case, as shown by the above derivation, but in fact it holds for the much more general case M/G/c/c, with any general (G) distribution. This means that one can use the Erlang table (or a PC program) to determine any type of server behavior. As long as the arrival of the calls follows an exponential distribution then, regardless of the distribution of the calls' duration (the meaning of service time in this context), one can employ this machinery. More information on Erlang B models can be found in Section 5.3.3.

5.1.7 M/M/∞ Model

This model is easily solved, because of the limiting nature of the equations. Here one has "infinitely" many servers. Such a model would apply to any self-service system in which a large population employs the resources. For example, a large supermarket in which shoppers take goods from the shelves and then queue prior to reaching the cash registers is an example of a series-of-queues, which will be discussed below.

One finds that:

$$p_n = (\lambda/\mu)^n \, e^{-(\lambda/\mu)}/n!$$
$$L_q = 0$$
$$L = \lambda/\mu$$
$$W_q = 0$$
$$W = 1/\mu$$

5.1.8 Finite Source Queues

All the models discussed thus far assume an infinite population from which service requests can originate. In reality, the population is never infinite. Formulas can be derived for all the above models under the finite population condition. These equations are somewhat "messy" but are still algebraic, and can fairly easily be programmed on a PC. Generally, if the population exceeds 250—and certainly if it exceeds 1,000—and the number of servers is correspondingly small, one can employ the formulas for an infinite population to derive a good approximation. When the population is below 50, one should employ the finite population formula. The interested reader can consult [9] and [12] for detailed information. Section 5.3.11 provides a teletraffic perspective on finite population queues.

5.1.9 Queues With State-Dependent Service

There are situations in which the service rate is not constant. For example, servers could speed up as the queue becomes longer, spending less time on each customer (e.g., the time spent by a manager on each individual item of incoming mail may decrease when there is a big backlog of unread mail, such as after a long vacation). On the other hand, the servers could become bogged-down when too many customers demand service, and actually slow down. Other examples of variations in service rate could be based on the time of day.

Gross & Harris [15] report some results in this area for the interested user. These models are generally approached with the Birth-Death C-K equation method.

5.1.10 Queues With Two Types of Arriving Traffic

Situations with two or more types of incoming customers are very common, particularly in a communications environment. For example, the traffic streams arriving at a private ATM switch—from internal and external voice users, from asynchronous and synchronous data users, and from file transfer requests from LAN interfaces—have fairly different characteristics and should be modeled as different classes of users [3].

Cooper [16] reports some results in this area for the interested user. Several of the available models have algebraic solutions that can be run on a PC.

5.1.11 Queues With Impatience

A customer is said to be impatient if the customer only tends to join the queue when a short wait is expected. Such a customer tends to remain in line only if the wait is sufficiently short; in other words, if the customer encounters an excessive wait, he/she becomes impatient and leaves before receiving service. This behavior affects the profitability of the service-providing establishment. The manager of the establishment would want to ensure that the queue is not so long as to prompt customers to leave.

Impatience is very common in telecommunications systems. For example, how long is a PBX user in a least cost routing environment willing to wait to find an available trunk that is cheaper than DDD? How long is a customer willing to wait on a camp-on line for the party to complete the call in progress? How long will a PBX user wait for a dialtone, before hanging up and redialing? How long will a data user who has just pressed the Return key on the workstation wait for a computer response before starting to press the Return key in succession?

Generally, an impatient user creates, by his/her own action, additional delays to himself/herself and to other users because a certain amount of resources will be invested by the system just to manage these overhead activities.

Three forms of impatience have been studied. One is balking, or the reluctance of a customer to join a queue upon arrival. Another type is reneging, or the reluctance to remain in line after joining and waiting (see Section 5.3.8 below). The third type is jockeying, or switching lines in a multiserver environment.

Gross & Harris [15] provide some models of these three factors. The models can be programmed on a PC.

5.1.12 Erlangian Models (M/E$_k$/1 and E$_k$/M/1)

Before discussing queues with more general arrival and service distributions, two models involving the Erlang-k distribution are surveyed. The Erlangian distribution is similar to the exponential distribution M considered thus far, but it is more general and more flexible in its attempt to model real-life situations (see Table 4.2). This is partially related to the fact that this distribution has two parameters instead of just one, as in the case of the exponential. The parameters are μ and k, which control the mean arrival/service time and the variance of the arrival/service time, respectively. Here $E(X) = 1/\mu$ and $V(X) = 1/(k)(\mu)^2$.

	Sample	Distribution	Mean	Variance
Erlang-k	any positive number	$(\mu k)^k x^{k-1} e^{-k\mu x}/(k-1)!$ μ positive; k is an integer	$1/\mu$	$1/k\mu^2$

Note that the exponential distribution has a mean of $E(X) = 1/\mu$ and a variance of $V(X) = 1/(\mu)^2$. Obviously this distribution can be molded more easily into a real-life problem because the analyst is able to fit not only the mean but also the variance. When $k = 1$, both distributions are identical.

For example, a telecommunications analyst would like to start an ATM networking design effort. He/she begins by trying to assess the type of traffic that will be involved. The telecommunications manager knows that only a sample of the data (not the totality) must be collected. The manager randomly obtains the following data (in a real example, the manager should collect at least 1,000 samples):

Length of calls (min)
9
1
17
9
2
15
7
13
9
11

Does this data fit the exponential distribution, so that the Erlang B table can be used? To answer this question in an intuitive way, one calculates the mean and variance of the collected data:

$$E(X) = (9 + 1 + 17 + 10 + 1 + 15 + 7 + 25 + 2 + 18)/10 = 10.5$$
$$E(X^2) = (81 + 1 + 289 + 100 + 1 + 225 + 49 + 625 + 4 + 324)/10 = 169.9$$
$$V(X) = E(X^2) - E(X)^2 = 169.9 - (10.5)^2 = 67.75$$

If this data came from an exponential distribution with mean of 10.5, then one should see a variance of 111, since an exponential distribution with the mean $1/\mu = 10.5$ should have a variance of $1/(\mu)(\mu) = 110$. Here, however, the variance is only 67. One can deduce that the message length is approximately Erlangian, with a mean of 10.5 and $k = 2$; this would correspond to a variance of 55, which is much closer to the observed data.

The $M/E_k/1$ model that would be required here has the following performance characteristics:

$$W_q = [(k + 1)/(2k)] \, [\lambda/(\mu)(\mu - \lambda)]$$
$$L_q = (\lambda)W_q \text{ (from Little's result)}$$

Note that, for $k = 1$, one obtains the previous results for the M/M/1 model, as expected.

The $E_k/M/1$ model is somewhat more complex (see [15]); some approximate results can be derived from the G/M/1 model below.

5.2. ADVANCED QUEUEING SYSTEMS

A number of telecommunications situations require a more advanced model involving distributions other than the exponential or Erlangian PDFs discussed thus far. The C-K equation method is no longer applicable and the researcher must deal with the concept of embedded Markov chains. Fortunately for the practitioner, fairly simple measures of effectiveness can be derived with the Pollaczek-Kintchine (P-K) method that is described below.

5.2.1 M/G/1

A general expression for the probability of n customers in the system is available; however, this is an integral equation and generally cannot be solved in closed form. What is of value to the practitioner is the P-K result, as described below.

Let s_B^2 be the variance of the service distribution. Since the practitioner, in principle, knows the service distribution, then he/she can easily calculate the variance with the equation

$$s_B^2 = V(B) = E(B^2) - E(B)^2$$

Then the P-K equation states that

$$L = (\rho) + [(\rho)^2 + (\lambda)^2(s_B^2)]/[2(1 - \rho)]$$
$$W = L/(\lambda)$$
$$W_q = W - 1/(\mu)$$
$$L_q = L - (\lambda)/(\mu)$$

This is a fairly powerful result, since it states that one is able to derive the queue's measures of performance based on knowing just the mean ($1/\lambda$) and the variance (s_B^2) of the service distribution.

For example, a telecommunications manager is designing a least cost routing system for a PBX using call-queueing when the trunks in question are occupied. The problem facing this manager is that there are data as well as voice calls going through the PBX, and so the conventional wisdom of assuming exponential call duration is not defensible. To proceed, the manager measures the mean and variance of the calls, which is easily accomplished, and determines that

$$\text{Mean} = 1/\mu = 1 \text{ min } (\mu = 1)$$
$$\text{Variance} = s_B^2 = 5 \text{ min}$$

The variance is high because of the data calls. The manager notes that the distribution is not exponential (if it were, the variance would have been 1), and is not Erlangian (if it were, the variance would have been less than 1). The only choice is to use the P-K equation. The manager knows that $1/\lambda = 4$, so that $\rho = 0.25$. Therefore, the delay to obtain access to the one (and only) tie trunk to London, England, is

$$L = (0.25) + [(0.25)^2 + (0.25)^2(5)]/[1.5] = 0.5$$
$$W = L/(\lambda) = (0.5)/0.25 = 2 \text{ min}$$

If the variance was higher, such as 20, the delay would be 4.5 min.

In another example, packetized voice systems through Ethernet LANs are starting to appear. A telecommunications manager knows that if the intrapacket delay exceeds 0.25 sec, then the speech quality will be very poor. Here, one has a M/D/1 situation, because all packets are of the same length; this model can be solved with the method above. In the deterministic situation, the variance is zero so that

$$L = (\rho) + [(\rho)^2]/[2(1 - \rho)]$$
$$W = L/(\lambda)$$

from which the designer can easily carry out the assessment.

5.2.2 M/G/c/∞ and M/G/c/c

One may wish to use a more generic model with c servers instead of a single one. The resulting formulas are somewhat complicated. The interested practitioner can consult [15–16] for information on how to solve this model.

It should be recalled at this juncture that the Erlang B solution discussed earlier under the M/M/c/c model is actually applicable to the more general M/G/c/c situation.

5.2.3 G/M/1

In the G/M/1 situation, one would like to solve a queueing problem with general arrival rate and exponential service time. This is a very important model in telecommunications and data communications, because in the real world the arrival rate of customer's service requests is actually not exponential in nature. The reason why so much attention is paid to the exponential model is that it is easy to solve; therefore one assumes that the exponential arrival would be a reasonable approximation—sometimes this is true, but many times it is not. Therefore, solutions to the G/M/1 queue are of interest.

An example of G/M/1 model is when a telecommunications manager has decided to employ a software-defined network to connect two PBXs in a networking arrangement, with overflow to DDD when more than SDN-provided resources are available. It is difficult to assess the characteristics (distribution) of the traffic that overflows out of the SDN; overflow traffic is filtered, and is almost always impossible to describe in precise Poissonian terms. Therefore the manager decides to employ the G/M/1 technique.

Solutions to this model exist and can be found in any text book (see [16], for example); unfortunately the complexity of the solution is beyond the scope of this discussion. The interested reader may consult any of the references listed at the end of this chapter.

5.2.4 G/G/1

The G/G/1 model by nature has the widest possible applicability to all sorts of communications and noncommunications problems because both the arrival distribution and the service distribution are assumed to be general. The following quote form Kleinrock's text [18] will, however, put the problem in perspective:

> this difficult system (whose mean wait cannot even be expressed simply in terms of system parameters) is studied through the use of the spectral solution to Lindley's integral equation

Fortunately, there are approximation methods, discussed below, that can be employed to obtain some reasonably accurate results in this area.

5.2.5 Other Models

The previous sections have concentrated on fairly standard queueing models. There are many other models that should be of interest to a telecommunications and data communications professional since these find wide applicability in many communications environments encountered daily. Some of these models include:

- Queues in which the arrivals are serviced in ways other than first-in-first-out (FIFO); this may be typical of how a PBX treats calls;
- Queues in which customers are treated based on a priority scheme; this is typical of many of the data and voice communications systems that carry different types of traffic;
- Queues in series, particularly when the departure distribution is not exponential; all data communications and telecommunications networks are actually queues-in-series (from which an exact analysis of a data communications/telecommunications situation should really start, not from the simpler models that are popularized by the trade press);
- Queues found in complex teletraffic applications; these are found in applications involving the internals of a voice network (e.g., a public network, a private voice network, or a software-defined network);
- Approximation methods when very little information is known a priori; these techniques can be applied to any queueing situation, including the G/G/1 model discussed above.

The reader interested in some results for these types of queues can consult the following references:

Topic	Reference
Reference non-FIFO queues	[16]
Priority queues	[19]
Queues-in-series	[15]
Nonexponential departures	[17]
Advanced teletraffic	[9, 13]
Approximations	[18]

Most of the research in the nonexponential departure models has been done recently under the thrust of data communications and telecommunications. Information on this topic has not yet been exhaustively collected in one book, but can be found various journals.

Table 5.1 provides a summary of the key queueing models discussed in Sections 5.1 and 5.2.

Table 5.1

Summary of Results (L = Average length of queue; W = Average delay)†

Model	Result
M/M/1	$L = \lambda/(\mu - \lambda)$ $W = 1/(\mu - \lambda)$
M/M/1/K	$p_n = (\rho)^n (1 - \rho)/[1 - (\rho)^{K+1}]$, when $\rho < 1$ $p_n = 1/(K + 1)$, when $\rho = 1$ $L = (\rho)(g/h)$, with $g = [1 - (K + 1)(\rho)^K + K(\rho)^{K+1}]$ $h = [1 - (\rho)^{K+1}](1 - \rho)$ $W = L/[(\lambda)(1 - p_K)]$
M/M/c	$\rho = \lambda/(c)(\mu)$ $p_n = (\lambda)^n p_0/[n!(\mu)^n]$, when n is between 1 and c $p_n = (\lambda)^n p_0/[(c)^{n-c} c! \, (\mu)^n]$, when n exceeds c $p_0 = 1/\left[\left(\sum_{n=0}^{c-1} r^n/n! \right) + c r^c/c!(c - r) \right]$ $W = \{ r^c(\mu)/(c - 1)![c(\mu) - \lambda]^2 \} p_0 + 1/\mu$ $L = (\lambda)W$
M/M/c/K	$r = \lambda/\mu$ $s = \lambda/(c)(\mu) = \rho$ $p_n = [1/n!] (r)^n p_0$, when n is between 1 and $c - 1$ $p_n = [1/(c)^{n-c} c!](r)^n p_0$, when n is between c and K $p_0 = 1/\left\{ \left[\sum_{n=0}^{c-1} (r)^n/n! \right] + [r^c/c!] \, [1 - s^{K-c+1}]/[1 - s] \right\}$, when s is not equal to 1 $p_0 = 1/\left\{ \left[\sum_{n=0}^{c-1} (r)^n/n! \right] + (r^c/c!)(K - c + 1) \right\}$, when s is equal to 1 $L_q = \{ p_0[(c)(\rho)]^c \rho \} \{ 1 - (\rho)^{K-c+1} - (1 - \rho)(K - c + 1)(\rho)^{K-c} \}/\{ c!(1 - \rho)^2 \}$ (L, the algebraic expression, is too long to show here, but is approximately $L_q + c$) $W_q = L_q/[(\lambda)(1 - p_K)]$
M/M/c/c (Erlang B)	$p_c = \{ [(c\rho)]^c/c! \}/\left\{ \sum_{n=0}^{c} [(c\rho)]^n/n! \right\}$ $\rho = (\lambda)/[(c)(\mu)]$
M/E$_k$/1	$W_q = [(k + 1)/(2k)] \, [\lambda/(\mu)(\mu - \lambda)]$ $L_q = (\lambda)W_q$ (from Little's result)
M/G/1	$L = (\rho) + [(\rho)^2 + (\lambda)^2(s_B^2)]/[2(1 - \rho)]$ with $s_B^2 = V(B) = E(B^2) - E(B)^2$ $W = L/(\lambda)$ $W_q = W - 1/(\mu)$ $L_q = L - (\lambda)(\mu)$

† See the next chapter for areas of applicability.

5.3 TELETRAFFIC MODELS

Before proceeding with these models, some terms and a number of related issues that have a bearing on these models are reviewed.

5.3.1 Traffic Terms

The following terms should be noted, particularly for circuit-switched systems, [4]:

Call-Hour (CH or ch). A unit of traffic density. One call hour is the quantity represented by one or more calls having an aggregate duration of one hour:

$$CH = 36 \text{ CCS} = 60 \text{ Cmin} = 3600 \text{ Cs}$$

Call-Minute (Cmin). A unit of traffic density (intensity). It is the quantity represented by one or more calls having an aggregate duration of one minute.

Call-Second (Cs). A unit of traffic density (intensity). One Cs is the quantity represented by one or more calls having an aggregate duration of one second.

CCS (cent = hundred Call Second). An older unit of traffic intensity used primarily in the United States and Canada. One CCS is the quantity represented by a 100-s call or by an aggregate of 100 Cs of traffic:

$$CCS = 0.02777 \text{ E}$$

Erlang (E). The erlang is the internationally accepted (and best) dimensionless unit of traffic intensity. One Erlang is the intensity of traffic in a resource (e.g., a trunk) that is continuously occupied (e.g., carrying 1 CH per hour or 1 Cmin per minute):

$$E = 36 \text{ CCS}$$

5.3.2 Offered Traffic/Carried Traffic

The amount of *traffic offered* to a trunk bundle or other telecommunications system may not be equal to the *traffic carried* by the system. Some of the traffic may be blocked (or potentially delayed). If T_o is the offered traffic, T_c is the carried traffic, and b is the blocking, the following relationships hold:

$$T_c = (1 - b) \times T_o$$
$$b = (T_o - T_c)/T_o$$

The blocked (overflow) traffic must be handled by a secondary system.

5.3.3 Erlang B

The Erlang B is the most common teletraffic model. It corresponds to the blocked calls lost paradigm of communications. This model was already covered in Section 5.1.6, but is revisited here from another perspective. The probability of a call being blocked, given an offered traffic of A erlangs to N full-availability channels is

$$P(N,A) = (A^N/N!)/(1 + A^1/1! + A^2/2! + A^3/3! + ... + A^N/N!)$$

with

$$N! = (N) \times (N - 1) \times (N - 2) \times (N - 3) \times ... \times 2 \times 1$$

For example, $5! = 5 \times 4 \times 3 \times 2 \times 1 = 120$. This is called the factorial function. Because $N!$ grows very rapidly, it is not practical to apply the definition directly to obtain the desired values, because of the roundoff errors accumulated by the software. For small values of N (i.e., N is less than 200) one may consult standard tables.

Tables are not very practical for automated PC-based calculations. Instead, one can employ the following iterative method, which is not affected by roundoff errors:

$$P(1, A) = A/(1 + A), \text{ from the above definition}$$
$$P(k, A) = [A \times P(k - 1, A)]/[k + A \times P(k - 1, A)]$$

For example, if $A = 4$,

$$P(1, 4) = \text{Probability of blocking given a single tie line}$$
$$= 4/(1 + 4) = 0.8 \text{ (from the first equation)}$$
$$P(2, 4) = \text{Probability of blocking given two tie lines}$$
$$= 4 \times 0.8/(2 + 4 \times 0.8) = 3.2/5.2 = 0.615$$
$$P(3, 4) = 4 \times 0.615/(3 + 4 \times 0.615) = 0.451 \text{ and so on}$$

This methodology can be easily incorporated into a PC program (Until recently, prepared tables were the method of choice. They were parametrized on the availability number blocking, offered traffic, and they provided the number of required trunks. Tables generally covered traffic to 250 erlangs).

However, the PC method may become slow for large values of N, for example $N = 1000$, or even $N = 10,000$ (a voice storage model solved by this author for a commercial voice storage system involved calculating the above Erlang terms for N upwards of 20,000). Reference [5] provides a method for calculating of these terms, if needed. To produce a rough approximation when N is greater than 1,000, see below.

The purpose of this model is not only to calculate the blocking probability, but to derive the number of necessary channels to achieve a desired grade-of-service, such as

$b = 0.01$ (this is typical of a public switched network; $b = 0.05$–0.10 may be more typical of a private voice network). In this case, one proceeds by calculating the blocking at the given offered traffic for one, two, and three channels, and so on, until the targeted grade of service is obtained. For example, for 4 erlangs of traffic (i.e., engineering an inter-PBX trunk bundle capable of supporting four simultaneous voice conversations) and a blocking of 0.01, one has

$$P(1, 4) = 0.80$$
$$P(2, 4) = 0.61$$
$$P(3, 4) = 0.45$$
$$P(4, 4) = 0.31$$
$$P(5, 4) = 0.19$$
$$P(6, 4) = 0.11$$
$$P(7, 4) = 0.06$$
$$P(8, 4) = 0.03$$
$$P(9, 4) = 0.013$$
$$P(10, 4) = 0.053$$

Thus, 10 trunks would be required. Note the following interesting fact: probability is an elegant and internally conservative discipline. We are asking a model that assumes a lot of ignorance about the real environment to predict the number of channels that it would take to support four simultaneous calls. Clearly, four trunks should suffice to carry that traffic if one knew the exact fashion in which those four calls originated. But the model must somehow "protect" itself and therefore demands that 10 trunks be provided. This reinforces the argument that the more actual data available, the better. In other words, it may "pay" to invest some effort up front to obtain exact data because it may lead to a less expensive solution.

Another point immediately evident is that the higher the grade-of-service one wishes to provide, the more expensive the solution. For example, for four simultaneous calls: $b = 0.05$ would require 8 tie lines (at full availability), $b = 0.01$ would require 10 tie lines, and $b = 0.001$ would requrie 12 tie lines. The same approach could be used between ATM switches at a macro level.

To obtain a rough approximation of the Erlang B for large values of N, one may use the following small table, which can easily be incorporated in a PC program (see also [5–6]):

	$b = 0.01$	$b = 0.10$
$A = 100$	$N \approx 117$	$N \approx 97$
$A = 200$	$N \approx 222$	$N \approx 188$
$A = 500$	$N \approx 540$	$N \approx 455$
$A = 1,000$	$N \approx 1,040$	$N \approx 920$

	$b = 0.01$	$b = 0.10$
$A = 2,000$	$N \approx 2,025$	$N \approx 1,810$
$A = 5,000$	$N \approx 5,010$	$N \approx 4,510$
$A = 9,000$	$N \approx 9,005$	$N \approx 8,100$

5.3.4 Traffic Overflow

For least cost routing (LCR) and virtual networks, it is important to know the distribution of traffic across a trunk bundle (assuming straightforward trunk bundle management). Once again, all assumptions discussed earlier apply.

Given a full-availability trunk bundle that is searched sequentially, the distribution of traffic of the original A erlangs on the kth trunk is

$$a_k = P(k, A) \times \{k/(1 - P(k, A)) - A\}$$

For example,

$$a_1 = P(1, A) \times \{1/(1 - P(1,A)) - A\}$$

now

$$P(1, A) = A/(1 + A)$$

and

$$1 - P(1, A) = 1/(1 + A)$$

from which

$$a_1 = A/(1 + A) \times \{(1 + A) - A\} = A/(1 + A)$$

The other terms are calculated similarly. Note that, by plotting these terms for a given offered traffic A, the traffic carried by each successive trunk in the bundle decreases. For the above example of 4 erlangs, one has:

$$a_1 = 0.80 \times [(1/.20) - 4] = 0.80$$
$$a_2 = 0.61 \times [(2/.39) - 4] = 0.68$$
$$a_3 = 0.45 \times [(3/.55) - 4] = 0.65$$
$$a_4 = 0.31 \times [(4/.69) - 4] = 0.55$$
$$a_5 = 0.19 \times [(5/.81) - 4] = 0.41 \text{ and so on}$$

he five trunks would carry 0.80 + 0.68 + 0.65 + 0.55 + 0.41 = 3.09 erlangs of traffic the other 0.91 erlangs would overflow to the 6th trunk). See [7] for a computer program o calculate these overflow terms.

The Erlang B model formula remains accurate for any probabilistic distribution of the message holding time (i.e., at least one of the assumptions made in the derivation of his model is not catastrophic). Reference [4] contains ready-made overflow tables.

.3.5 Erlang C

:ather than blocking calls altogether, the PBX, server, or data switch may queue the calls or future access to the resource. Given the same general assumptions of the Erlang B model, one obtains the following expressions (valid for N exceeding A):

- Probability of congestion with N trunks:

  = Probability that an arriving call will have to be queued

  $$= \frac{N \times P(N, A)}{(N - A + A \times P(N, A)}, \text{ which is approximately } P(N, A) \times [N/(N - A)]$$

- Average number of calls on queue:

  $$= \frac{N \times P(N, A}{N - A + A \times P(N, A)} \times [A/(N - A)]$$

- Total probability that the delay for a call will exceed a given value t (assuming a FIFO queue management discipline and an average call holding time of h):

  $$= \frac{N \times P(N, A)}{N - A + A \times P(N, A)} \times e^{-(N-A) \times t/h}, \text{ with } e = 2.718 \ldots$$

(Note that all calls are assumed to be of the same kind: one cannot have in this model calls of average holding time h_1 and calls of average holding time h_2).

- If a call is known to be delayed, the probability that the delay exceeds t:

  $$= e^{-(N-A) \times t/h}$$

hese formulas are for full-availability trunks. The last two formulas only apply to xponential call holding time; other distributions lead to different results. (This was not the case with the Erlang B model, for which the blocking formula held for any message ength distribution.) Also, the delay distribution (but not the average delay) depends

on the queue management discipline; the above formulas only apply to FIFO queu
management.

In this scenario, one wants to calculate the number of trunks N, given an offere
traffic A, so that the probability that a call has to wait for more than, for example, $t = 1$
sec would be less than 0.05. In the past, one had to rely on graphical charts such as thos
found in [8]. Now, one can easily program the third equation on a PC to obtain the desire
answer.

Consider the following example: if $A = 4$ and N is less than 4, the delay will b
infinite. Assuming an average call holding time $h = 1000$ sec, one finds that

$N = 4$: Probability delay exceeds 10 sec
$$= 4 \times 0.31)(4 - 4 + 4 \times 0.31) \times e^0 = 1$$
$N = 5$: Probability delay exceeds 10 seconds
$$= (5 \times 0.19)/(5 - 4 + 4 \times 0.19) \times e^{-(5-4)\times0.01} \approx 0.53$$
$N = 6$: Probability delay exceeds 10 seconds
$$= (6 \times 0.11)/(6 - 4 + 4 \times 0.11) \times e^{-(6-4)\times0.01} \approx 0.27$$
$N = 7$: Probability delay exceeds 10 seconds
$$= (7 \times 0.06)/(7 - 4 + 4 \times 0.06) \times e^{-(7-4)\times0.01} \approx 0.12 \text{ and so on}$$

With seven trunks, a traffic arrival of four simultaneous calls, and an average holdin
time of 1,000 sec, one would expect about 12% of the arriving calls to wait for mor
than 10 sec to obtain a trunk.

Two variants that attempt to factor some realism into the Erlang C model ar
constant holding time and random service.

5.3.6 Constant Holding Time

The formulas presented above are valid for exponentially distributed, or memoryless, ca
length (i.e., if you call someone to make four points, and after two minutes you hav
only discussed the first point, you can be sure that the future portion of the call i
not memoryless). Constant (fixed) length calls are representative of a network carryin
packetized, framed, or cellularized information (e.g., data, voice, or video). In additio
certain subsets of hardware, such as common control devices, have holding time that i
independent of the actual caller behavior and approximately constant. Constant holdin
time is the antithesis of the memoryless situation: if calls all have fixed duration, the
the past duration of the call totally determines the remaining future duration (e.g., 1,00
bit packets flowing through a 9,600 bps channel require 104 ms, so if we know that 7
ms have passed since the beginning of the call, then exactly 34 ms remain). Thus, ther
is the possibility of using these two distributions—exponential and constant—to provid
some optimistic and pessimistic estimates for a number of variables of interest.

As an approximation, the probability of congestion at steady state is the same a
in the exponential case listed above (i.e., if the bundle consists of a single trunk, the tw

expressions coincide). The probability of delay at steady state is less under with a constant holding time, since there is more order in the system (i.e., given a call, one is able to anticipate the time of its departure). Figure 5.2 provides a comparison for a small set of values. For example, with five trunks and 0.5 erlangs of traffic per trunk, the probability of the delay exceeding the holding time is around 0.001 in the constant case and 0.01 in the exponential case. These observations hold for a Poisson arrival rate and FIFO queue management. Reference [9] will point the interested reader to research papers that discuss these issues in detail.

In Figure 5.3, observe that four trunks would suffice to guarantee delay of one holding time with probability 0.01 if one knows that all calls have constant length, five trunks are required if one only knows that the calls have exponential length. The more information one has available about the type of traffic serviced by the switch, system, or network, the tighter the design; this results in fewer trunks, which saves money for the organization.

5.3.7 Random Service

The delay distribution depends on the call queue management (the average delay is the same, regardless of the discipline). One may conceivably program a PBX in such a way that all stations with extension 1xxx (corresponding to executive management users) receive priority service. Similar priorities may be programmed into a data server or other communications system.

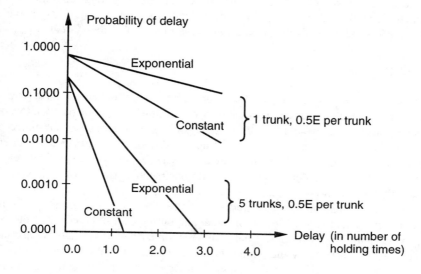

Figure 5.2 Constant holding time.

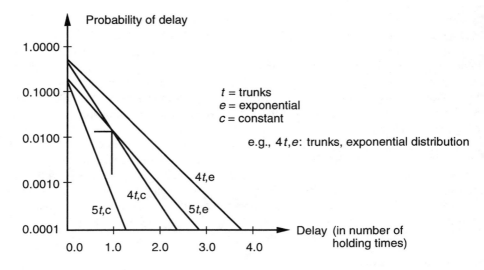

Figure 5.3 Required number of resources.

Queueing in strict order of arrival (FIFO) may not be altogether efficient. Other methods such as scanning in cyclic order, gating (i.e., calls are admitted in batches and then served in random order), or random selection from the queue may be simpler and better. If all calls approximately equivalent in length, then FIFO and random service are nearly the same. If a significant percentage of the calls are very long (common in a data environment) and the balance very short, then random selection is more equitable as it tends to spread out long calls that would otherwise monopolize the system.

5.3.8 Call Defections

The Erlang C model assumes that a caller is prepared to wait for service for a long time, even forever. In practice, long delays cause a proportion of calls to be abandoned and may incite unusual user behavior (e.g., redialing in rapid succession or an unnecessary request for dial tone). If the system is well-designed and the queueing delay is small, defection should not be a problem since few users will become impatient. Call defection may become significant under heavy load conditions (such as file transfer situations in a voice/data PBX) or in a fault situation.

Under heavy defections, the grade-of-service for a user depends on both the individual user's reaction to the delay problem and on the overall behavior of the rest of the users. When a user is willing to "hang on" for some time, fewer calls are abandoned and more traffic is carried by the bundle in question. One might say that the efficiency increases at the expense of service—a classical tradeoff. In turn, this hanging-on implies that the probability of congestion increases, so that an impatient user will be more likely o eventually defect if the entire population itself is patient. If the population as a whole s impatient, more defections occur, thus the route becomes less congested and the impatient ser can get through.

Of course, the refined model that takes into account this effect is somewhat complicated. However, the formulas listed below can once again be fairly easily programmed into a PC.

Defining $1/L$ as the average time an user will wait before defection (in terms of average holding time), one obtains for an infinite population:

- Probability that all N available trunks are busy:

$$E_D = [K \times P(N, A)]/[1 + (K - 1) \times P(N, A)] \text{ with}$$

$$K = [(N/L) \times e^{A/L} \times G(N/L, A/L)]/(A/L)^{N/L} \text{ with}$$

$$G(N/L, A/L) = \int_0^{A/L} t^{(N/L)-1} e^{-t} dt$$

(This is the incomplete Gamma function; it can be found in tables or calculated numerically with a PC program.)

- Probability that a call does not have to wait for a trunk:

$$P = [N/A] \times [1/K + A/N - 1] \times E_D$$

- Average waiting time (averaged over all calls):

$$A \times [N/L] \times [1/K + A/N - 1] \times E_D$$

- The probability that a call that has already waited t time will have to wait more:

$$p(\text{Wait} > t) = E_D \times G(N/L, Ae^{-t}/L)/G(N/L, A/L)$$

It can be verified that if $L = \infty$, these formulas reduce to a loss system without defection. f $L = 0$, they reduce to a delay system without defection). The formula for a finite number f sources is much more complicated; see [9].

We are not suggesting that these somewhat complicated formulas must be employed; y listing them, we hope that the reader will appreciate why a design based on a simplified methodology may fail to provide the desired grade-of-service.

.3.9 Other Variants

The assumption up to now was infinite queue capacity. Reference [9] provides some models for finite queues, systems with simple priority schemes, and limited availability.

5.3.10 Effect of Call Retries

Another factor not considered by the classical models is the behavior and treatment of the overflow traffic. These models simply assume that if the traffic is blocked on the first try, it disappears forever. This is hardly the case in real life. When the blocking is small (e.g., 0.001 to 0.01), then the overflow/blocked traffic is small and it can perhaps be ignored. However, if the blocking is around 0.05 to 0.10, as may be the case in some private networks, then it should be considered in the design. This traffic reappears in the system, requiring new service. Even if the trunk occupancy may not always be directly affected, there may be an impact on other components of the system (e.g., common control), including overflows. All circuit-switched services, including frame relay and cell relay, are subject to blocking and, hence, retries.

The amount of blocked traffic that overflows to a DDD, WATS, or virtual network is important to consider in calculating traffic-sensitive costs incurred over and above the fixed tie trunk expenditures.

A number of approaches have been developed to address this problem, two of which are briefly discussed below. All methods have two factors in common: (1) they postulate a certain behavior on the part of the population in case of blocking, which may be mostly an analytical nicety to obtain a solution; (2) the behavior is parametrized in terms of certain variables that, at best, must be quantified and, at worst, are difficult to pin down. The suggested approach is to actually study recall behavior through the real data made available by the PBX, router, or switch, and employ this numerical characterization in the design process.

Simplest Method

This approach assumes that the interval between successive attempts is very long and that an unsuccessful call has a fixed probability of being retried. If r is the average number of retries per call, then it can be shown with these two assumptions that the blocking with N trunks would be $P(N, A \times r)$, with $P(N, A)$ being the Erlang-B term defined above. This simple model states that retries increase the average rate, and thus the offered traffic, by the factor r (note that r was averaged over all calls, not just those that were blocked). The problem with this model is not only the question of the the validity of the assumptions, but that of measuring or calculating r. A more refined model can be found in [9] and [23].

Extended Erlang B (EEB)

Jewett has published an approximate method and related tables [10, 11] in which the blocked traffic is recycled back into the first-attempt traffic until the overflow traffic i

ffectively zero. The recycling does not necessarily correspond to the physical mechanism
that would occur in a PBX system, since these events are temporally shifted; the method
oes through a synthetic, a priori cycling process and derives the number of trunks. What
he EEB designates as first-attempt traffic and recalls on each subsequent cycle are not
he exact pure calls and recalls that are being connected and unconnected; however, the
nd result of using first-attempt traffic and approximating the overflow with this techniques
ive a first-order estimation of total line usage. This is important for traffic-sensitive
onfigurations.

The method assumes that blocked traffic looking for trunk resources overflows to
 DDD, or similar arrangement, with probability p_1; it dies (i.e., is never retried and
isappears) with probability p_2; and it reappears into the switch for trunk retry with
robability $1 - p_1 - p_2$. Two problems with this method are: (1) the overflow traffic is
gain assumed to be Poisson, when that is not the case; and (2) evaluation of p_1 and p_2.

To obtain the first-attempt traffic, one needs the percentage of calls or service
equests that overflow, that retry, and that legitimately disappear from the system. This
nformation is not traditionally collected, but it can be measured (to an extent). To calculate
rst-attempt traffic, all attempted calls to a channel must be known. To collect this data,
ll calls from particular station numbers are posted to a database the first time that a
pecific destination is dialed from a given station. If a call is blocked and later is retried
rom the given station to the same remote destination, it would not be included in the
ally. Blocked calls can be similarly tabulated to determine those overflowing, retrying
he destination again, or abandoning (a judgment must be made on the length of the
nterval for the decision window). Studies indicate that this data can be measured and
nalyzed in mechanized form using a computer.

Analysis of blocked traffic is a necessity, particularly for systems that have high
nitial blocking. The Extended Erlang B is, at least, a refinement on the classical model
hat discounts this traffic. Tables are available for the EBB based on typical values of p_1
nd p_2, but they are fairly expensive. Alternately, a simple PC program can be constructed,
sing the information supplied in [10] and [11].

.3.11 Finite Sources

o improve the traditional models, one can factor in the finite nature of the user population.
f the population is over 1,000, the infinite model does not introduce a substantial
berration, in this respect. However, if the population is smaller, the impact can be marked.
Note that the population is not the size of the organization; it is the size of the group
ikely to use the facilities in question. This number could be small indeed (e.g., a mail
lerk in a branch office in Albany is not likely to need to call the corporate headquarters
n Houston).

Blocked Calls Cleared (Erlang B)

The formulas to use in this case are:

$$a = A/[(M - A \times (1 - B)]$$
$$B_N = [(M - N) \times a \times B_{N-1}]/[N + (M - N) \times a \times B_{N-1}] \text{ with}$$
$$N = \text{number of trunks}$$
$$B_N = \text{blocking with } N \text{ trunks}$$
$$M = \text{number of users}$$
$$A = \text{offered traffic}$$

This is called a *system of equations* (i.e., they must be solved simultaneously), not a explicit formula. Methods exist to solve a *linear* set of equations. However, this set i not linear and therefore must be solved iteratively and numerically. (References [12] an [26] present a more complex formula, but it is also implicit and must be solved iteratively The way to proceed is as follows:

1. Having calculated $B1$ for given values of a and M, other B_N terms can be obtaine by iteration, and A can be calculated in terms of a, M, and B_N;
2. A numerical relationship (table) for B_N against A for a given M can then b constructed, eliminating the variable a (which, in practice, is hard to measure an quantify).
3. One continues to calculate these terms until the value B_N is just below a pre established threshold value (e.g., 0.01), with N being the required number c channels.

This procedure can be programmed on a PC with some effort. Convergence mus be carefully designed into the program. References [12] and [26] provide some table but they are mostly given in terms of the variable *a*, not *A* (the offered traffic), an therefore hard to use. Although this approach is more correct and accurate than the Erlan B method, it is somewhat more complicated and thus has not been used.

It will result in a design with fewer trunks, thereby saving money for the organization For example, for 12 erlangs of traffic, one has:

Number of Users	Required Trunks (P = 0.001)	Required Trunks (P = 0.01)
12	12	12
18	17	16
25	20	18
∞	24	20

Saving seven trunks on a New York–Chicago trunk bundle, presuming one know that only 18 users could possibly be requiring said facilities at a 0.001 grade-of-servic would result in an approximate yearly savings of $100,000. Note that if there are exactl

2 users generating 12 erlangs of traffic (i.e., 12 simultaneous calls), 12 trunks suffice ince there is no one left to contend for these resources; on the other hand, if there are ,000 people generating the same 12 simultaneous calls on average, then 24 trunks are equired because of the probabilistic chaos generated by people joining and abandoning ne system.

locked Calls Delayed, Finite Sources

hese formulas are very complex. The interested reader may consult [12], [13], and [26].

.3.12 Non-Poisson Traffic

1ost real-life traffic is non-Poisson in nature in spite of assertions to the contrary. Examples f non-Poisson traffic include any types of buffering, multistage filtering, overflows, onmemoryless users, and data (particularly when aggregated from many users such as n a "production" LAN). As discussed in Chapter 4, random process are described in :rms of probability distributions.

A Poisson distribution with a mean $\beta = 2$ would have the following distribution:

Arrivals	Probability
0	0.135
1	0.270
2	0.270
3	0.180
4	0.090
5	0.036
6	0.012
7	0.003
8	0.001
...	...

Recall the meaning of probability: if you repeated the experiment 1,000 times or lore, then 135 times you would encounter 0 arrivals. Given a single experiment, however, ne is not able to make any statement. For example, even if one established that the -rival pattern between 9 a.m. and 10 a.m. on Monday morning was exactly Poisson with 1 average of two calls, then one could say nothing at all about the traffic on September , 1993, or September 15, 1993, or September 22, 1993. All one could say is that if one 1easured the number of arrivals for Monday mornings for 20 years (i.e., 1,000 xperiments), one could relatively certain, assuming a totally time-invariant situation, that le average number of calls would turn out to be 2, despite the fact that one Monday lorning one could have 0, another could have 27, another could have 1, another could ave 0, and so on. In turn, a seven-trunk design based on this model of two calls on

average would provide reasonable service on average. In other words, the system woul‹
be adequate when one got 0,1, or 2 calls, but not on the days when one got 27 calls. Thi
would be true in spite of the model pathology that requires seven trunks just to guarante
that the system will be able to accommodate two simultaneous calls, on the average.

A different distribution might be what is called binomial. In this case, for the sam‹
average arrival of two calls ($n = 20$, $p = 0.1$):

Arrivals	Probability
0	0.121
1	0.272
2	0.285
3	0.191
4	0.089
5	0.031
6	0.008
7	0.002
8–20	<0.001 each term
>20	impossible

Note that here only 12.1% of the experiments would result in a 0 arrival, compare‹
to 13.5% in the Poisson case. Another distribution could be the following:

Arrivals	Probability
0	0.1
1	0.1
2	0.1
3	0.1
4	0.1
5	0.1
6	0.1
7	0.1
8	0.1
9	0.1

A precise characterization of the probabilistic nature is given by specifying th‹
entire distribution, as we have done above. This, however, involves many numbers. /
less comprehensive, but still useful, description is based on the ratio of the mean of th‹
distribution to the variance of the distribution. The formula is

$$a = \{E(X^2) - [E(X)^2]\}/E(X)$$

This is a single number. When this ratio is less than 1, the traffic is said to b‹
smooth; at 1 the traffic is called random, though this is a misnomer; when the ratio exceed‹
1, the traffic is called rough or peaked. Distributions with longer tails, which correspon‹

rough traffic since the variance is much higher than the mean, require more trunks or sources than distributions with shorter tails. Ratios in the 0.5 to 2.0 range are typical PBX systems (a ratio of 1 corresponds to the Poisson distribution). Similar information not readily available for other equipment (e.g. routers or broadband/multimedia users). o fully describe a distribution mathematically would require specifying the infinite list "moments," of which the mean and variance are the first and the second.

An interesting family of distributions is the Gamma distribution. This distribution a generalization of the exponential and affords more realism in arrival process. Two arameters, r and a, describe the arrival. The more parameters available, the more realistic e description. (An analogy is that trying to express a thought just using words beginning ith the letter A would be difficult. If you are allowed to use words that begin with A d B, it is a little easier. If you are allowed to use words that begin with A, B, C, D, , and F, it is much easier. This indicates that as the number of parameters increases, alism increases. The exponential distribution with a single parameter cannot describe a mplex, multidimensional world.). See Figure 5.4.

A method called equivalent random method, from Wilkinson, may be employed for e cases where the ratio is not equal to 1. The approach states that for a given offered affic of mean A and a variance of V, a corresponding, equivalent Poisson traffic load ith mean A' offered to a trunk bundle with S trunks will produce an overflow traffic ith moments A and V. If the load A' and the value of S can be derived, then the number servers t required to meet the stated grade of service can be ascertained. The number trunks to provide the same grade of service to the A, V traffic is the difference between and t.

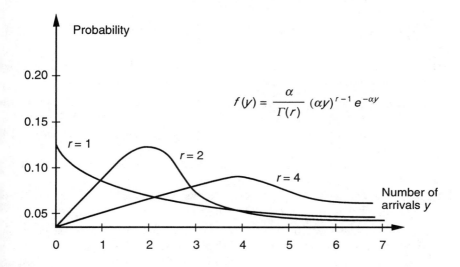

$$f(y) = \frac{\alpha}{\Gamma(r)} (\alpha y)^{r-1} e^{-\alpha y}$$

gure 5.4 Gamma distribution.

Computation of A' and S are difficult in analytical form, and one must again reso to approximations. One empirical simplification [14] is

$$A' \approx V + 3 \times a \times (a - 1)$$
$$S \approx A \times [(A + a)/(A + a - 1)] - (1 + A)$$
$$a = V/A$$

For example if $A = 10$, $V = 14$, then $a = 1.4$. Using this empirical formula,

$$A' \approx 15.68$$
$$S \approx 6.2$$

Using an Erlang-B table (or program) one sees that it takes 25 trunks to provi 0.01 blocking; 19 trunks would be (empirically) required to service the 10 non-Poiss erlangs (versus only 15 trunks to serve 10 erlangs of straight Poisson traffic). Th highlights a possible cause of performance degradation should a PBX system be designe with a simple Erlang B table. Reference [9] provides additional information on this subjec

5.3.13 Conclusion on Classical Models

In this chapter, we have looked at the popular models, and how the six factors characterizir a congestion system may affect the solution methodology. Whenever possible, one shou try to employ the more accurate techniques. These will produce more robust designs th can weather traffic overloads and stress in a more reliable way.

5.4. SIMULATION

While literally thousands of models have been solved analytically, one may find that the models suffer from the following limitations:

1. The practitioner needs to solve a problem, but he/she does not know if that particul model has already been solved before, and where the solution might be found;
2. The model can be found in the literature, but the solution is not in terms of algebraic equation;
3. The model can be found in the literature, but the solution is too complicated attempt.
4. Though a similar model has been solved before, this model does not exactly fit th situation at hand.

One way to circumvent these limitations of the analytical models is to empl simulation. Simulation is a well-developed discipline that allows the practitioner to bui a microcosm of the real world on the computer and then let the computer search f the solution.

Simulation requires expert designers, programmers, and a nontrivial amount of computer time. Yet it is often employed to obtain solutions to very complicated problems.

Simulation can be written in any high-level programming language; however, there actually are computer languages explicitly designed for simulation. The most well-known and commercially available are: General Purpose Simulation System (GPSS, an IBM product) and SIMSCRIPT. Several other languages also are available. See [15] and [16] for additional information and references on simulation.

REFERENCES

[1] Minoli, D., "Queueing Fundamentals for Telecommunications," DataPro Report MT30-405-202, January 1987.

[2] Minoli, D., "Engineering PBX Networks: Part 1—Design Models," DataPro Report MT30-315-101, September 1986.

[3] Minoli, D., and E. Lipper, "Mixed Classes of Traffic Obeying Different Queueing Rules with Reference to Integrated Packet Switched Networks," Record of 1978 Can. Conf. on Comm. and Power, pp. 1–4.

[4] Roger, F.R., *Reference Manual for Telecommunications Engineering*, New York: Wiley Interscience, 1985.

[5] Dill, G. D., and G. D. Gordon, "Efficient Computation of Erlang Loss Functions," *Comsat Technical Review*, Vol. 8, No. 2, Fall 1978.

[6] Akimaru, H., et al., "Truncated Error of Asymptotic Expansion for Erlang Loss Function," *Transactions of the IECE of Japan*, Vol. E66, July 1983.

[7] Minoli. D., "Getting the Most WATS for Every Communications Dollar," Data Communications, September 1980.

[8] ITT-SEL, *Teletraffic Engineering Manual*, Germany: Ernst Klett Buch, 1966.

[9] Bear, D., *Principles of Telecommunication Traffic Engineering*, England: Peter Peregrinus, 1974..

[10] Jewett, J. E., "Extended Erlang B Approach to Long Distance Network Design: Without Upping or Queueing," *BCR*, May/June 1976.

[11] J. E Jewett, "Extended Erlang B Approach to Long Distance Network Design: Without Upping or Queueing," *BCR*, July/August 1976.

[12] Beckmann, P., *ABC of the Telephone, Elementary Queueing Theory and Telephone Traffic*; Lee's ABC of the Telephone Publisher, Geneva, IL.

[13] Syski, R., *An Introduction to Congestion Theory in Telephone Systems*, London: Oliver and Boyd, 1960.

[14] Briley, B. E., *Introduction to Telephone Switching*, Reading, MA: Addison-Wesley, 1983.

[15] Gross, D., and C. M. Harris, *Fundamentals of Queueing Theory*, New York: John Wiley, 1974.

[16] Cooper, R. B., *Introduction to Queueing Theory*, MacMillan, 1972.

[17] Cohen, J. W., *The Single Server Queue*, Amsterdam: North Holland, 1969. Kleinrock, L., *Queueing Systems*, Vol. I and II, New York: Wiley-Interscience, 1975.

[18] Kleinrock, L. *Queueing Systems*, Volumes 1 and 2, John Wiley, New York, 1975.

[19] Jaiswal, N. K., *Priority Queues*, New York: Academic Press, 1968.

[20] Whit, W., "Blocking When Service is Required From Several Facilities Simultaneously," *AT&T Technical Journal*, October 1985.

[21] Minoli, D., "Engineering Two-Ways Foreign Exchange Trunk Bundle Systems," *Computer Communications*, Vol. 3, No. 2, April 1980.

[22] Bakmaz, M., "A Procedure for Optimal Dimensioning of Trunk Groups While Serving Two Traffic Loads With Different Grade of Service," IEEE Trans. on Comm, June 1983.

[23] Bretschneider, G., "Repeated Calls With Limited Repetition Probability," *Proc. of 6th International Teletraffic Congress*, 1970, pp. 434/1–5.

[24] Lawson, R. W., *A Practical Guide to Teletraffic Engineering and Administration*, Chicago: Telephony Publishing Corp., 1983.

[25] Hills, M. T. Seven-part series on engineering issues, *Business Communications Review*, Nov/Dec 1982–Nov/Dec 1983.

[26] Beckmann, P., Lee's ABC of the Telephone Publisher, Geneva, IL.

Chapter 6

Putting It All Together: A Performance Analysis Guide for Lower Layer Protocols†

6.1 INTRODUCTION

This chapter applies the general queueing methods described in the previous two chapters to the study of data communications networks. The goal is to supply ready-made formulas for the assessment of the performance of a number of typical data networking environments, guided by the functional layering of the open systems interconnection reference model (OSIRM). The chapter is pragmatic in nature, and the formulas supplied are as simple as they can be. In most cases, references are provided to indicate the open-literature source of the equations. Figure 6.1 depicts the series of queues that are encountered by transactions as they make they way through the protocol stack, typically from an application, toward the physical communications link (this does not include any end-system delays, such as getting the data from a database server).

Typically the tools provided in this chapter are

1. Simple analytic formulas derived from queueing or teletraffic theory;
2. Results of measurement, extended to a generic formula;
3. Results of a discrete-event simulation model, extended to a generic formula.

These tools are for use by communications planners who need to ascertain that mission-critical corporate networks operate as expected to maintain workforce productivity, but who do not have the resources and/or inclination to commission a multiple staff-year study tailored to their specific environment. The tools are designed to assist practitioners on a macro-level of planning.

---

† This chapter was supplied by R. Leighton, U S WEST Advanced Technologies.

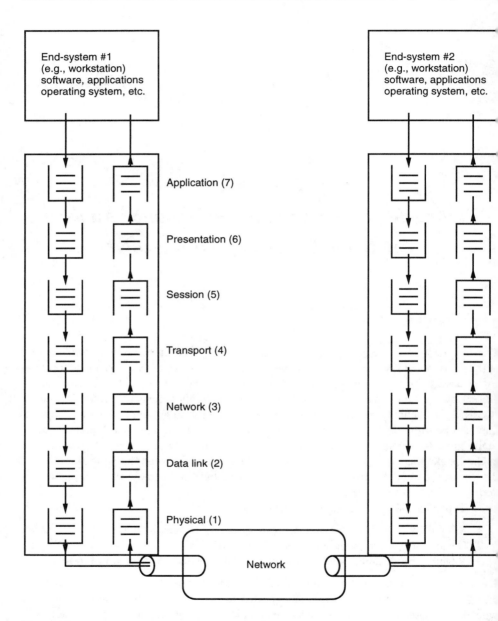

Figure 6.1 Transmission delays mapped to the OSIRM.

Although use of the analytic tools of this chapter do not require special skills, the explanations and assumptions may be given in formal terms (e.g., queueing theory), particularly in the listed references. The material presented in this chapter is not over-simplified models so much as it is simplified estimates taken from sophisticated work described in the open literature.

A performance analysis can result in substantial savings over the lifecycle of a project. Sometimes this type of analysis is not undertaken because of the perception that such efforts must necessarily be very complicated, resource intensive, and time consuming. There are many documented cases in which a simple, high-level analysis in the development stage of a project would have prevented problems that required changes later in the project, resulting in significant monetary losses.

Listed below are some situations in which a cost-performance analysis on a high level is recommended in the initial stages of development

- The project is in the early phase of design or planning in which a broad sense of performance and cost is all that is necessary;
- There is a need for many scenarios and/or topologies to be tested; for example, determining the cost of different service levels, such as the difference between completing 90% of the transactions within 5 seconds versus within 3 seconds;
- Detailed operations data are not available, which is a common real-life situation. For example, why complicate the analysis by taking into account the variance of a component (e.g., message length) when variance data are totally lacking? A high-level, sensitivity analysis often justifies and prioritizes the extra effort to obtain additional operations data;
- The workload of the application is not yet known or has not been characterized in any detail;
- Management will not approve a long, expensive study (such as the development of a detailed, discrete-event simulation model) that requires skills not readily available. In fact, a high-level study often justifies the need for such a longer study;
- The expertise to do a detailed analysis is simply not available;
- There is an advantage for the person directly involved in the systems analysis or planning of the project to do the simplified analysis. By doing the analysis, he/she gets a "feel" for the required infrastructure, which does not always happen when outside, skilled assistance or a mechanized tool is used.

Because pertinent assumptions need to be stated for any mathematical model, two of the most common ones employed to derive the results listed below are discussed in communications terms. The first assumption often made concerns the nature of the transaction arrivals. In this chapter, it almost always is assumed that these arrivals follow a Poisson probability distribution. The second assumption concerns the probability distribution of the service times. This relates to communications work in the form of the transmission times or, in other words, the probability distribution of message lengths (transmission time = message length/transmission or data rate). Usually, the probability distribution is assumed to be either deterministic (fixed) or exponential. This assumption essentially defines the variation or amount of variance in the message length. In traditional low-speed data communications networks, experience shows that the variance may fall between the above two distributions. In practical terms, this means that using a deterministic distribution will give an optimistic result and using an exponential distribution will give a pessimistic result [1]. Traffic patterns for new, high-speed applications—such as multimedia, imaging, and video conferencing—have yet to be determined; they will become better known in the next few years.

There are several other complications that must be addressed. First, a given function that has performance implications, may occur in several OSIRM layers and be implemented in different ways. For example, check summing may be implemented in the data link layer in hardware, or it may exist in the transport layer in software (there are other variations as well). The ramifications of these two alternatives are of major significance to the performance of the protocols.

The second complication concerns the "queue decomposibility" of the individual layers or even the functions being performed within them. Figure 6.1 shows that communications consists of a series-of-queues. In this chapter, each layer and the functions within it is analyzed as an independent decomposable system, which can be solved one at a time. In most situations, the series-of-queues is not decomposable, and therefore must be treated as an interconnected ensemble. The performance equations for a model that takes into account the lack of decomposibility are very complicated; they sometimes must be solved by iteration or the model must be analyzed by use of discrete-event simulation. Furthermore, this approach is most difficult if not impossible to use in practical engineering planning work. Reference [2] discusses a model that accurately describes queues within most of the OSIRM layers that are not independent, that is, the performance equations cannot be solved by themselves.

The following treatment is organized on the basis of OSIRM layers, with the network layer information presented first followed by the data link and MAC layers. The network, link, and MAC sections identify the transmission protocol performance data for their respective layers, when these are of individual interest.

6.2 A COST-PERFORMANCE ANALYSIS METHODOLOGY

This section presents a pragmatic methodology for using the equations listed in Sections 6.4 through 6.9 to estimate cost/performance (i.e., delay and throughput) figures for an end-to-end communications system.

We suggest that a formal procedure be followed throughout the methodology with regard to the assumptions made in the analysis. These assumptions encompass both the details of the models and the validity of the data. This procedure is particularly recommended if it becomes desirable to add more detail to the models being used (as discussed below). The basic procedure is to simply, but rigorously, document each assumption made as the analysis proceeds, and to attach two attributes to each assumption. The first attribute is the importance or priority of the assumption. This usually can be determined by examination or, if necessary, by sensitivity analysis. The second attribute is the confidence that the analyst places in the assumption, which is often subjective. An example of such an assumption might be the length of messages being transmitted on a frame relay WAN. The chances are that these values will contribute greatly to the overall transit time, given that the transmission rates are usually relatively lower in a WAN. If it becomes necessary to refine performance results and if confidence is low in the message lengths supplied, it is clear that more effort will be needed to obtain more precise message-length data.

The overall methodology is relatively simple. The costs for shared resources are computed by determining the ratio of the utilization of the resource indicated by the test case (or architecture) to the maximum utilization chosen for the resource and multiplying it by the cost of the resource. This assumes that there is enough work in the rest of the system to "load up" this sharable resource to maximum utilization. Obviously, this assumption could be abused if one considers a resource too large for the situation and then takes advantage of its lower unit cost. However, with a reasonable selection of infrastructure, the assumed level of utilization will be governed by its use in calculating either the transit times (a high utilization will yield higher transit times) or the costs (a high utilization will yield lower unit costs). The steps in the cost-performance methodology are given below.

1. Determine the performance service level to be achieved.
2. Determine the infrastructure to be tested and include the end-systems that contain the upper OSIRM layers (the end-system is most likely a sharable resource). The transit time of an application running over the OSIRM layers must be accounted for if it is included in the transit time under evaluation.
3. Select the transit time and throughput equations given in the next few sections; for the first iteration, the basic building blocks are probably sufficient.
4. Determine the parameters required from the above equations and acquire the needed data (e.g., the lengths of messages are almost always required).
5. Develop the maximum values of utilization for nonsharable resources. These values usually would be calculated from parameters such as message volume and message lengths. The costs of these resources would, of course, be fully "owned" by the architecture being "costed out" (in contrast to the sharable resources that are discussed in Step 6).
6. Develop the maximum values of utilization for sharable resources. These values may come from physical constraints (e.g., the maximum throughput—or utilization—for CSMA/CD probably should not exceed 40%) or they may be assumed. The values will be adjusted as the performance and costs are iterated. If the chosen values are too high, the queueing on the resource and subsequently the calculated transit time will increase significantly. If the chosen utilization values are too low, the cost allocated to this architecture will be too high.

7. Calculate the expected transit time (see below).

8. If the transit time exceeds the chosen performance service level, the capacity of the infrastructure must be increased or the load on the shared or nonshared resource (i.e., the throughputs or utilizations assumed in Steps 5 and 6) must be decreased. In either case, it will reduce the transit time and increase the cost. Note that this is a simple interactive process, but some logical sensitivity tests will hasten the convergence to the optimum cost-performance solution. For example, it would be logical to: (a) compute the transit time and the cost of each component in the architecture, (b) examine the component with the largest transit time, (c) compute the difference in cost per change in the transit delay ratio, and (d) compare the ratio with the similar ratio for the next-largest time element. From this type of comparison, the least expensive way of decreasing the transit times may be computed.

Common sense will minimize much of the calculation load. For example, LANs usually operate in the hundreds of microseconds range, the processing times for the OSIRM layers on a 10 Mips workstation are in the tens of milliseconds, and the usual WANs and the applications running on end-systems are in the tenths of seconds to several second range for narrowband services. If the situation calls for reducing the transit time by seconds, LANs are not a likely area in which to start. Note, however, that for broadband services, the WAN delay will be considerably less. For example, in SMDS one can navigate the network in 20 milliseconds.

There are two steps that should be performed at about this point in any modeling effort. They are the verification and validation of the abstraction that is used as the model. Verification involves a process, similar to code-checking in programming, in which the analyst verifies that the analytical or discrete-event model is indeed the intended abstraction. Validation involves determining how close the model or abstraction is to reality. In the latter process, a number of techniques have been used and debated for years; the most widely accepted method is to validate against known data, if available.

At this point, it will become apparent if more detailed models or more precise data are necessary. An example of this iteration would be if one is comparing architectures and the results are relatively close (i.e., within 20 to 30% for very high-level analysis). If so, the assumptions and their respective attributes should be examined. It should be obvious that assumptions with a high-priority and a low-degree of confidence should be addressed first, regardless of whether these assumptions concern models or data. It may also be necessary to switch to a discrete-event modeling technique at this point in which case all of the assumptions involving data should also be reexamined.

In any system development or planning effort, high-level calculations are merely a starting place. The analysis of cost and performance should be an ongoing activity. After the project is underway and the high-level analysis is finished, the next step should be performing a more detailed analysis as more information becomes available. This type of analysis (for performance) could be accomplished either by discrete-event simulation or possibly through the use of commercial performance tools. Also, measurement and operations data gathering should be continued to support the analysis and validate the results. Eventually, the analysis tools that are developed should be used and refined in the prototype and production environments. Capacity planning is one category of user for these tools. Table 6.1 shows a typical, phased scenario for the use of simple analytic (called back-of-the-envelope, or BOE), discrete-event simulation (DES), and measurement tools. (Measurement includes data gathering, measurement experiments in the laboratory, and measurement in the operations environment.)

6.3 MEASURES OF INTEREST

6.3.1 Transit Delay

End-to-end transit delay can be obtained by assuming layer independence (or decomposition of all queueable resources) and summing the delays in each individual layer (or on each queueable resource) from the end-system on one end through the end-system on the opposite end.

(Note that these are macro-level estimates that consider primarily physical components or infrastructure such as data transmission rates, the power of processors, and so forth. In general, tuning considerations are assumed to be optimal. For example, window sizes in all applicable layers are assumed to be tuned to the point at which there is no delay waiting for an acknowledgment. It is recognized that this contradicts, to an extent, the infrastructure guideline because proper window sizes certainly might imply the need for added real memory for buffers. It also is recognized that the lack of this infrastructure can cause lost packets of data, which can lead to extreme performance degradation. Reference [3] includes an example of lost data reducing throughput by a factor of six.)

6.3.2 Throughput

The end-to-end throughput is assumed to be the minimum of each of the individual layer throughputs (i.e., the layer with the smallest throughput) calculated via the following sections.

Table 6.1
Project Phases versus Tools

Phase	Tools
Application design	BOE
Coding/testing	BOE, DES, measurement
Prototype	DES, measurement
Production (various versions)	DES, measurement

Throughput analysis is complicated not only at the analytical level, but also at the philosophical level. As an illustrative example, studies have been conducted on the throughput of a 10BASE-T LAN. Although the throughput of the media is 10 Mbps, the throughput of the individual layers (i.e., MAC, LLC, IP, and transport) may be lower, particularly in the case of less-than-optimal implementations. Some studies have been published that claim low MAC and TCP/IP throughput. Other studies (labeled as "well designed") show that under optimal conditions, Ethernet can have a throughput relatively close to the theoretical limit of 10 Mbps [4]. Similar results have been found with TCP/IP, with some studies have showing that TCP/IP can support gigabit-per-second rates [5–7]. Usually hardware bottlenecks limit the maximum potential performance of a protocol. *To be practical, however, these hardware limitations must be taken into account in real-life.* They cannot be dismissed, as some would have it, with the simplistic statement that "there is nothing wrong with the protocol—it's all in the implementation."

For example, assume that a study shows that the MAC protocol would provide a 99% throughput compared to the maximum theoretical value if it has a 4MB RAM cache available to it. The questions to consider are:

- Does a typical $200 Ethernet board have a 4MB RAM cache? What is the actual throughput of a typical—not an ideal—business installation? What is the impact of reducing the cache to the size found on typical equipment (possibly zero)?
- Furthermore, many protocols have *implementation* or *intrinsic* inefficiencies. As an example of the former, consider what would happen—regardless of the power of the underlying hardware—if a designer makes a certain timer too long or a window too short. A protocol has an *intrinsic inefficiency* when it is too complex; for example, compare X.25 packet protocols to frame relay protocols.

Sometimes a protocol that has operated at a certain speed X for a number of years, could, in the light of new user requirements, be stretched to operate at 10X (e.g., some designers talk about extending Ethernet from 10 Mbps to 100 Mbps). However, the question is not whether the particular protocol can be made to run at 10X, but rather which protocol is best for use at speed of 10X. In other words, which protocol runs at its optimum level at 10X? A protocol may operate at 10X, but it may not operate efficiently. For example, is Ethernet technology the best way on which to deliver 100 Mbps to the desktop? TCP/IP has traditionally operated at 10 Mbps. Some have shown that TCP/IP could also operate at gigabit rates [8–11]. Is TCP/IP the best way to deliver gigabits per second, or would it be more advantageous to develop a whole new protocol from the bottom up? Can one push X.25 PLP to run at T1 rates or is it better to replace it with frame relay-based protocols?

6.4 NETWORK LAYER

6.4.1 Transit Delay—X.25

The following analysis applies to transit delays calculated for the portion of the packet network specified in each heading. Two delays are considered: service time and queueing time. The server may be either a node or a transmission link. Service times are therefore either the time it takes to process the packet in the node or the time it takes to transmit the packet across the circuit. The queueing time is the time the packet waits for the server, whether node or circuit. Obviously, the utilization of the server is necessary to calculate the queueing value. Furthermore, timing components, such as propagation delay and the effect of window sizes, are not considered [12].

Terminal to PAD Link

$$\text{Service time} = \frac{L}{R} = \frac{1}{R}$$
$$\text{Queueing time} = 0$$

where

L = length of the input message = 1 byte;
R = transmission rate in bits or bytes per-unit-time.

The terminal input circuit is assumed to be a dialup or dedicated line so that: (1) there is no queueing, and (2) only the transmission of the last byte on input or the first byte on output needs to be completed.

PAD to Switch Link

$$\text{Service time} = \frac{L_i}{R_{pad}}$$
$$\text{Queueing time} = \frac{\rho_{pad}}{1 - \rho_{pad}} \times E \; (L_{pad})/R_{pad}$$

where

L_i = average packet length (either input or output);
R_{pad} = rated speed of the PAD in bytes/unit-time;
ρ_{pad} = estimated utilization of the PAD; and
$E(L_{pad})$ = expected length of the packets being processed by the PAD. This includes the packets being transmitted both to and from the terminals attached to the PAD.

Any Node-Node Link

$$\text{Service time} = \frac{L_{packet}}{R_{link}}$$
$$\text{Queueing time} = \frac{\rho_{link}}{1 - \rho_{link}} \; E(L_{link})/R_{link}$$

where

L_{packet} = average packet length (either input or output);
R_{link} = transmission rate of the link in bits or bytes per-unit-time;
ρ_{link} = estimated utilization of the link; and
$E(L_{link})$ = expected length of the packets (In this case, this includes the nine-byte ACKs (acknowledgments) being sent in response to the packets traveling in the opposite direction on this link.)

Switching Node

$$\text{Service time} = \frac{1}{R_{switch}}$$

$$\text{Queueing time} = (1/2)\, \frac{\rho_{switch}}{1 - \rho_{switch}}\ (\text{switch service time})$$

where

R_{switch} is the rated capacity of the switch in packets per-unit-time;
ρ_{switch} is the estimated utilization of the switch.

Estimating Total Transmit Time

If the timing of the individual hops across the backbone are approximately the same, the total message time across the backbone can be approximated as follows:

$$\text{Message transit time} = (N_{hops} - 1 + N_{ppm}) \times \frac{T_{total}}{N_{ppm}}$$

where

T_{total} = the total time (on link and node) for one hop;
N_{hops} = the number of hops across the backbone; and
N_{ppm} = the number of packets per message.

The average time on the link and node (T_{total}) is computed using the equations described in the beginning of this section.

6.4.2 Throughput—X.25

Because of the complexity involved in analyzing the throughput of a packet network, the throughput can be assumed to be the minimum of any of the packet network edge component throughputs, (e.g., the circuits or switches immediately adjacent to the end-nodes, whether terminals or hosts) [13].

6.5 DATA LINK LAYER

6.5.1 Delay (Interactive or Inquiry-Response Transactions)

1. Calculate the data transmission time by summing the estimates for the expected values of input and output message lengths. Use this figure as the value of L.

$$t_t = \frac{L}{R} = \frac{L_i + L_0}{R}$$

where

L_i = length of the input message;
L_0 = length of the output message; and
R = transmission rate in bits or bytes per-unit-time.

2. Calculate the circuit utilization ρ for a given message arrival rate. Increase this calculated value by 10% for synchronous data link control (SDLC) or by 20% for binary synchronous protocol (BSC). This added percentage accounts for factors such as protocol handshaking and terrestrial propagation time (however, if satellite communications are used, this estimate is invalid).

$$\rho = (\lambda \times t_t) \times 1.1 \text{ (or 1.2 for BSC)}$$

where λ = arrival rate in transaction per unit time, and t_t is defined above.
3. Calculate the waiting or queueing time, t_w, using the M/M/1 model.

$$t_w = \frac{\rho}{(1 - \rho)} E(t_t)$$

where is ρ defined above

$$E(t_t) = \text{the average or expected transmission time} = \frac{L}{2}$$

4. To calculate the interactive response time, t_{resp}, sum up the data transmission time (from Step 1), the waiting time (from Step 3), and the supplied host time. Multiply this value by 1.1 (or 1.2 for BSC) to allow for time elements that have not been considered:

$$t_{resp} = 1.1 \text{ or } 1.2 \ (t_t + t_w + t_{host})$$

5. If the resulting response time is significantly different from the required service level, adjust the message arrival rate in Step 2 and recalculate the response time. To calculate delay for a simple one-way link, merely sum the transmission and waiting times.

6.5.2 Throughput

Assume the maximum throughput is the reciprocal of the expected transmission time (t_t) [14].

6.6 MAC LAYER

6.6.1 Delay

Usually, calculating the transit delay in the media access layer is not given much consideration because the delay is insignificant in comparison to upper-layer software computation times (except if the applied load exceeds the maximum throughput limits discussed below). This delay, however, can become important new broadband applications, such as multimedia. In general, though, it is more than sufficient in for engineering planning to follow the throughput limits to prevent excessive delays. In those traditional cases in which it is necessary to estimate the transit times, it is possible to develop estimates as shown [15–17].

IEEE 802.3

The transit delay can be estimated for IEEE 802.3 by summing the transmission time, and an estimate of the rest of the CSMA/CD mechanism, including the probability of collision and recovery. The calculation for transit time is the standard equation:

$$\text{transmission time} = t_t = \frac{L}{R}$$

where

L = the total length of the message or frame, including overhead, in either bits or bytes;
R = the data transmission rate at 10 Mbps.

The estimate of the rest of the delay, including propagation time and the collision mechanism, is obtained by adjusting the basic equation for M/M/1 queueing. (Note that this technique provides a reasonable estimate only because the shape of the delay curve approximates the M/M/1 delay curve when the asymptotes are adjusted for the extreme values of the relative propagation value a.) The delay is:

$$t_w = \frac{\rho}{(1 - \rho)} t_t$$

where

ρ = is the circuit utilization adjusted as shown below for a:
t_t = transmission time calculated above;
for $a = .1$ (usually the case of the smaller packets), divide the utilization by 0.6;
for $a = .01$ (usually the case for the largest packets), divide the utilization by 0.8.

IEEE 802.5

An estimate can also be made for the token ring protocol by the same method. In this case, summing of the two components above without adjustment is sufficient to develop a reasonable estimate for the total transit time.

6.6.2 Throughput

IEEE 802.3

The IEEE 802.3 protocol can achieve a maximum throughput utilization of 60% to 80%. The smaller frame sizes achieve the lower limit. A more general—and more optimistic—equation using the value a is [14, 18]:

$$\text{throughput} = S = \frac{1}{1 + 2a(1 - A)/A}$$

$$a = \frac{\text{propagation time}}{\text{transmission time}}$$

where

$$A = (1 - 1/N)^{N-1}$$

$$N = \text{number of stations}$$

One has

$$a = \frac{d/V}{L/R} = \frac{Rd}{VL}$$

where

R = transmission rate in bits or bytes per-unit-time
d = length (distance) of media
V = propagation velocity in medium
L = length of frame

However, since the equation very quickly converges on an asymptotic value as N increases, a simple equation can be used as N approaches infinity can be used:

$$\lim_{N \to \infty} S = \frac{1}{1 + 3.44a}$$

See [4] for a complete discusion of this topic.

IEEE 802.5

$$\text{throughput} = S = \begin{cases} \dfrac{1}{1 + a / N} & \text{for } a < 1 \\[3mm] \dfrac{1}{a(1 + 1 / N)} & a > 1 \end{cases}$$

where a and N have been defined above.

As in the case of 802.3, the equations can be simplified for the case of a large N (i.e., more than 10 stations). This should be applicable for all practical examples:

$$\lim_{N \to \infty} S = \begin{cases} 1 \text{ for } a < 1 \\[3mm] \dfrac{1}{a} \text{ for } a > 1 \end{cases}$$

It should be emphasized that, as in the case of IEEE 802.3, these equations are a "best possible" (i.e., optimistic) solution for throughput values.

6.7 MULTIPLE LAYER DEVICES

This section covers those devices or classes of devices that span several of the OSIRM layers. The class discussed is a generic model of a bridge/router. In a pure sense, bridges are considered to be in the data link layer, with routers in the network layer. However, it is possible to present a generic performance model that, for the purposes of macro-level analysis, will suffice for both devices [19–20]. Furthermore, the two devices are being functionally merged by vendors; witness the brouters, trouters, and so forth.

6.7.1 Delay

This generic model of a bridge can be used as a macro-level model of either a local bridge, a remote bridge, or a router:

$$t_{delay} = t_{w-proc} + t_{e-proc} + t_{w-trans} + t_{t-trans}$$

where

t_{delay} = total delay

t_{w-proc} = waiting time for the processor

$$= \frac{\rho_{proc}}{(1 - \rho_{proc})} t_{e-proc}$$

t_{e-proc} = execution time in processor

$$= \frac{1}{(R_{fwd})}$$

$t_{w-trans}$ = waiting time for transmission

$$= \frac{\rho_{trans}}{(1 - \rho_{trans})} t_{trans}$$

$t_{t-trans}$ = expected transmission time on LAN/WAN

$$= \frac{L_{packet}}{(R_{trans})}$$

The individual parameters in the above equations are defined as follows:

ρ_{proc} = the utilization of the bridge processor

$$= \frac{\lambda_{fwd}}{(R_{fwd})}$$

λ_{fwd} = the actual packet forwarding rate

R_{fwd} = the maximum bridge packet forwarding rate

ρ_{trans} = the estimated utilization of the second LAN or circuit on the bridge's output port

L_{packet} = the average length of the packet

R_{trans} = the LAN or circuit transmission rate

6.7.2 Throughput

As an approximation, the advertised forwarding rate can be used as the throughput rate for bridge-type devices; similarly, the advertised throughput rate can also be used for routers. It should be noted, however, that the throughput is a more complex function than that which is expressed by a single metric. In fact, [3] indicates that two metrics are needed: one is a function of the speed with which the device can process the packets (the load is the instruction path length needed to process a packet, and the power is the processing speed, e.g., Mips); the second indicates the volume of bits that can be processed (in this case, the power may be memory-bandwidth or bus speed).

REFERENCES

[1] Ellis, R. *Designing Data Networks*, Englewood Cliffs, NJ: Prentice-Hall, 1986.

[2] Paterok, M., and O. Fisher, "Feedback Queues with Preemption-Distance Priorities," *Performance Evaluation Review*, Vol. 17, May 1989, pp. 136–145.

[3] Clark, D. D., and D. L. Tennenhouse, "Architectural Considerations for a New Generation of Protocols," ACM 089791-405-8/90/0009/0200.

[4] Boggs, D. R., et al., "Measured Capacity of an Ethernet: Myths and Reality," *Computer Communications Review*, Vol. 18, No. 4, August 1988.

[5] Jacobson, V. Course notes, SIGCOMM, 1990.

[6] Clark, D. D., et al., "An Analysis of TCP Processing Overhead," *IEEE Comm.*, Vol. 27, June 1989, pp. 23–29.

[7] Schroeder, M. D., and M. Burrows, "Performance of Firefly RPC," 12th ACM Symposium on Operating System Principles, ACM SIGOPS, December 1989.

[8] Partridge, C., "How Slow is One Gigabit Per Second?" *Computer Communications Review*, ACM SIGCOMM, Vol. 20, No.1, December 1989, pp. 44–53.

[9] Borman, D. A., "Implementing TCP/IP on a Cray Computer," *Computer Communications Review*, ACM SIGCOMM, Vol. 19, No.2, April 1989, pp. 11–15.

[10] McKenney, P., and K. Dove, "Efficient Demultiplexing of Incoming TCP Packets," Proc. ACM SIGCOMM '92, August 1992, pp. 269–279.

[11] Feldmeiner, D. C., "Improving Gateway Performance with a Routing Table Cache," Proc. IEEE INFOCM 1988, March 1988, pp. 298–307.

[12] Fernandez, J., and D. E. Liddy, "Don't Just Guess: How to Figure Out Delays in Private Packet Networks," *Data Communications*, March 1988, pp. 197–210.

[13] Fernandez, J., and D. E. Liddy, "Is Your Packet Network a 'Model' of Response-Time Efficiency?" *Data Communications*, May 1988, pp. 139–153.

[14] Stallings, W., *Data and Computer Communication*, 2d ed., New York: Macmillan, 1988.

[15] Bhargava, et al., "Experimental Analysis of Layered Ethernet Software," Proc. 1987 Joint Computer Conference, pp. 559–568.

[16] Stallings, W., "Local Network Performance," *IEEE Comm.*, Vol. 22, No. 2, February 1984, pp. 27–36.

[17] Schwartz, M., *Telecommunications Networks: Protocols, Modeling and Analysis*, Reading, MA: Addison-Wesley, 1987.

[18] Metcalfe, R., and D. Boggs, "Ethernet: Distributed Packet Switching for Local Computer Networks," *Communications of ACM*, Vol. 19, No. 7, July 1976, pp. 67–81.

[19] Rickert, J. B., "Evaluating MAC Layer Bridges: Beyond Filtering and Forwarding," *Data Communications*, May 1990, pp. 117–122.

[20] Hawe, et al., "Transparent Interconnection of Local Area Networks with Bridges," J. *Telecommunication Networks*, Vol. 3, No. 2, Summer 1984, pp. 116–130.

Chapter 7

The Impact of Source-Dependent Traffic

Source dependency is a fact of life; yet it has generally been ignored by the researchers because of its lack of elegance. Using a specific example, this chapter demonstrates that dependency can have severe implications on system performance [1]. The effects of dependency should certainly be considered for critical networks (e.g., military networks, networks for nuclear plant monitoring, fly-by-wire LANs aboard commercial and military planes, and commercial networks with tight response-time requirements).

7.1 INTRODUCTION

As mentioned in Chapter 4, the vast majority of published models designed to derive system performance (delay or throughput) assume that the constituents of the community under study are totally independent of each other. There are two reasons for this often-debilitating assumption:

1. Mathematical simplicity for model solution;
2. The uniqueness of the independence condition. Dependence is not expressible in a unique formula, and may have infinitely many representations related to the underlying mechanism. One has:

   a. Independence: $\mathrm{Prob}(A \ \& \ B) = \mathrm{Prob}(A) \times \mathrm{Prob}(B)$
   b. Dependence: $\mathrm{Prob}(A \ \& \ B) = f(\mathrm{Prob}(A), \mathrm{Prob}(B))$,
      for any admissible $f(x, y)$.

Yet, many systems exhibit deep, intrinsic dependencies. Even systems that in theory could be classified as independent (e.g., telephone traffic arrival to a toll switch from unrelated customers), lose their independence status under many circumstances. Examples include "Mother's Day," natural emergencies, announced 900-xxx-yyyy call-ins for polling purposes, and major sale promotions.

There are three goals of this chapter:

- To analyze the possible effect of dependence on throughput in some specific communications examples;
- To sensitize the user community to the need to study and include dependence in modeling efforts;
- To advocate that the user community demand that researchers who present "yet-another-performance-model" include real-life assumptions.

Because dependence is not uniquely expressible, one is not able to derive general and elegant results. Nonetheless, since dependence is part of most communications systems (as already discussed in Section 4.6.1), one should consider it regardless of whether elegant results are obtainable. Surprisingly, once the dependence function is specified, the mathematical analysis is fairly simple; the challenge is in expressing the nature of the dependence itself for a given system.

The dependence is hereby considered in the context of VSAT technology; fairly similar results apply directly to other contention systems such as LANs and wireless LANs, as well as traditional non-contention systems. Figure 7.1 depicts the environment of the financial industry in which this particular study originated [1]. All 2,000 nationwide account executives (AEs, or stockbrokers) at a large Wall Street firm are connected with a private-broadcast audio channel (generated by the company) that provides real-time quick-action tips on buying and selling securities. The AEs have computer terminals connected to the centralized "computerized trading" system in the New York City vicinity. Portions of this network may use VSATs, as shown in Figure 7.1. Additionally, the premises connectivity for those sites with several AEs may consist of a LAN.

7.2 ANALYSIS

We analyze a slotted Aloha system and follow established nomenclature [2–6]. Two types of dependencies are examined. The first is established by a functional description, in other words, by the representation of the joint probability distribution. This approach is easily tractable at the mathematical level; however, one cannot get an intuitive feeling and/or model the dependency mechanics. The second model follows a Markov Chain formulation. The Markov Chain permits the description of fairly intuitive system behavior into the model, but generally requires more algebra to solve for the desired steady-state probabilities.

7.2.1 Functional Model

Consider j users supplying packets at each Aloha slot. Let G be the population's offered traffic and let S be the successful traffic. $U_i = n$ means that user i has no packet in the given slot, while and $U_i = y$ means that user i has a packet. We assume a stationary system so that the user's probability of supplying a packet in any slot is time-invariant and, without loss of generality, that all users are uniform:

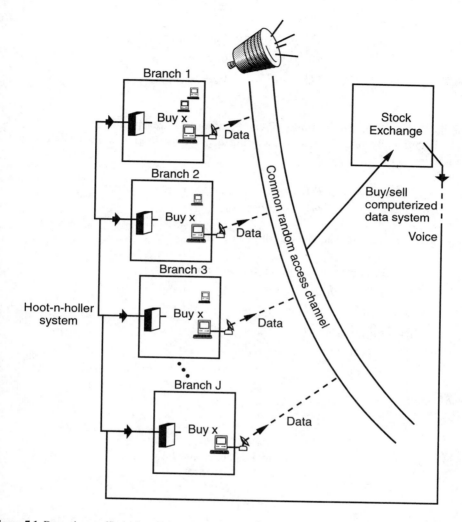

Figure 7.1 Dependent traffic in financial services industries.

$$P(U_1 = y, \ U_2 = n, \ U_3 = n, \ ...) =$$
$$P(U_1 = n, \ U_2 = y, \ U_3 = n, \ ...) =$$
$$P(U_1 = n, \ U_2 = n, \ U_3 = y, \ ...) = ...$$
$$= P([y, \ n, \ n, \ ...])$$

as well as all other multiple combinations, for example,

$$P(U_1 = y, \ U_2 = y, \ U_3 = n, \ ...) =$$
$$P(U_1 = y, \ U_2 = n, \ U_3 = y, \ ...) =$$
$$P(U_1 = n, \ U_2 = y, \ U_3 = y, \ ...) = ...$$
$$= P([y, \ y, \ n,...])$$

The number of users can be finite, or can be allowed to reach infinity.

Traditionally, one proceeds by factoring the joint distribution under the independenc assumption, so that

$$P(U_1 = x_1, \ U_2 = x_2, \ U_3 = x_3, \ ...) =$$
$$P(U_1 = x_1)P(U_2 = x_2)P(U_3 = x_3) \ ...$$

Thus, given a Bernoulli mechanism of p, one has

$$S = \text{Prob (exactly one user supplies a packet)} =$$
$$P(U_1 = y)P(U_2 = n)P(U_3 = n) \ ... \ +$$
$$P(U_1 = n)P(U_2 = y)P(U_3 = n) \ ... \ +$$
$$P(U_1 = n)P(U_2 = n)P(U_3 = y) \ ... \ + \ ... = jp(1 - p)^{j-1}$$
$$G = \text{expected number of arrivals}$$
$$= 1 \times P(1 \text{ arrival}) + 2 \times P(2 \text{ arrivals}) + 3 \times P(3 \text{ arrivals}) + \ ... = jp$$

from which

$$S = G(1 - p)^{j-1}$$

If $jp \rightarrow G, j \rightarrow \infty$, simple mathematical calculations show that

$$S = Ge^{-G}$$

which is the standard result.

Without the independence assumption (and with or without Bernoulli mechanism) one has

$$S = P(U_1 = y, \ U_2 = n, \ U_3 = n, \ ...) +$$
$$P(U_1 = n, \ U_2 = y, \ U_3 = n, \ ...) +$$
$$P(U_1 = n, \ U_2 = n, \ U_3 = y, \ ...) + \ ...$$
$$= jP([y, \ n, \ n,...])$$

where $P([y, \ n, \ n,...])$ is the uniform joint probability that exactly one user supplies packet and no other users have a packet.

$$G = 1 \times \{P(U_1 = y, U_2 = n, U_3 = n \ldots) +$$
$$P(U_1 = n, U_2 = y, U_3 = n \ldots) +$$
$$P(U_1 = n, U_2 = n, U_3 = y\ldots) + \ldots\} +$$
$$2 \times \{P(U_1 = y, U_2 = y, U_3 = n \ldots) +$$
$$P(U_1 = y, U_2 = n, U_3 = y \ldots) +$$
$$P(U_1 = n, U_2 = y, U_3 = y \ldots) + \ldots\} +$$
$$3 \times \{\ldots\} + 4 \times \{\ldots\} + \ldots$$
$$= 1 \times \binom{j}{1} P([y, n, n, \ldots]) + 2 \times \binom{j}{2} P([y, y, y, \ldots]) +$$
$$3 \times \binom{j}{3} P([y, y, y, \ldots]) + \ldots$$

because of the uniformity condition.

Note that

$$\sum_{x_1=y}^{n} \sum_{x_2=y}^{n} \sum_{x_3=y}^{n} \ldots \sum_{x_j=y}^{n} P(U_1 = x_1, U_2 = x_2, U_3 = x_3, \ldots) = 1$$

or

$$P([n, n, n, \ldots]) + \binom{j}{1} P([y, n, n, \ldots]) + \binom{j}{2} P([y, y, n, \ldots])$$
$$+ \binom{j}{3} P([y, y, y, \ldots]) + \ldots = 1$$

Again, j can approach ∞. S and G provide the required formulation for the dependent case.

7.2.2 Examples

Example 1

Let $G(x) = p(1 - p)^x$ be the probabilities of the geometric distribution. Let

$$P([n, n, n, \ldots]) = P(U_1 = n, U_2 = n, U_3 = n \ldots) = 1 - \sum G(i)$$

$$P([y, n, n, \ldots]) = G(1)/\binom{j}{1}$$

$$P([y, y, n, \ldots]) = G(2)/\binom{j}{2}$$

$$\ldots$$

$$P([y, y, y, \ldots y]) = G(j)/\binom{j}{j}$$

Then

$$G = \text{expected number of arrivals}$$
$$= 1 \times G(1) + 2 \times G(2) + 3 \times G(3) + \dots + j \times G(j)$$
$$S = \text{successful traffic} = G(1)$$

As $j \to \infty$,

$$G = (1 - p)/p$$
$$S = p(1 - p)$$

Table 7.1 obtains S as a function of G, parametrized on p. The standard S, per the equations developed by Abramson, is also obtained from G. Figure 7.2 shows that for most values of G, the throughput of the system is lower than that expected in an independent-sources case.

One can easily see that this environment differs from the standard Bernoulli/binomial case because the higher terms of the joint distribution cannot be factored in predefined factors.

Example 2

Let $P(x) = e^{-a}a^x/x!$ be the Poisson terms. Let

$$P([n, n, n,\dots]) = 1 - \sum_{i=1}^{j} P(i)$$

$$P([y, n, n,\dots]) = P(2)/\binom{j}{1}$$

$$P([y, y, n,\dots]) = P(1)/\binom{j}{2}$$

$$P([y, y, y,\dots]) = P(3)/\binom{j}{3}$$

$$P([y, y, y, y\dots]) = P(4)/\binom{j}{4}$$

$$\dots$$

$$P([y, y, y,\dots, y]) = P(j)/\binom{j}{j}$$

At infinite j, one has

Table 7.1
S and G in a Source-Dependent Situation, Example 1

p	G	S	$S_{ABR} = Ge^{-G}$
0.1	9	0.09	0.00
0.2	4	0.16	0.04
0.3	2.3	0.21	0.23
0.4	1.5	0.24	0.33
0.5	1.0	0.25	0.36
0.6	0.66	0.24	0.33
0.7	0.42	0.21	0.27
0.8	0.25	0.16	0.19
0.9	0.11	0.09	0.09

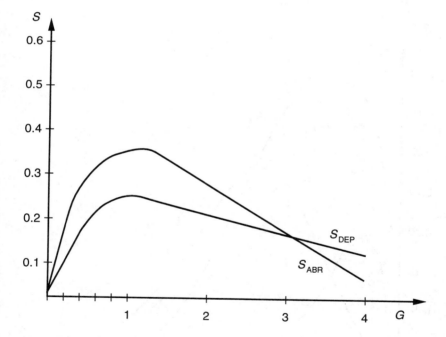

Figure 7.2 Decreased throughput in a source-dependent scenerio.

$$G = 1 \times P(2) + 2 \times P(1) + 3 \times P(3) + 4 \times P(4) + \dots$$
$$= E(\text{Poisson}) + P(1) - P(2) = a + e^{-a}a - e^{-a}a^2/2$$
$$S = 1 \times P(2) = e^{-a}a^2/2$$

Table 7.2 and Figure 7.3 show again that the throughput is lower compared to both slotted and unslotted Aloha environment under independent arrival. Thus, a result

Table 7.2
S and G in a Source-Dependent Situation, Example 2

p	G	S	$S_{\text{slotted}} = Ge^{-G}$	$S_{\text{unslotted}} = Ge^{-2G}$
0.2	0.35	0.01	0.24	0.17
0.4	0.61	0.05	0.32	0.18
0.6	0.83	0.09	0.35	0.16
0.8	1.01	0.14	0.37	0.13
1.0	1.18	0.18	0.27	0.13
2.0	2.0	0.26	0.27	0.03
3.0	3.07	0.22	0.14	0.007
4.0	4.07	0.14	0.07	0.001
5.0	5.04	0.07	0.03	0.0002

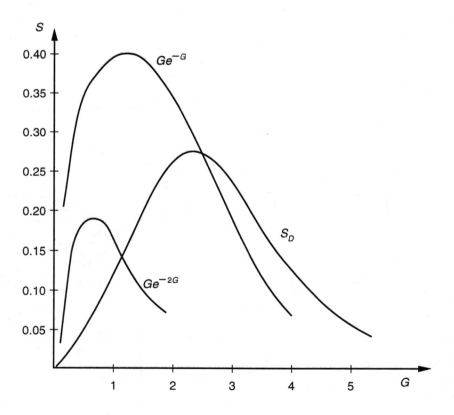

Figure 7.3 Performance, Example 2.

obtained by Sant [7.7] for a general non-Poisson but independent arrival does not hold in the source-dependent case.

Example 2.1

Assume all factors of Example 2, except that

$$P([y, n, n, ...]) = P(1)/\binom{j}{1}$$

$$P([y, n, n, ...]) = P(2)/\binom{j}{2}$$

Then

$$G = 1P(1) + 2P(2) + 3P(3) + ... = a$$
$$S = P(1) = ae^{-a}$$

for infinite j. Here one recaptures $S = Ge^{-G}$ the independence condition, or factorization. Contrasting this with Example 2, we see that even a minor perturbation of the independence status leads to channel degradation.

Example 3

Given j users (j is finite), let

$$P([n, n, n,...]) = 1 - jp, p \leq 1/j$$

$$P([y, n, n,...]) = p/\binom{j}{1}$$

$$P([y, y, n,...]) = p/\binom{j}{2}$$

$$...$$

$$P([y, y, y,...,y]) = p/\binom{j}{j}$$

One obtains

$$G = p + 2p + 3p + \ldots + jp = pj(j - 1)/2$$
$$S = p$$

For $j = 2$, Figure 7.4 compares the joint distribution of the independent case with a dependent case that is a variant of Example 3. Figure 7.5 shows that if the sources have very little traffic to offer (G is less than $1/2$), then the throughput is less in the dependent case. From the joint distribution of Figure 7.4, one intuitively knows that in the dependent case there is a higher chance that the state $U_1 = y$, $U_2 = y$ occurs, due to the "copycat" behavior of the two sources.

Example 4

Based on empirical observation on a small number of AEs, we believe that a "trading floor" follows a model similar to the following example,

$$P([n, n, n,\ldots]) = 0.4$$
$$P([y, n, n,\ldots]) = p$$
$$P([y, y, n,\ldots]) = 0.2 - p$$
$$P([y, y, y,\ldots y,]) = 0.4$$
$$0 \le p \le 0.2$$

One has $S = p$ and $G = 0.4(j + 1) - p$, with j as the number of AEs. When $p = 0$, $G = 0.4(j + 1)$, $S = 0$; when $p = 0.2$, $G = 0.4(j + 1) - 0.2$, $S = 0.2$. For the same G, the classical model would obtain the following results

U_2	U_1	y	n
y		p^2	$p(1 - p)$
n		$p(1-p)$	$(1 - p)^2$

Independent Case

U_2	U_1	y	n
y		$p/2$	$p/2$
n		$p/2$	$1 - (3/2)p$

Dependent Case

$G = 2p$ $\qquad S = 2p(1 - p)$ $\qquad G = 2p$ $\qquad S = p$

Figure 7.4 Joint distributions (variant of example 3).

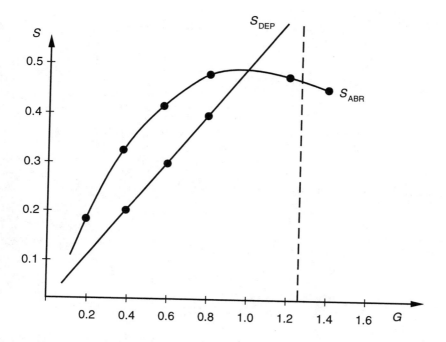

Figure 7.5 Channel throughput, finite number of sources.

$$\text{when } G = 0.4(j + 1)$$
$$p' = 0.4(j + 1)/j \quad \text{and}$$
$$S' = jp'(1 - p')$$
$$\text{when } G = 0.4(j + 1) - 0.2,$$
$$p' = [0.4(j + 1) - 0.2]/j \quad \text{and}$$
$$S' = jp'(1 - p')^{j-1}$$

with $j = 4$, $S/G = 0$ at p = 0, and $S/G = 0.11$ at $p = 0.2$ while $S'/G = 0.125$ at $p = 0$ ($p' = .5$), and $S'/G = 0.16$ at $p = 0.2$ ($p' = .45$) We see in Table 7.3 that the throughput s lower in the correlated case. As j approaches infinity, S'/G again tends to e^{-1}.

For some VSAT systems put in place in the late 1980s, one had the following arameters:

Aloha slot: 1 ms;
Channel: 32 kbps;
Packet length: 32 characters;
Traffic sources: 60/channel;
Traffic rate: 4 packets/source/min

Table 7.3
Another Example of Throughput Degradation

p	G_{DEP}	S_{DEP}	G_{ABR}	S_{ABR}
0.1	0.2	0.1	0.2	0.16
0.2	0.4	0.2	0.4	0.32
0.3	0.6	0.3	0.6	0.42
0.4	0.8	0.4	0.8	0.48
0.5	1.0	0.5	1.0	0.50
0.6	1.2	0.6	1.2	0.48

This results in 4 packets per second per channel and

$$\text{Prob (1 packet per slot)} = 1/250$$

In conjunction with an empirical model, one has

$$P([n, n, n, ...]) = (249/250) + (4.5/10)(1/250)$$
$$P([y, n, n,...]) = (1/10) (1/250)$$
$$P([y, y, n,...]) = (4.5/10) (1/250)$$

with all other terms equal to zero. Here, one finds $S = (1/10)(1/250)$, $G = 1/250$ and $S/G = 0.1$. Under the independent scenario, $p = 1/(250 \times 60)$, $G = nj = 1/250$ $S = 0.36(1/250)$, and $S/G = 0.36$.

Thus, a network designer would have to realize that the effective throughput is lower than anticipated, and make necessary provisions by augmenting the channel capacity.

Conclusion

The examples discussed above indicate that the expected throughput S is generally less in a dependent environment than in an independent environment. The uniformity assumption in the derivation above was introduced only for nomenclature and computational simplicity. In general, one could employ a computer program and dispense with this assumption. However, the nature of the dependence mechanism is far from clear. A Markovian approach permits the user to incorporate a specific dependency mechanism.

7.3. MARKOVIAN APPROACH

Once again, the aim of this section is to present a methodology, assess the general impact and motivate the need for further inclusion of dependency in network models. We thus proceed with a simplified environment and some specific situations.

Some dependencies may involve a "copycat" behavior, in which both users do the same thing with high probability; or, the entrance into definitive states in which the system goes through compulsory activities; or, a semipredicatable environment where the system is quiescent for a random time, but then enters into a deterministic sequence in which all users are expected to perform certain pre-established tasks. See Figure 7.6. We choose to avoid the more sophisticated behavior, and proceed with a four-states chain for two users, as in Figure 7.7. Specific values of the transition probabilities recapture the independent scenario, as a convolution of two Bernoulli chains (transition values would be p^2, $p(1 - p)$, and $(1 - p)^2$).

Computation of S and G

One computes the probability that a packet is successful as follows:

$$P(\text{succ|state } A) = p_{AB} + p_{AD}$$
$$P(\text{succ|state } B) = p_{BD} = p_{BB}$$
$$P(\text{succ|state } C) = p_{CD} = p_{CB}$$
$$P(\text{succ|state } D) = p_{DB} = p_{DD}$$

so that the steady-state value of S is

$$S = \Pi(A)(p_{AB} + p_{AD}) + \Pi(B)(p_{BD} + p_{BB}) + \Pi(C)(p_{CD} + p_{CB})$$
$$+ \Pi(D)(p_{BD} + p_{DD}) = \Pi(B) + \Pi(D)$$

G has distribution

$$0 \text{ if in state } A$$
$$1 \text{ if in states } B \text{ or } D$$
$$2 \text{ if in state } C$$

from which

$$G = \Pi(B) + \Pi(D) + 2\Pi(C)$$

Standard case

The transition matrix for the independent scenario is

$$
\begin{bmatrix}
(1 - p)^2 & p(1 - p) & p^2 & p(1 - p) \\
(1 - p)^2 & p(1 - p) & p^2 & p(1 - p) \\
(1 - p)^2 & p(1 - p) & p^2 & p(1 - p) \\
(1 - p)^2 & p(1 - p) & p^2 & p(1 - p)
\end{bmatrix}
$$

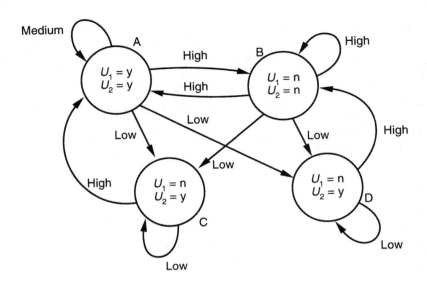

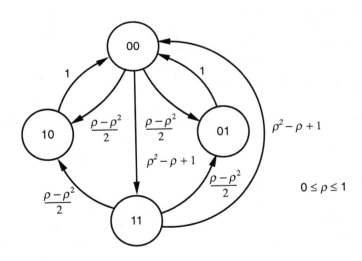

$$S = \frac{L(2-L)}{2+L-L^2} \qquad G = \frac{2-L^2}{2+L-L^2} \qquad L = \rho - \rho^2$$

(a)

Figure 7.6 Markovian dependencies (a) Copycat sources.

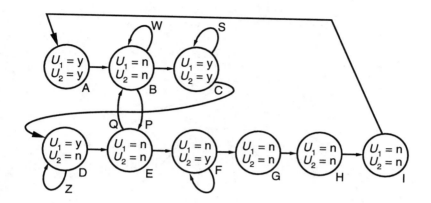

(b)

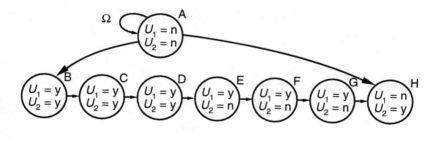

(c)

Figure 7.6 continued. (b) Definitive states. (c) semipredictable behavior.

Then,

$$S = \Pi(A)[2p(1-p)] + \Pi(B)[2p(1-p)] + \Pi(C)[2p(1-p)] + \Pi(D)[2p(1-p)]$$
$$= 2p(1-p)$$
$$G = \Pi(B) + \Pi(D) + 2\Pi(C)$$
$$= p(1-p) + p(1-p) + 2p^2 = 2p$$

after solving for the steady state value.

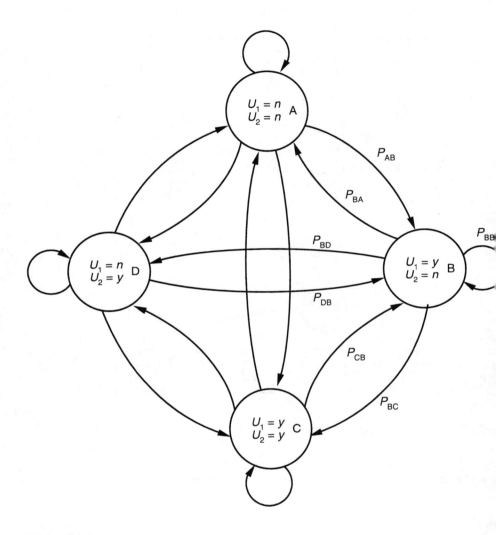

Figure 7.7 Modeled chain for two users.

Example 1

Consider the transition matrix

$$\begin{bmatrix} 1 - 3b & b & b & b \\ a & 1 - 2a & 0 & a \\ 0 & a & 1 - 2a & a \\ a & a & 0 & 1 - 2a \end{bmatrix}$$

with $b < 1/3$, $a < 1/2$. After considerable algebra one has

$$\Pi(A) = 2a/(2a + 7b)$$
$$\Pi(B) = 3b/(2a + 7b)$$
$$\Pi(C) = b/(2a + 7b)$$
$$\Pi(D) = 3b/(2a + 7b)$$
$$S = 6b/(2a + 7b)$$
$$G = 8b/(2a + 7b)$$

or

$$S = (3/4)G$$

In this case, the throughput is greater than in the independent case. For example, at $a = 0.1$ and $b = 0.2$, $G = 1$ and $S = 0.75$. One knows that, in this ordered environment, the two users remain in unblocking states B and D for a significant portion of the time.

Example 2

Consider the following transition matrix

$$\begin{bmatrix} 0 & p & 1 - 2p & p \\ 0 & 1 - p - b & b & p \\ 1 - b & 0 & b & 0 \\ 0 & p & b & 1 - p - b \end{bmatrix}$$

with $p < 1/2$ and $1 - p - b > 0$. The parameter b represents a blockage transition to state C.

$$\Pi(A) = b(1 - b)/[2p(1 - b) + 2b - b^2]$$
$$\Pi(B) = p(1 - b)/[2p(1 - b) + 2b - b^2]$$
$$\Pi(C) = b/[2p(1 - b) + 2b - b^2]$$
$$\Pi(D) = p(1 - b)/[2p(1 - b) + 2b - b^2]$$
$$S = [2p - 2pb]/[2p(1 - b) + 2b - b^2]$$
$$G = [2p + 2b - 2pb]/[2p(1 - b) + 2b - b^2]$$

or

$$S = G - [2b]/[2p(1 - b) + 2b - b^2]$$

For appropriate values of b and p, the throughput is totally bounded by a value less than Ge^{-G}. An inspection of the Markov Chain shows that the collision state C can be reached with any desired regularity by picking system parameters p and b. Figure 7.8 depicts another example of reduced throughput.

It is easy to get decreased throughput situations with the functional model; it is harder to obtain parameters for the Markovian approach. The latter appears more intuitive as a possible mechanical model of system behavior. The functional model is more abstract and pathological. Should one conclude that in real-life systems, the achievement of a functional relationship for dependence is an unlikely mechanism and that it is not a natural phenomenon? This remains to be seen, as literature on dependency becomes more available.

7.4 CONCLUSION

Source-dependent traffic is likely to occur in many communications networks, including data networks and multimedia networks. Network performance in the form of delay and throughput should be expected to degrade under such pattern of arrival. An effort should be made by the network designer to assess and model the impact, and to make necessary provisions with additional channel capacity or larger trunk bundles.

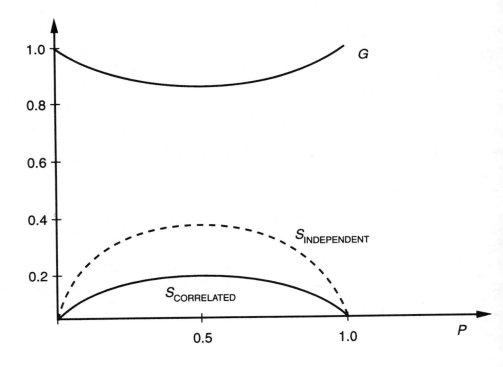

Figure 7.8 *S* versus *G*.

REFERENCES

[1] Minoli, D., "Aloha Channels Throughput Degradation Under Dependent Sources," 1986 Computer Networking Symposium Conference, pp. 151–159.

[2] Abramson, N. "Packet Switching with Satellites," 1973 National Computer Conference, AFIPS Conference Proceedings 42, pp. 675–702.

[3] Kleinrock, L., *Queueing Systems*, Vol. 2, New York: John Wiley, 1976.

[4] Abramson, N., Personal communication with author, 1985.

[5] Minoli, D., et al., "Analytical Models for Initialization of Single Hop Packet Radio Networks," *IEEE Trans. on Comm.*, Vol. COMM-27, 1979, pp. 1959–1967.

[6] Minoli, D., "Exact Solution for the Initialization Time of Packet Radio Networks with Two Station Buffers," National Computer Conference, AFIPS Conference Proceedings, Vol. 48, pp. 875–885.

[7] Sant, D., "Some models of Packet Broadcasting Networks," Ph.D diss., University of Hawaii, February 1981.

Chapter 8

Relaxation Theory Methods for the
Study of the Management of Quality-of-Service
Parameters in Broadband Networks

his chapter provides methodologies which can be used to study quality of service (QOS) adeoffs in broadband networks, and derives some practical results. A sophsiticated new neory based on classical analysis, which we call *relaxation theory* (RT), is developed nat allows the designer to study tradeoff between delay, cell/frame loss, number of system uffers, and trunk bandwidth.

Since the entire RT discipline needs to be developed from the ground up, this hapter is dedicated to that task (in this case one cannot rely on an existing methodology uch as Queueing Theory or Stochastic Processes and move directly to develop a model sing such theory—the theory itself needs to be developed). The mathematics is solvable i closed and/or numerical form. The process which is embodied in RT more closely esembles the procedure undertaken by a switch to process cells than other statistical-ased emulation models. Obviously, the methodology needs actual traffic data in order) provide valid information. Chapter 9 provides an example of application.

Section 8.1 provides an intuitive motivation and summary of some RT results to rovide the reader a practical sense of the mathematics to follows. Section 8.2 develops ie mathematical theory, including the case where there are two service classes. RT ssumes a time-dependent traffic requirement function and proceeds to calculate the 'engineering'' level for the trunk bandwidth required to meet per-cell (or per-frame) elay requirements. In doing so, the number of instantaneous buffers needed to meet the)OS requirement emerges (as a derivative parameter). There is a clear tradeoff between ie number of lost cells (or frames), the number of buffers, trunk bandwidth, and the cceptable (required) delay goal. The analysis also allows the designer to specify the number of resources below what the analysis predicts, and then infer what the cell (c frame) loss implications are. Or, the designer can bound the number of buffers an determine what the delay/loss performance will be.

8.1 BACKGROUND

8.1.1 Introduction

Assume that $f(t)$ represents the service requirement to a facility in terms of some appropriat unit.[1] For example, the facility could be a switch and $f(t)$ represents cells arriving at tim t requiring processing. $f(t)$ can represent either the requirement from a single user or from a population of users. Assume that $f(t)$ is defined over an appropriate interval of interes [a,b]. See Figure 8.1.

Given this requirement, one needs to determine an engineering level, $L(f, \epsilon)$ for th facility in order to meet a defined quality of service [8.1]. For this analysis, the engineerin

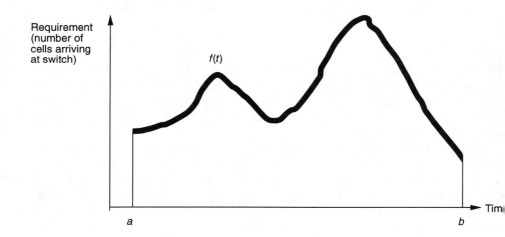

Figure 8.1 Requirement function $f(t)$.

[1] For the majority of this chapter $f(t)$ is assumed to describe the acutal arrival in determinate form. RT, howeve can be applied more generally in the following cases.

- The time-dependent arrival can only be approximated in stochastic form, the variance $V(X_t(s))$ is sma and $f(t)$ represents the expected value over time, i.e. $f(t) = E(X_t(s))$.
- The time-dependent arrival can only be approximated in stochastic form, but regardless of the value c $V(X_t(s))$, $f(t) = E(X_t(s))$.
- The time-dependent arrival can only be approximated in stochastic form and $f(t)$ represents the valu where the cumulative function achieves 0.95 (or some other specified value close to 1).
- The time-dependent arrival can only be approximated in stochastic form, and a stochastic-based answe is sought (this case is addressed in Section 8.2.6).

level will equate to the number of cell-length (TDM) slots in a combined pool of (SONET) trunk bandwidth, in order to be able to place the incoming cells, potentially after some buffering, onto the trunk, without additional loss or delay. Figure 8.2 depicts the modeled switch behavior.

The approach is initially nonstochastic[2] in the sense that it assumes a specified time-variant requirement, and that once properly engineered at the value $L(f,\epsilon)$, there will be allocated bandwidth without contention or randomized queueing. Extensions to stochastic environments are also provided. While the theory ostensibly would appear to be related to deterministic queueing theory, in fact it goes well beyond it. At least, it achieves the equivalent of setting up a simulation of cell arrival and then proceeds to "solve the simulation" in closed form. However, since the requirement function can be as complex as a continuously differentiable function, RT is much more powerful than a discrete simulation.

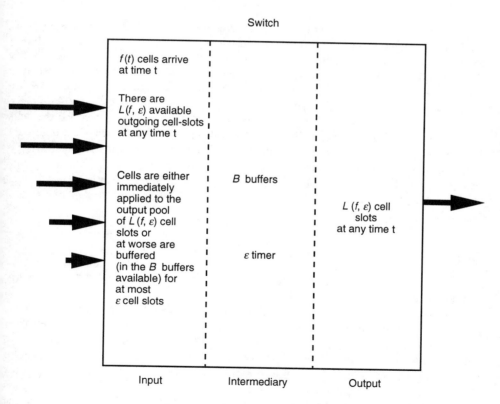

Figure 8.2 Modeled switch operation.

---

[2] See footnote 1.

There are other teletraffic-based methods to model and study the ATM performance problem. RT is presented as one possible alternative or complement to these routine approaches. RT itself is independent of any application, and can be developed on its own merit.

8.1.2 Approach

If there were no grade of service constraints on how to service the cells that present themselves to the switch according to the arrival function, then, in general terms, one could design the system using the average of $f(t)$, namely,

$$A(f, b - a) = \frac{1}{(b - a)} \int_a^b f(x)dx$$

This is the equivalent of spreading the "requirement mound" left and right (as a mound of sand, for example) into both the past and the future. Clearly this is not possible in practice, because at a given point in time one cannot push work back into the past. Another way to say this is, that given a specific requirement accumulation, it does not matter from a traditional averaging perspective where the requirement accumulation is within interval [a,b]: the average is always the same.

However, often there are grade of service constraints on how to service the cells which arrive to the switch according to the arrival function $f(t)$. Typically an important criterion is to delay each cell no more than a specified interval of time ϵ.

Then one is interested in obtaining the engineering level $L(f,\epsilon)$ such that if the switch is provisioned with this number of transmission resources, then no cell will ever be delayed more than ϵ units of time. $L(f,\epsilon)$ is called the generalized average of $f(t)$. See Figure 8.3. Clearly,

$$L(f,0) = \max_{[a,b]} f(t)$$

namely, if the switch is not allowed to delay any cell and is not allowed to discard any cell then one must design for the peak rate.

When $\epsilon = b - a$, then $L(f,\epsilon) = L(f, b - a) \approx A(f, b - a)$, namely,[3] the designer can average the traffic over the period in question and design for that level. Note, however that this approach may also require a large number of buffers B. In the top part of Figure 8.4, ten cells arrive at time 1 of a 10-time-unit window. If there are not constrains on how quickly the cells have to be moved along, then the designer could put in place a trunk resource passing (servicing) 1 cell per unit time. At the end of the 10 time-units interval, all 10 cells would have been transmitted. Ten buffers are required to store the

---

[3] $L(f, b - a) \geq A(f,b - a)$. In some specific cases the equality holds; this occurs when $f(t)$ is monotonically decreasing on [a,b], as shown later.

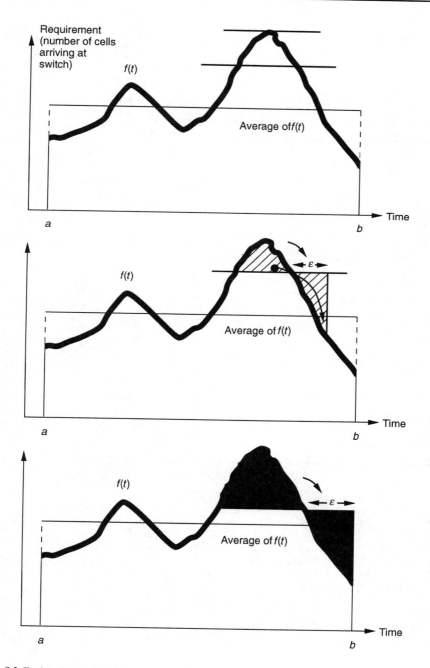

Figure 8.3 Engineering level *L(f,e)*.

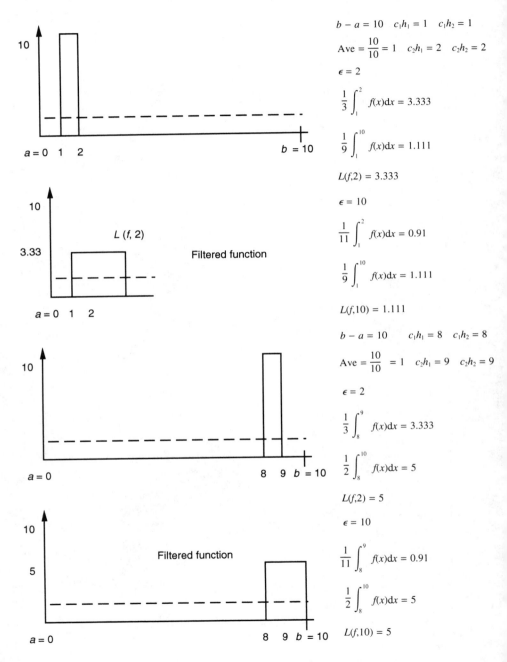

Figure 8.4 The generalized average is stronger than the average to meet QOS.

cells until they can be gracefully discharged. The fact that the average method is not a useful approach (because work is aposteriori pushed into the already gone past), is demonstrated by the fact that if ten cells arrive at time 8 of a 10-time-unit window, the average is still 1, telling the designer to put in place a trunk resource passing (servicing) 1 cell per unit time. However, by time $t = 10$, only two cell would have been sent out, and 8 cells remain unsent. This forces designers to perform the averaging over shorter intervals, say the "busy hour;" however, the approach remains flawed.

With the $L(f,\epsilon)$ approach, arriving work can only be postponed into the future (up to ϵ units away). By construct, the unfinished work at b is zero. Additionally no cell is allowed to be delayed beyond the set criterion by appropriately deriving $L(f,\epsilon)$. The number of buffers will also be lower.

Figure 8.4 depicts the $L(f,\epsilon)$ for the arrival function $f(t)$ (later sections will show how this is obtained). While the average of the function is one, $L(f,2) = 3.333$, if the arrival occurred early (cells can only be delayed at most two cell times), and $L(f,3) = 5$, if the traffic arrived late and must still be moved out before the expiration of the observation period. Figure 8.4 also shows what the "filtered function" looks like (e.g., for $\epsilon = 2$, $L(f,2) = 3.333$). This means that, if the output trunk pool is made to absorb (transmit) 3.3 cells per unit time and 10 cells came in at time $t = 1$, then on the output side 3.3 cells will be dispensed at time $t = 1$, 3.3 cells at time $t = 2$, and 3.3 cells at time $t = 3$. No cell shall have been delayed by more than 2 time units (filtering is discussed in Section 8.2.5).

8.1.3 Examples

Table 1.1 depicts an example that is worked out numerically; here $L(f,1) = 6$. Two other cases are also shown in Table 8.1 when the engineering level is less that 6. Figure 8.5 shows the example graphically.

Table 8.1
Example of Engineering Level, Buffer Size, and Cell Loss, $\epsilon = 1$

t	$f(t)$	$h\rightarrow4$		$h\rightarrow5$		$h\rightarrow6$[†]	
		$O(a)$	Loss	$O(a)$	Loss	$O(a)$	Loss
1	5	1	0	0	0	0	0
2	5	2	0	0	0	0	0
3	9	7	3	4	0	3	0
4	9	12	5	8	3	6	0
5	2	10	0	5	0	2	0
6	2	8	0	2	0	0	0
7	1	5	0	0	0	0	0
8	1	2	0	0	0	0	0
Total	34		8		3		0

[†] $L(f,1)$

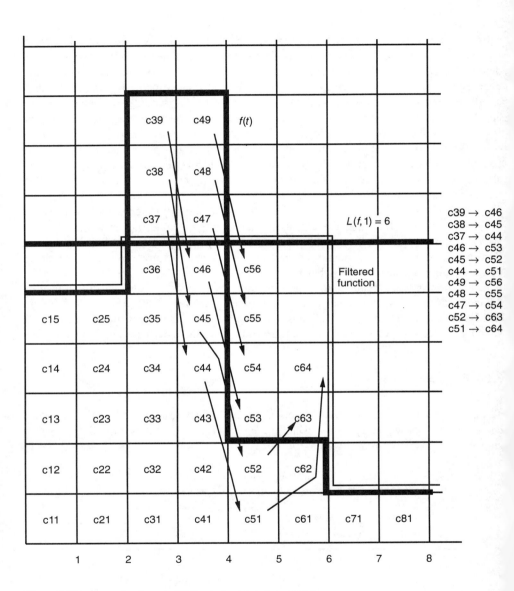

Figure 8.5 An example of $e = 1$. (Cells can be delayed one unit.)

Table 8.2 shows what happens when the work (cells) can be buffered for two units of time; now $L(f,2) = 4.67$. Here cells can now be appropriately pushed into the future in such a way as to *reduce* the required engineering level compared with the previous value. An additional case is also shown in Table 8.2 when the engineering level is less than 4.67. Figure 8.6 shows the example graphically.

Table 8.2
Example of Engineering Level, Buffer Size, and Cell Loss $\epsilon = 2$

t	$f(t)$	$h \rightarrow 4.5$		$h \rightarrow 4.67^{\dagger}$	
		$O(a)$	Loss	$O(a)$	Loss
1	5	1	0	0.33	0
2	5	2	0	0.66	0
3	9	7	0	4.99	0
4	9	12	4	9.32	0
5	2	10	0	6.65	0
6	2	8	0	3.98	0
7	1	5	0	0.31	0
8	1	2	0	0	0
Total	34		4		0

$^{\dagger}L(f,2)$

When $f(t)$ is continuously differentiable (i.e. it is a smooth continuous function), then the calculus procedures described in Section 8.2 must be employed to derive $L(f,\epsilon)$; if $f(t)$ takes only a finite number of discrete values, then a numerical procedure exemplified in the Tables 8.1 and 8.2 can be employed. Note that in general ϵ can be any (fractional) value, but for these simple examples it is kept as an integer. Also, for these examples, $f(t)$ has only one extrema ($df/dx = 0$), but in general it can be any (integrable) function.

Figures 8.5, 8.6, and 8.7 show how work requirements (cell ij (c_{ij})), can be postponed into the future, but within the specified constraint. In Figure 8.5 (corresponding to Table 8.1), the cells can only be delayed one unit. In Figures 8.6 and 8.7 (corresponding to Table 8.2), the cells can be delayed up to two units.

The tables show unfinished work, $O(x)$, indicating how it builds up and various points (here, one). When the engineering level is selected correctly, the unfinished work at the end of the interval is 0. Note that in Table 8.1 (with allowed delay up to one unit), up to six buffers are required when the engineering level is selected (correctly) to be 6. In fact, when engineering at the level $L(f,\epsilon)$, the needed buffers, B, will be $B = \epsilon L(f,\epsilon)$. If a lower engineering level is selected, the number of buffers can be higher. The table's loss column represents the number of cells lost. The tables also show what would happen if an inadequate engineering level is used. For example, assume that the switch could only process 4 cells per unit time for the case $\epsilon = 1$. The third and fourth columns of the table show that at the end of the cycle there would be two cells left over which could not be moved out. Also note that there is a relatively high buildup of cells which have to buffered since the switch is "slow" (i.e. only processed 4 cells per unit time). At $t =$, 12 cells would have to be buffered (unless they are flushed from the system, when they age beyond the stipulated ϵ delay requirement). Worse yet, a number of cells incur more than one unit of delay.

Figure 8.8 depicts what happens to cells when the engineering level is not properly selected. Figure 8.8 displays graphically the data of Table 8.1 (columns 3 and 4), for a selected engineering level of $h = 4$. At time $t = 3$, 3 cells will be "lost" (i.e. have aged

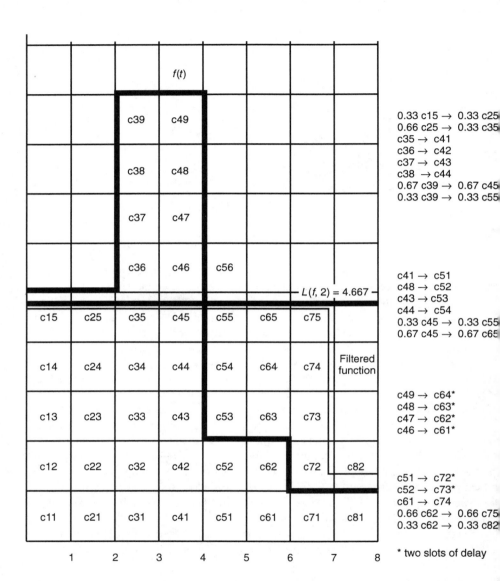

Figure 8.6 An example of $e = 2$. (Cells can be delayed two units.)

beyond the desired limit); at $t = 4$, 5 cells will be lost; etc., for a total of 8 lost cells over the time window of interest. For example, at $t = 3$ the switch already already had two cells which were being buffered for one unit time and hence should be immediately transmitted, (i.e. $O(2) = 2$) when 9 more cells arrive, for a total of 11. At this point,

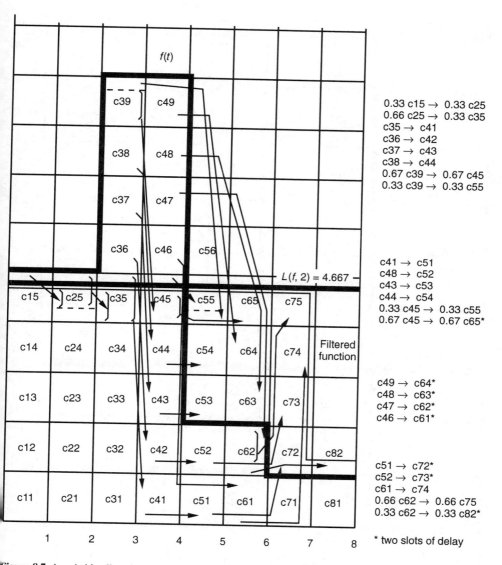

Figure 8.7 A switch's allocation of work to meet a delay requirement of two units at the correctly specified engineering level predicted by RT.

cells can be transmitted, 4 can be buffered for one unit time, and 3 must go unattended (i.e. lost). Raising the engineering level to $h = 5$ reduces the lost cells to 3, and raising t to $L(f,1)$ implies that no cells at all are lost. Lowering the engineering value to $h = 3$ implies that more cells are lost. In fact, as Figure 8.9 shows, 13 cells are lost.

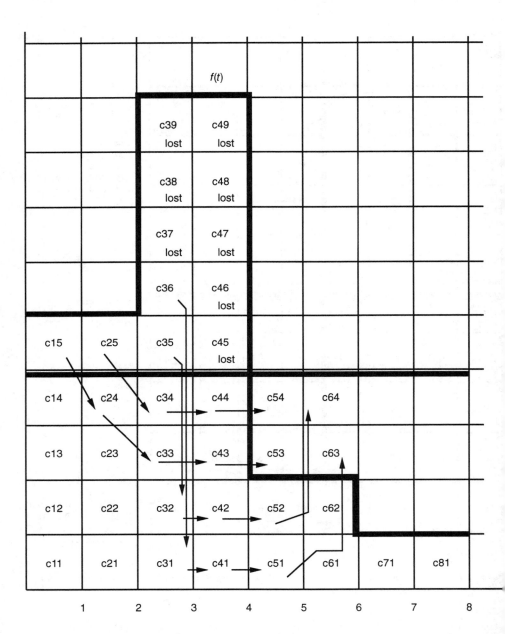

Figure 8.8 Lost cells when engineering level is selected below what is predicted by RT. Here the level is se
to $h = 4$. Cells can only be delayed one unit, by assumption. Eight cells are lost.

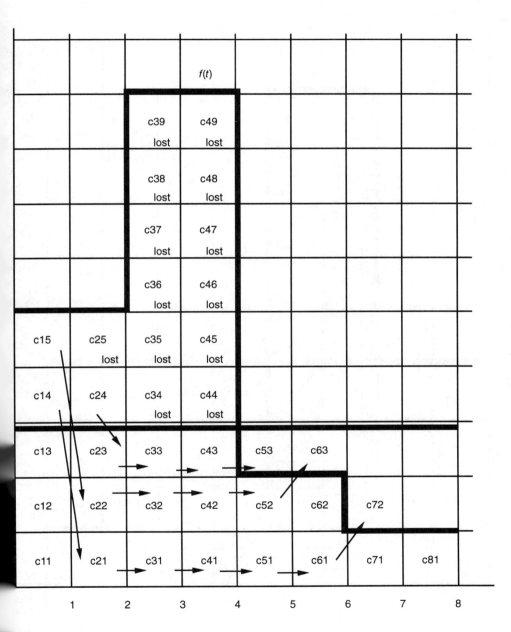

Figure 8.9 Lost cells when engineering level is selected below what is predicted by RT. Here the level is set to $h = 3$. Cells can only be delayed one unit, by assumption. Thirteen cells are lost.

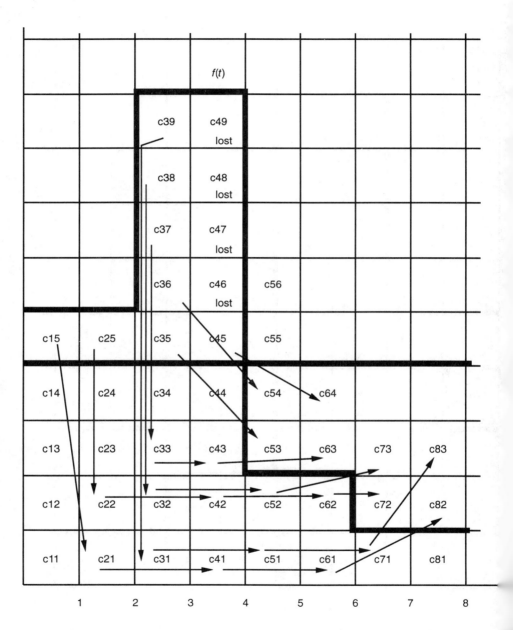

Figure 8.10 Lost cells when engineering level is selected below what is predicted by RT. Here the level is set to $h = 4$. Cells can be delayed by two units, by assumption. Only four cells are lost.

Figure 8.10 shows the same example of Figure 8.8, (i.e. the engineering value is selected below what the theory predicts: $h = 4$ instead of $L(f,1) = 6$ and instead of $L(f,2) = 4.67$), but the cells are allowed to be delayed for two units. As would be expected less cells are lost in this case: only four cells are lost, rather than 8 as in the case of Figure 8.8.

Note that the time scale in cells per second for a first-generation ATM switch will be 1.45 Mcps, i.e. assuming a STS-12c interface. Over a 3,600-second window this means a very large number of cells *per user*.

These examples (tables and figures) have been included to motivate some of the complex RT mathematical derivations which follow.

Section 8.2 derives closed form expressions for any generic arrival function $f(t)$, including the case where there are two types of customers (low- and high-priority). Chapter 9 applies the theory to some typical ATM environments.

8.2 RELAXATION THEORY

8.2.1 Introduction

Let $f(t) \geq 0$ for all t represent a requirement function (in terms of cells arriving at the switch), defined over [a,b]. Assume that all arrivals must be processed within an interval $\epsilon \leq b - a$. The interval [a,b] represents a time window of interest, for example the "busy hour," a generic hour, the "busy day," a generic day, and so on. Assume that $f(t)$ is Reimann-Stieltjes integrable over [a,b] (i.e. $f(t)$ can have finitely many discontinuities). Also assume that $f(t)$ has compact support on [a,b] (i.e. $f(t)$ is zero outside the interval [a, b]).

The goal is to find an engineering level $L(f,\epsilon)$, such that at time b the unfinished work $O(b) = 0$, and at no point z in the interval [a,b], $O(z) > L(f,\epsilon)\epsilon$.

If there were no time constraints in providing the required services, and all such requests and associated work could be queued as long as necessary (in an infinite size buffer) then, in generalities, the average of $f(t)$ on [a,b],

$$A(f, b - a) = \frac{1}{(b - a)} \int_a^b f(x)\mathrm{d}x$$

is an approximation for the engineering level (this is actually true only in very specific cases, because work cannot be moved aposteriori into the past). Suppose on the other hand that the service must be provided within ϵ from the request of service ($\epsilon \leq b - a$) because of contractual (tariff) stipulation, grade of service requirements, or simply because the buffering facilities are not available. The goal is to derive the appropriate engineering level for this general situation. Once a generic formula for $L(f, \epsilon)$ is obtained, the problem can be "relaxed" to any value of ϵ, all the way to the average of $f(t)$; hence, we refer to this technique as relaxation theory.

The problem is rather difficult, and even after a general procedure is delineated the computation in closed form of a specific level is relatively laborious. If $f(t)$ only attains a finite number of values (i.e. the time domain is discrete) then the problem can always be solved with numerical methods.

In this section we first provide a general recursive procedure for the computation of $L(f,\epsilon)$ (Section 8.2.2). We then provide several examples and closed form computation for various classes of functions (Section 8.2.3). A closed form solution for *any* function $f(t)$ is provided next (Section 8.2.4). The filter of the function $f(t)$, when subjected to the effect of the generalized averaging procedure, is provided in Section 8.2.5. We then briefly address the case where the request function is stochastic in nature (Section 8.2.6). An initial assessment of the techniques required to solve the problem in a prioritized environment is given in Section 8.2.7. Finally, some approximations are presented in Section 8.2.8, for the cases where one wants to avoid a closed form solution.

The following generic results of the generalized average will be evident from the theory:

(1) *Boundedness of the generalized average*

Let

$$\Pi(v) = \frac{1}{(b-v)} \int_v^b f(x)\mathrm{d}x$$

and

$$\Pi = \max_{v \in [a,b]} \Pi(v)$$

Then, $L(f,\epsilon) \geq \Pi \geq \Pi(v)$ for all v in the interval [a,b]. In particular $L(f,\epsilon) \geq \Pi(a)$, where $\Pi(a) = A(f, b - a)$.

(2) *Linearity of the generalized average*

$$L(af,\epsilon) = aL(f,\epsilon)$$

(3) *Subadditivity of the generalized average*

$$L(f+g,\epsilon) \leq L(f,\epsilon) + L(g,\epsilon)$$

(4) *Equality with the average*

If $f(t)$ is monotonically decreasing in the interval [a,b], then $L(f,b-a) = A(f,b-a)$.

(5) *Numerical calculation of $L(f,\epsilon)$*

If $f(t)$ acquires only a finite number of values in [a,b], then $L(f,\epsilon)$ can be calculated by recursive numerical techniques. Otherwise, infinitesimal calculus techniques are required.

(6) Relationship with burstiness of f(t)

Define burstiness of a function in the interval [a,b] as

$$\beta = \frac{\underset{[a,b]}{max} f(s)}{A(f, b - a)}$$

Then, as β increases, $L(f,\epsilon)$ increases.

8.2.2 Definition of Generalized Average

Consider fixed real numbers $h \geq 0$, $\epsilon \geq 0$ and a sequence

$$V = \{x_n \text{ in } [a,b], \text{ with } x_0 = a \text{ and } x_m = b, \max d(x_{n-1}, x_n) = \Delta\}$$

Recursively define the infinitesimal quantity

$$S(\epsilon, h, V, \Delta) = [O(x_n)|x_n \epsilon V, O(x_n) = \begin{cases} \max \{0, O(x_{n-1}) + \int_{x_{n-1}}^{x_n} \min (0, f(s) - h)ds\} + \\ \qquad \int_{x_{n-1}}^{x_n} \max (0, f(s) - h)ds \quad \epsilon \neq 0 \\ \int_{x_{n-1}}^{x_n} \max (0, f(s) - h)ds \qquad \epsilon = 0 \end{cases}$$

with $O(a) = 0$. Now define the limiting quantity (if it exists)

$$L(f, \epsilon, \Delta) = \inf h$$
$$O(x_n) \leq h\epsilon \text{ for all } n$$
$$O(b) = 0$$

namely, the smallest h such that the unfinished work at b is zero, and at each x_n, it is less that what can be accomplished in the next time slot, that is, $h\epsilon$. We call

$$L(f, \epsilon) = \underset{\Delta \to 0}{\text{Lim}} L(f, \epsilon, \Delta)$$

the *generalized average* of $f(t)$. Note that $O(x) \geq 0$ for all x.

The term

$$\int_{x_{n-1}}^{x_n} \max\, (0, f(s) - h)\mathrm{d}s$$

represents the new work which accumulates between x_{n-1} and x_n; namely, the integration of the service requests exceeding the level h. Note that if the value h is not exceeded over the interval in question, this new work is zero, because of the maximum function within the integral sign. The term

$$\int_{x_{n-1}}^{x_n} \min\, (0, f(s) - h)\mathrm{d}s$$

represents the net amount of accumulated work which can be accomplished between x_{n-1} and x_n (potentially by postponing some of the new work to some future time—within an ϵ). If $f(t)$ exceeds h, no net work can be accomplished, but only a postponement of current work, in order to take care of old work. Note that the integral is negative, thus subtracts from the total work carried over from x_{n-1}, i.e. $O(x_{n-1})$, the amount of total work (excluding new work) which can be accomplished in the interval (x_{n-1}, x_n).

The quantity

$$0\, (x_{n-1}) + \int_{x_{n-1}}^{x_n} \min\, (0, f(s) - h)\mathrm{d}s$$

represents the amount of old work which could not be accomplished in $(x_{n-1}, x_n]$; this work could never be negative, hence, the maximum function (i.e. no future work can be done at any point, even if excess capacity exists, only old work). Finally,

$$\max\, \{0,\, O(x_{n-1}) + \int_{x_{n-1}}^{x_n} \min\, (0, f(s) - h)\mathrm{d}s\} + \int_{x_{n-1}}^{x_n} \max\, (0, f(s) - h)\mathrm{d}s$$

is the total work that spills over into the interval $(x_{n-1}, x_n]$. In each case it must be less than $h\epsilon$. In summary, two conditions must be met:

1. $O(x_n) \le h\epsilon$ for all x_n; and
2. $O(b) = 0$.

It can be shown that an equivalent definition for $O(x_n)$ is

$$O(x_n) = \max\, \{0,\, O(x_{n-1}) + \int_{x_{n-1}}^{x_n} f(s)\mathrm{d}s - (x_n - x_{n-1})\, h\}$$

However, we will use the first definition since it is easier to obtain closed form expressions from that formulation.

Figure 8.11 depicts one example of how a calculation can be carried out. Note that $(f,1) = 3$. Since $\epsilon = 1$, work represented by cell A and B can only be postponed one time unit into the future; they can be moved to cell D and E respectively. Cells C, D, and E must then be moved over to cells F, G, H. Note in this example how the integral

$$\int_{x_{n-1}}^{x_n} \min (0, f(s) - h)ds$$

represents the net accumulated work which can be accomplished in $(x_{n-1}, x_n]$; many times this is zero. For $h = 2$, $O(1)$ and $O(2)$ exceed $h\epsilon$, thus disqualifying this choice of h. The correct engineering level is 3.

2.3 Computation of $L(f,\epsilon)$ for Simple Functions

The closed form computation of $L(f,\epsilon)$ is laborious even for simple functions. In this section we carry out several such computations.

2.3.1 $\epsilon = 0$

$\epsilon = 0$ then

$$O(b) = \int_b^a \max (0, f(s) - h)ds;$$

now,

$$O(b) \le (b - a)z$$

with

$$z = \max_{[a,b]}(0, f(s) - h)$$
$$= \max (0, (\max (0, f(s))) - h).$$

Therefore, we satisfy $O(b) = 0$ if and only if $h \ge \max f(s)$ on the interval $[a,b]$. Then,

$$L(f,0) = \max_{[a,b]} f(s).$$

See Figure 8.12.

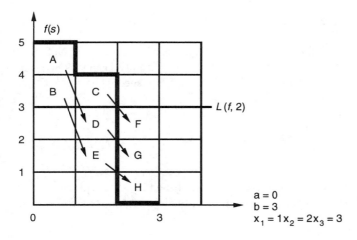

	h = 4			h = 3			h = 2		
	$x_1 = 1$	$x_2 = 2$	$x_3 = b = 3$	$x_1 = 1$	$x_2 = 2$	$x_3 = b = 3$	$x_1 = 1$	$x_2 = 2$	$x_3 = b = 3$
$v_1 = O(x_{n-1})$	0	1	1	0	2	3	0	3	5
$v_2 = \int_{x_{n-1}}^{x_n} \min\{0, f(s) - h\}ds$	0	0	-4	0	0	-3	0	0	-2
$v_3 = \max(v1 + v2)$	0	1	0	0	2	0	0	3	3
$v_4 = \int_{x_{n-1}}^{x_n} \max\{0, f(s) - h\}ds$	1	0	0	2	1	0	3	2	0
$0(x_n) = v3 + v4$	1	1	0	2	3	0	3	5	3

Figure 8.11 An example of computation using the calculus method.

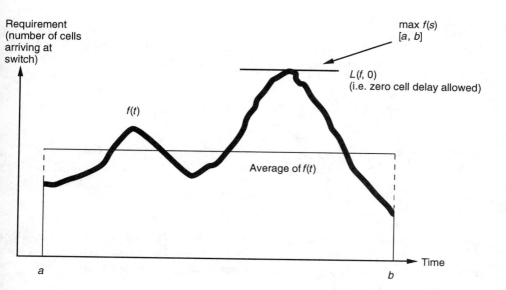

Figure 8.12 $L(f,0)$.

8.2.3.2 $L(f, \epsilon) \geq f(b)$

We want to show that for any function $f(s)$, $L(f,\epsilon) \geq f(b)$. We have

$$O(b) = \max \left[0, O(b - \epsilon) + \int_{b-\epsilon}^{b} \min (0, f(s) - h)ds \right] + \int_{b-\epsilon}^{b} \max (0, f(s) - h)ds$$

Then

$$O(b) \geq \int_{b-\epsilon}^{b} \max (0, f(s) - h)ds$$

since we are ignoring a positive term (max term). Now, if h satisfying the condition were less than $f(b)$ (i.e $h < f(b)$), the integral above would exceed 0, resulting in the situation

$$O(b) \geq \int_{b-\epsilon}^{b} \max (0, f(s) - h)ds > 0$$

or $O(b) > 0$, which is not allowed. Hence, $L(f,\epsilon) \geq f(b)$.

8.2.3.3 f(s) Monotonically Decreasing on [a,b]

Here, we want to show that, if function $f(t)$ is monotonically decreasing on [a,b] the $L(f, b - a) = A(f, b - a)$. As seen in Figure 8.13, for any z_h one has, in this case,

$$O(x_n) = \max\left[0, O(x_{n-1}) + \int_{x_{n-1}}^{x_n} \min(0, f(s) - h)ds\right] + \int_{x_{n-1}}^{x_n} \max(0, f(s) - h)ds$$

$$= \max\left[0, O(z_h) + \int_{z_h}^{b} \min(0, f(s) - h)ds\right] + \int_{z_h}^{b} \max(0, f(s) - h)ds$$

$$= \max\left[0, \int_{a}^{z_h}(f(s) - h)ds + \int_{z_h}^{b}(f(s) - h)ds\right]$$

since (a) the unfinished work up to z_h is nothing more than the area above a line at heigh h and below $f(t)$; (b) the third term is zero in the interval $[z_h, b]$; and (c) the second ter is negative in the interval $[z_h, b]$ (hence the minimum function disappears).

In turn this equates to

$$O(x_n) = \max\left[0, \int_{a}^{b}(f(s) - h)ds\right]$$

$$= \max\left[0, -(b - a)h + \int_{a}^{b}f(s)ds\right]$$

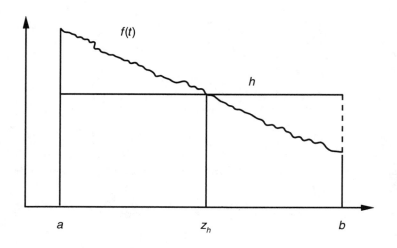

Figure 8.13 Monotonically decreasing requirement function.

Now at $x_n = b$ one must have $O(b) = 0$. This means

$$0 = -(b - a)L(f, b - a) + \int_a^b f(s)ds$$

or

$$L(f, b - a) = \frac{1}{(b - a)} \int_a^b f(s)ds = A(f, b - a)$$

8.2.3.4 If max $f(s) = f(b)$, then $L(f, \epsilon) = f(b)$

First we show that, if $L(f, \epsilon)$ is set equal to $f(b)$, then $O(b) = 0$; and then we show that if $L(f, \epsilon) = f(b) - \delta$ then $O(b) > 0$.

For a small σ note that

$$O(b) = \max\left[0, \; 0\,(b - \sigma) + \int_{b-\sigma}^b \min\,(0, f(s) - f(b))ds\right] + \int_{b-\sigma}^b \max\,(0, f(s) - f(b))ds$$

Since on $[b - \sigma, b]$, $f(s) \leq f(b)$, the second integral is zero, while the first integral is a *negative number*, subtracting from the $O(b - \sigma)$ term; therefore

$$O(b) \leq O(b - \sigma).$$

Now,

$$O(b - \sigma) = \max\left[0, \; 0(b - 2\sigma) + \int_{b-2\sigma}^{b-\sigma} \min\,(0, f(s) - f(b))ds\right]$$

$$+ \int_{b-2\sigma}^{b-\sigma} \max\,(0, f(s) - f(b))ds$$

Since on $[b - 2\sigma, b - \sigma]$, $f(s) \leq f(b)$, the second integral is zero, while the first integral is a *negative number*, subtracting from $O(b - 2\sigma)$; therefore

$$O(b - \sigma) \leq O(b - 2\sigma)$$

Continuing this process we obtain

$$O(b) \le O(b - \sigma) \le O(b - 2\sigma) \le O(b - 3\sigma) \le \dots \le O(a) = 0$$

Next we want to show that if $L(f,\epsilon) = f(b) - \delta$ then $O(b) > 0$. Now, for some small σ

$$O(b) = \max\left[0,\ O(b - \sigma) + \int_{b-\sigma}^{b} \min\ (0, f(s) - f(b) + \delta)ds \right]$$
$$+ \int_{b-\sigma}^{b} \max\ (0, f(s) - f(b) + \delta)ds$$

The second integral is now positive (>0), while the first integral is zero. This implies that $O(b) = O(b - \sigma) +$ a positive number, that is $O(b) > 0$.

8.2.3.5 As Burstiness Increases so Does L(f,e)

We wish to show that as the burstiness increases so does $L(f,\epsilon)$ as long as $\epsilon \le \epsilon_0$ (i.e. for a relatively small ϵ). Burstiness is defined here as:

$$\beta = \frac{\max_{[a,b]} f(s)}{A(f,\ b - a)}$$

While this is true in general, we examine in detail only the case where the average of the function remains the same, but the maximum increases, as shown with the examples of Figure 8.14. Additionally, for proof's simplification we only demonstrate the condition explicitly for the case shown in Figure 8.15. We wish to show that $L(f_1,\epsilon) < L(f_2,\epsilon)$.

Assume that this were not the case, namely $L(f_1,\epsilon) = L(f_2,\ \epsilon) = L$. We show that this is not possible.

Define ζ_L and ζ_R as the points where $f_1(\zeta_L) = L(f_1,\epsilon) = L$ and $f_1(\zeta_R) = L(f_1,\epsilon)$. Also define μ_L and μ_R as the points where $f_2(\mu_L) = L(f_2,\epsilon) = L$ and $f_2(\mu_R) = L(f_2,\epsilon)$. Also let $f_1(\alpha_L) = f_2(\alpha_L) = K$ and $f_1(\alpha_R) = f_2(\alpha_R) = K$. Two cases exist: (1) $L \le K$; and (2) $L > K$. For f_1 one has

$$O(\zeta_R) = \max\left[0,\ O(\zeta_L) + \int_{\zeta_L}^{\zeta_R} \min\ (0, f_1(s) - h)ds \right] + \int_{\zeta_L}^{\zeta_R} \max\ (0, f_1(s) - h)ds$$

In the interval in question, the first integral is zero. Then

$$O(\zeta_R) = O(\zeta_L) + \int_{\zeta_L}^{\zeta_R} (f_1(s) - h)ds$$

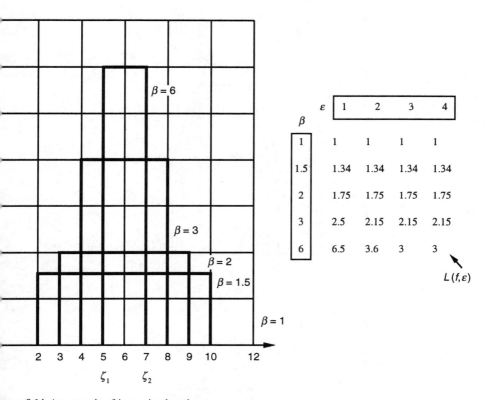

gure 8.14 An example of increasing burstiness.

imilarly,

$$O(\mu_R) = O(\mu_L) + \int_{\mu_L}^{\mu_R} (f_2(s) - h)\mathrm{d}s$$

fact, by definition and because of the form of $f(s)$,

$$O(\zeta_R) = \int_{\zeta_L}^{\zeta_R} (f_1(s) - h)\mathrm{d}s$$

$$O(\mu_R) = \int_{\mu_L}^{\mu_R} (f_2(s) - h)\mathrm{d}s$$

y definition $f_2(\mu_R) = L(f_2,\epsilon)$ and $O(\mu_R) = \epsilon L(f_2,\epsilon)$. Also $f_1(\zeta_R) = L(f_1,\epsilon)$ and $O(\zeta_R) = \epsilon L(f_1,\epsilon)$. ince by assumption $L(f_1,\epsilon) = L(f_2,\ \epsilon) = L$, it follows that $O(\zeta_R) = O(\mu_R) = O(\mu_R)$, or

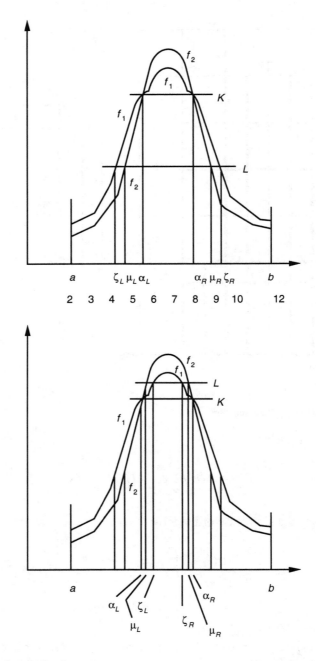

Figure 8.15 Functions analyzed.

$$\int_{\mu_L}^{\mu_R} (f_2(s) - h)ds = \int_{\zeta_L}^{\zeta_R} (f_1(s) - h)ds$$

r, by simplification

$$L[(\mu_L - \zeta_L) + (\zeta_R - \mu_R)] + \int_{\mu_L}^{\mu_R} f_2(s)ds = \int_{\zeta_L}^{\zeta_R} f_1(s)ds$$

ow, since the average of f_1 and f_2 are the same, we have

$$\int_a^{\zeta_L} f_1(s)ds + \int_{\zeta_L}^{\zeta_R} f_1(s)ds + \int_{\zeta_R}^b f_1(s)ds = \int_a^{\mu_L} f_2(s)ds + \int_{\mu_L}^{\mu_R} f_2(s)ds + \int_{\mu_R}^b f_2(s)ds$$

y substituting the previous integral for f_1 over (ζ_L, ζ_R) we obtain

$$\int_a^{\zeta_L} f_1(s)ds + L[(\mu_L - \zeta_L) + (\zeta_R - \mu_R)] + \int_{\mu_L}^{\mu_R} f_2(s)ds + \int_{\zeta_R}^b f_1(s)ds$$

$$= \int_a^{\mu_L} f_2(s)ds + \int_{\mu_L}^{\mu_R} f_2(s)ds + \int_{\mu_R}^b f_2(s)ds$$

r,

$$\int_a^{\zeta_L} f_1(s)ds + L[(\mu_L - \zeta_L) + (\zeta_R - \mu_R)] + \int_{\zeta_R}^b f_1(s)ds = \int_a^{\mu_L} f_2(s)ds + \int_{\mu_R}^b f_2(s)ds$$

ase 1: $L \leq K = f_1(\alpha_L) = f_2(\alpha_L) = f_1(\alpha_R) = f_2(\alpha_R)$

his last expression is not possible because $f_2 < f_1$ over the interval (a, μ_L) and over the
tterval (μ_R, b); in fact, one has $f_2 < f_1$ over (a, α_L) and (α_R, b), as seen in Figure 8.15.

ase 2: $L > K = f_1(\alpha_L) = f_2(\alpha_L) = f_1(\alpha_R) = f_2(\alpha_R)$

his last expression derived above,

$$\int_{\mu_L}^{\mu_R} (f_2(s) - h)ds = \int_{\zeta_L}^{\zeta_R} (f_1(s) - h)ds$$

cannot be possible since the interval (ζ_L, ζ_R) is completely contained within the interval (μ_L, μ_R) and in that interval $f_1 < f_2$.

Hence we have concluded that as the burstiness increase, so does $L(f,\epsilon)$ for reasonably small ϵ. To demonstrate the last point, note that it was stated earlier that if $f(s)$ is monotonically decreasing in [a,b], then $L(f, b - a) = A(f,b - a)$. Now assume that the maximum of $f(s)$ increases but the average remains the same, as was the case in this discussion. Here, while the burstiness increases, $L(f,b - a)$ remains the same.

8.2.3.6 Polynodal Functions

A precise characterization of the functions we address is given in Section 8.2.4. Momentarily we refer to the functions of Figure 8.16 as a polynodal function. In the following subsections we will provide a closed form solution to each of these functions to pave the way for the general solution presented in Section 8.2.4.

Function Type A

As already covered, since the maximum of $f(s)$ occurs at b, $L(f,\epsilon) = f(b)$ for all ϵ.

Function Type B

Based on the definition of $L(f,\epsilon)$, a sequence with $\Delta = \epsilon$ suffices. Let $f(c) = h$ ($h = L(f,\epsilon)$ by postulate), and $j\epsilon < c \le (j + 1)\epsilon$. Then

$$O(\epsilon) = \int_a^\epsilon (f(s) - h)ds,$$

$$O(2\epsilon) = \int_a^{2\epsilon} (f(s) - h)ds,$$

$$\dots$$

$$O(j\epsilon) = \int_a^{j\epsilon} (f(s) - h)ds,$$

$$O(c) = \int_a^c (f(s) - h)ds$$

Because of the nature of $f(s)$, $O(c)$ is the largest unfinished work; in fact,

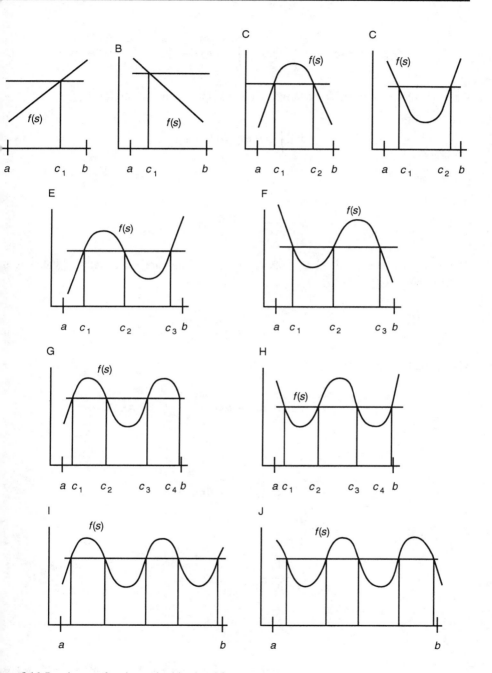

ure 8.16 Requirement functions solved in closed form.

$$O(c + \epsilon) = \int_a^c (f(s) - h)ds + \int_c^{c+\epsilon} (f(s) - h)ds < \int_a^c (f(s) - h)ds$$

since the second integral is negative. Thus we impose the constraint

$$\int_a^c (f(s) - h)ds > h\epsilon$$

or

$$\frac{1}{c - a + \epsilon} \int_a^c f(s)ds \le h$$

The unknown c is obtained by solving the following integral equation (which is not unreasonable in practice)

$$f(c) = \frac{1}{c - a + \epsilon} \int_a^c f(s)ds$$

The second constraint is that

$$O(b) = \max \left(0, \int_a^c (f(s) - h)ds + \int_c^b (f(s) - h)ds\right) = 0$$

or

$$\int_a^b (f(s) - h)ds \le 0$$

from which

$$\frac{1}{b - a} \int_a^b f(s)ds \le h$$

Finally,

$$L(f,\epsilon) = \max \left[\frac{1}{b - a} \int_a^b f(s)ds, \frac{1}{c - a + \epsilon} \int_a^c f(s)ds\right]$$

ith c given above. To be precise, we should write c_ϵ instead of c; we use the simpler otation for convenience.

Three numerical examples follow to illustrate the concepts before a set of completely losed form expressions are derived.

Consider the top example of Figure 8.17. Here the two components of the max term or h are equal; note that $O(c) = O(2) = 6 = h\epsilon$ is the largest unfinished work. Also note at $O(b) = 0$. Consider the second example of Figure 8.17. The "average" term dominates, nd $L(f,2) = 6$. Note that, if $h = 5.5$, the constraint $O(b) = 0$ is violated. Again, $O(c)$ is e largest unfinished work. Finally consider the third example of Figure 8.17. Here

$$\int_0^8 (8 - x) \, dx = 4$$

ow

$$\frac{1}{c + 1} \int_0^c (8 - x) dx = 8 - c$$

mplies

$$\frac{1}{c + 1} \{8c - c^2/2\} = 8 - c$$

r

$$c = 3.123 \text{ and}$$
$$\frac{1}{4.123} \int_0^{3.123} (8 - x) \, dx = 4.877$$

or $\epsilon = 1$; thus $L(f,1) = 4.877$ (it is also possible to derive a completely closed form olution, as we do below). Note that, for this selection of h, $O(c + 1) = h\epsilon$ and $O(b) =$. If we had used $h = 4$, then $O(2) > h\epsilon$, $O(3) > h\epsilon$, and $O(4) > h\epsilon$, all of which are nacceptable.

xample: Linear Functions. Let $f(s) = A - Bs$. Then the integral equation

$$\frac{1}{c - a + \epsilon} \int_a^c (A - Bs) ds = A - Bs$$

218

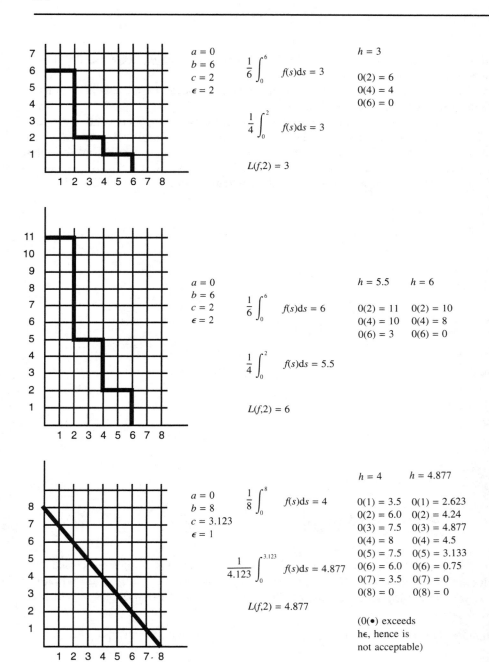

Figure 8.17 Examples solved in closed form.

leads to

$$c = (a - \epsilon) + \sqrt{\epsilon^2 - 2a\epsilon + 2A\epsilon/B}$$

and

$$h_1 = A - B(a - \epsilon) - \sqrt{B^2\epsilon^2 - 2B^2a\epsilon + 2A\epsilon B}$$

Also we have

$$h_2 = \frac{1}{b - a} \int_a^b (A - Bs)ds = A - (B/2)(a + b)$$

and

$$L(f, \epsilon) = \max(h_1, h_2)$$

It is clear that a cross point exists if we make ϵ sufficiently large, since h_2 is independent of ϵ. At $\epsilon = 0$, $h_1 = A - Ba$, $h_2 = A - (B/2) a - (B/2)b$; since $b > a$, $h_1 > h_2$, and $L(f, 0) = A - Ba$, as expected.

For the example of the bottom part of Figure 8.17, $A = 8$, and $B = 1$. Then $h_1 = 8 - (0 - \epsilon) - \mathrm{Sqrt}(\epsilon^2 - 0 + 16\epsilon)$ and $h_2 = 8 - 0.5(8) = 4$. Then

$$L(f, \epsilon) = \max(4, 8 + \epsilon - \mathrm{Sqrt}(\epsilon^2 + 16\epsilon))$$

The results are shown in Table 8.3.

Example: Exponential Functions. Let $f(s) = e^{-s}$, $a = 0$. Then the average of $f(s)$ is

$$\frac{1}{b} \int_0^b e^{-s}ds = (1 - e^{-b})/b = h_2$$

Solving for c and h_1 are obvious.

$$e^{-c} = \frac{1}{b + \epsilon} \int_0^c e^{-s}ds$$

$$e^{-c} = \frac{1}{b + \epsilon + 1} = h_1$$

Thus,

Table 8.3
Exact value of $L(f,\epsilon)$

ϵ	$L(f,\epsilon)$
1.00	4.877
1.25	4.606
1.50	4.377
1.75	4.177
2.00	4.000
2.25	4.000
2.50	4.000
2.75	4.000
3.00	4.000
4.00	4.000
5.00	4.000
6.00	4.000

$$L(f,\epsilon) = \max \left[\frac{1}{b + \epsilon + 1}, \frac{1 - e^{-b}}{b} \right]$$

or

$$L(f,\epsilon) = \frac{1 - e^{-b}}{b}$$

since this term exceeds $1/(b + \epsilon + 1)$ for all bs and ϵs.

Further Relationship with the Average. There exists ϵ^* such that

$$L(f,\epsilon^*) = \frac{1}{b - a} \int_a^b f(s)ds$$

This states that if ϵ is sufficiently large, the generalized average coincides with the average. We need

$$f(c) = \frac{1}{b - a} \int_a^b f(s)ds$$

Hence one would solve for c. Call this value $f^{-1} (A(f, b - a))$. Then

$$\epsilon^* = \frac{[b - f^{-1}(A(f,b - a))] \displaystyle\int_a^{f^{-1}(A(f,b-a))} f(s)ds + [a - f^{-1}(A(f, b - a))] \displaystyle\int_{f^{-1}(A(f,b-a))}^b f(s)ds}{\displaystyle\int_a^b f(s)ds}$$

For the earlier example of the bottom of Figure 8.17, $c = f^{-1}(4) = 4$. Then

$$\epsilon^* = \frac{(8 - 4)\displaystyle\int_0^4 f(s)ds + (0 - 4)\displaystyle\int_4^8 f(s)ds}{32} = 2$$

For comparison, if $\epsilon = 3$ (using the formula of the first example in this series), $h_1 = 11$ $-$Sqrt $(57) \approx 3.5$ (note however that $O(8) > 0$ if we used this value of h). Hence we have

$$L(f,0) = f(a)$$
$$L(f,\epsilon^*) = A(f, b - a) < f(a)$$
$$L(f,\epsilon) = A(f, b - a) \text{ if } \epsilon > \epsilon^*$$

Function Type C

Assume that $f(s)$ has the general shape of Figure 8.18, with a peak at z. Applying the definition of Section 8.2.2 we obtain

$$O(c_1(h_1)) = 0$$
$$O(c_2(h_1)) = \int_{c_1(h_1)}^{c_2(h_1)} (f(s) - h_1)ds$$

where $c_1(h_1)$ and $c_2(h_1)$ are the points where $f(s)$ intersects h_1. By the nature of $f(s)$, $O(c_2(h_1))$, is the largest unfinished work. In fact,

$$O(c_2(h_1 + \epsilon)) = \int_{c_1(h_1)}^{c_2(h_1)} (f(s) - h_1)ds + \int_{c_2(h_1)}^{c_2(h_1) + \epsilon} (f(s) - h_1)ds < \int_{c_1(h_1)}^{c_2(h_1)} (f(s) - h_1)ds$$

since the second integral is negative. Thus, we impose

$$\int_{c_1(h_1)}^{c_2(h_1)} (f(s) - h_1)ds < h_1\epsilon$$

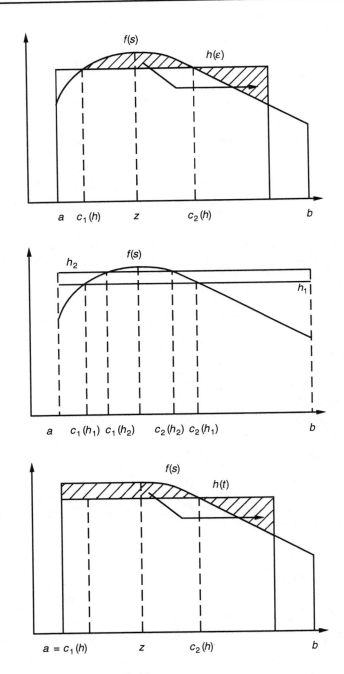

Figure 8.18 Function type C solved in closed form.

or

$$\frac{1}{c_2(h_1) - c_1(h_1)} \int_{c_1(h_1)}^{c_2(h_1)} f(s)ds < h_1\epsilon$$

We define

$$h_1 = \frac{1}{c_2(h_1) - c_1(h_1) + \epsilon} \int_{c_1(h_1)}^{c_2(h_1)} f(s)ds$$

The constants $c_1 = c_1(h_1)$ and $c_2 = c_2(h_1)$ are obtained by solving *simultaneously* the following two integral equations:

$$\begin{cases} f(c_1(h_1)) = \dfrac{1}{c_2(h_1) - c_1(h_1) + \epsilon} \int_{c_1(h_1)}^{c_2(h_1)} f(s)ds \\[2mm] f(c_1(h_1)) = f(c_2(h_1)) \end{cases}$$

The second constraint is obtained by requiring $O(b) = 0$ and by seeking a h_2 such that

$$O(b) = \max\left(0, \int_{c_1(h_2)}^{c_2(h_2)} (f(s) - h_2)ds + \int_{c_2(h_2)}^{b} (f(s) - h_2)ds\right) = 0$$

or

$$\int_{c_1(h_2)}^{b} (f(s) - h_2)ds) \leq 0$$

from which

$$\frac{1}{b - c_1(h_2)} \int_{c_1(h_2)}^{b} f(s)ds \leq h_2$$

We define

$$h_2 = \frac{1}{b - c_1(h_2)} \int_{c_1(h_2)}^{b} f(s)ds$$

The constant $c_1(h_2)$ is obtained by solving the integral equation

$$f(c_1(h_2)) = \frac{1}{b - c_1(h_2)} \int_{c_1(h_2)}^{b} f(s)ds$$

Note that if $h_1 \le h_2$, $c_1(h_2) \ge c_1(h_1)$, $c_2(h_2) \le c_2(h_1)$ by the nature of $f(s)$; therefore

$$\int_{c_1(h_2)}^{c_2(h_2)} (f(s) - h_2)ds \le \int_{c_1(h_2)}^{c_2(h_2)} (f(s) - h_1)ds \le \int_{c_1(h_1)}^{c_2(h_1)} (f(s) - h_1)ds \le h\epsilon$$

namely, the constraint

$$\int_{c_1(h_2)}^{c_2(h_2)} (f(s) - h)ds \le h\epsilon$$

is met.

If $h_1 > h_2$, $c_1(h_2) \le c_1(h_1)$, $c_2(h_1) \le c_2(h_2)$; then

$$\int_{c_1(h_1)}^{b} (f(s) - h_1)ds \le \int_{c_1(h_2)}^{b} (f(s) - h_1)ds \le \int_{c_1(h_2)}^{b} (f(s) - h_2)ds \le 0$$

Namely, the constraint

$$\int_{c_1(h_1)}^{b} (f(s) - h)ds \le 0$$

is met. Finally

$$L(f, \epsilon) = \max \left[\frac{1}{c_2(h_1) - c_1(h_1) + \epsilon} \int_{c_1(h_1)}^{c_2(h_1)} f(s)ds, \frac{1}{b - c_1(h_2)} \int_{c_1(h_2)}^{b} f(s)ds \right]$$

where the values of $c_2(h_1)$, $c_1(h_1)$, and $c_1(h_2)$ are obtained as discussed above. By the natur of $f(s)$

$$\frac{1}{b - c_1(h_2)} \int_{c_1(h_2)}^{b} f(s)ds \geq \frac{1}{b - a} \int_{a}^{b} f(s)ds$$

and

$$L(f,\epsilon) \geq h_2 \geq A(f, b - a)$$

As, in Figure 8.18(c),

$$f(s) = \begin{cases} f(c_1) & d = a \\ A & a < s \leq d \\ g(s) & d < s < b \end{cases}$$

with $g(s)$ monotonically decreasing and

$$\text{Lim}_{x \to d} g(x) = A$$

then we obtain $c_1 = a$ and

$$L(f,\epsilon) = \max \left[\frac{1}{b - a} \int_{a}^{b} f(s)ds, \frac{1}{c_2 - a + \epsilon} \int_{b}^{c_2} f(s)ds \right]$$

as we would expect from Section 8.2.3.6.2. Note that at c_2 we plunk down old area and pick up an equivalent amount of new area (work) to move; this replacement area, plus any new area must be accommodated within an ϵ.

Examples. Several examples follow to demonstrate the use of the formulas derived above.

In Figure 8.19 we compute $L(f,\epsilon)$ for various values of ϵ. For $\epsilon = 1$ and $\epsilon = 2$ the $1/(c_2 + \epsilon - c_1)$ term dominates; for $\epsilon = 3$ the average term $1/(b - c_1)$ dominates. Note that unless h is selected appropriately, either $O(b) = 0$ but $O(x) > h\epsilon$, or $O(b) > 0$. To make the example easy we used a function $f(s)$ such that $c_1(h_1) = c_1(h_2)$ and $c_2(h_1) = c_2(h_2)$. Note, however, that in general these constants may vary with ϵ and so must be obtained explicitly.

Figure 8.20 shows another example. Once again we have used a function for which $c_1(h_1) = c_1(h_2)$ and $c_2(h_1) = c_2(h_2)$, but only for $\epsilon = 1$ or $\epsilon = 2$. For $\epsilon = 3$, $c_1(h_1) \neq c_1(h_2)$ and $c_2(h_1) \neq c_2(h_2)$.

Figure 8.21 shows yet another example. Here $c_1(h_1)$ and $c_1(h_2)$ are determined analytically using the integral equations above (we have made $c_2(h_1) = c_2(h_2) = 4$ to simplify the problem slightly.) For $\epsilon = 1$ we have

$$\frac{1}{5 - c_1(h_1)} \int_{c_1(h_1)}^{4} f(s)ds = f(c_1(h_1))$$

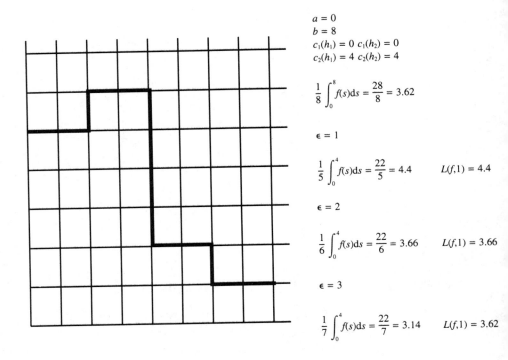

$a = 0$
$b = 8$
$c_1(h_1) = 0 \quad c_1(h_2) = 0$
$c_2(h_1) = 4 \quad c_2(h_2) = 4$

$$\frac{1}{8}\int_0^8 f(s)\,ds = \frac{28}{8} = 3.62$$

$\epsilon = 1$

$$\frac{1}{5}\int_0^4 f(s)\,ds = \frac{22}{5} = 4.4 \qquad L(f,1) = 4.4$$

$\epsilon = 2$

$$\frac{1}{6}\int_0^4 f(s)\,ds = \frac{22}{6} = 3.66 \qquad L(f,1) = 3.66$$

$\epsilon = 3$

$$\frac{1}{7}\int_0^4 f(s)\,ds = \frac{22}{7} = 3.14 \qquad L(f,1) = 3.62$$

	$\varepsilon = 3$			$\varepsilon = 3$			$\varepsilon = 3$		
x	h = 4	h = 34.4	h = 5	h = 3	h = 3.66	h = 5	h = 3	h = 3.62	h = 5
	O(x)	O(x)	O(x)	O(x)	O(x)	O(x)	O(x)	O(x)	O(x)
1	1.00	0.60	0.00	2.00	1.34	0.00	2.00	1.38	0.00
2	2.00	1.20	0.00	4.00	2.68	0.00	4.00	2.76	0.00
3	4.00	2.80	1.00	7.00[††]	5.02	1.00	7.00[††]	5.14	1.00
4	6.00[††]	4.40[†]	2.00	10.00[††]	7.36[†]	2.00	10.00[††]	7.52[†]	2.00
5	4.00	2.00	0.00	9.00[††]	5.70	0.00	9.00[††]	5.90	0.00
6	2.00	0.00	0.00	8.00[††]	4.04	0.00	8.00[††]	4.28	0.00
7	0.00	0.00	0.00	6.00	1.38	0.00	6.00	1.66	0.00
8	0.00	0.00	0.00	4.00[†††]	0.00	0.00	4.00[†††]	0.00	0.00

[†] $O(c_2) = h\varepsilon$
[††] $O(b) = 0$ but $o(x) > h\varepsilon$
[†††] $O(b) > 0$

Figure 8.19 A computations of $L(f,e)$.

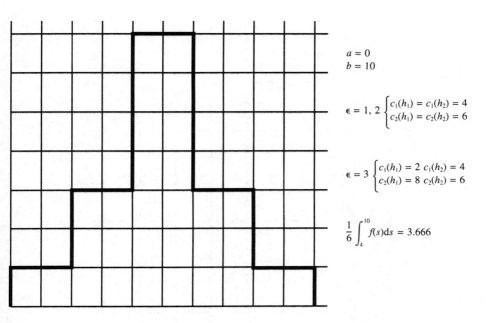

$a = 0$
$b = 10$

$\epsilon = 1, 2 \begin{cases} c_1(h_1) = c_1(h_2) = 4 \\ c_2(h_1) = c_2(h_2) = 6 \end{cases}$

$\epsilon = 3 \begin{cases} c_1(h_1) = 2 \ c_1(h_2) = 4 \\ c_2(h_1) = 8 \ c_2(h_2) = 6 \end{cases}$

$\dfrac{1}{6} \displaystyle\int_{4}^{10} f(s)\mathrm{d}s = 3.666$

$\dfrac{1}{3} \displaystyle\int_{4}^{6} f(s)\mathrm{d}s = 4.666$

$L(f,1) = 4.66$

$\epsilon = 2$

$\dfrac{1}{4} \displaystyle\int_{4}^{6} f(s)\mathrm{d}s = 3.5$

$L(f,1) = 3.666$

$\epsilon = 3$

$\dfrac{1}{9} \displaystyle\int_{2}^{8} f(s)\mathrm{d}s = 2.88$

Figure 8.20 A second computation of $L(f,e)$.

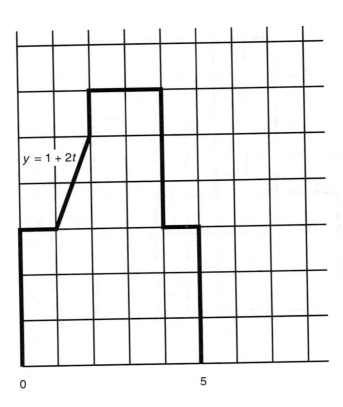

Figure 8.21 A third computation of $L(f,e)$.

or

$$\frac{1}{5 - c_1(h_1)} \left[\int_{c_1(h_1)}^{2} (1 + 2s)ds + \int_{2}^{4} 6ds \right] = 1 + 2\, c_1(h_1)$$

from which $c_1(h_1) = 1.535$, $h_1 = 4.07$. This value of h is determined by requiring $O(c_2(h_1)) \leq h\epsilon$. Indeed $O(4) = 4.07$. We now determine $c_1(h_2)$ as follows:

$$\frac{1}{5 - c_1(h_1)} \int_{c_1(h_2)}^{5} f(s)ds = 1 + 2\, c_1(h_2)$$

or $c_1(h_2) = 2$, $h_2 = 5$. This value of h is determined by requiring $O(b) = 0$. Finally $L(f,1) = 5$.

As a final example, consider the following function:

$$f(s) = \begin{cases} s & 0 \le s < 8 \\ 16 - s & 8 \le s < 16 \end{cases}$$

nd $\epsilon = 1$. We have

$$\int f(s)ds = \begin{cases} \dfrac{s^2}{2} & 0 \le s \le 8 \\ 16s - \dfrac{s^2}{2} & 8 < s < 16 \end{cases}$$

nd

$$c_1(h_1) = \frac{1}{c_2(h_1) - c_1(h_1) + 1}\left[\int_{c_1(h_1)}^8 f(s)ds + \int_8^{c_2(h_1)} f(s)ds\right] = 16 - c_2(h_1)$$

rom which (dropping the h_1) we get

$$\begin{cases} c_1(c_2 - c_1 + 1) = -64 - \dfrac{c_1^2}{2} + 16\,c_2 - \dfrac{c_1^2}{2} \\ \\ (16 - c_2)(c_2 - c_1 + 1) = -64 - \dfrac{c_1^2}{2} + 16\,c_2 - \dfrac{c_1^2}{2} \end{cases}$$

olving simultaneously for c_1 and c_2 we obtain

$$c_1(h_1) = 5.64, \quad c_2(h_1) = 10.36, \quad h_1 = 5.64$$

n the other hand, h_2 leads to

$$\frac{1}{16 - c_1(h_2)}\int_{c_1(h_2)}^{16} f(s)ds = c_1(h_2)$$

$_1(h_2) = 4.61$, $h_2 = 4.67$, $O(b) = 0$. Thus $L(f,1) = 5.64$. Note that $O(5.64) = 0$; $O(8) = 2.79$; $)(10.36) = 5.58$; $O(13.73) = 0$; and $O(16) = 0$. Thus, $O(16)$ is zero and the problem is etermined by $O(c_2) = h\epsilon$.

230

Function Type D

Assume that $f(s)$ has the general shape of Figure 8.22. Applying the theory developed in Section 8.2.2 we obtain

$$O(c_1) = \int_a^{c_1(h_1)} (f(s) - h_1)ds$$

We require $O(c_1(h_1)) \le h\epsilon$, or

$$h_1 \ge \frac{1}{c_1(h_1) + \epsilon - a} \int_a^{c_1(h_1)} f(s)ds)$$

since at this point we have the largest accumulated work. The constant is solved as

$$f(c_1(h_1)) = \frac{1}{c_1(h_1) + \epsilon - a} \int_a^{c_1(h_1)} f(s)ds$$

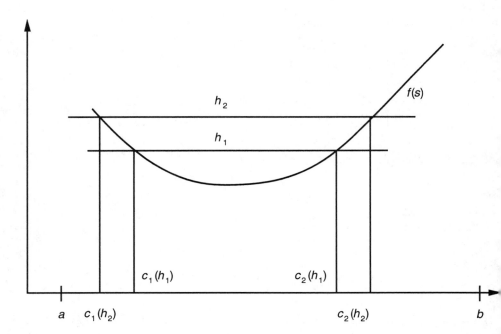

Figure 8.22 Function type D.

We also require $O(b) = 0$; now,

$$O(b) = \begin{cases} \displaystyle\int_{c_2(h_2)}^{b} (f(s) - h_2)ds & \text{if } O(c_2(h_2)) = 0 \\[2em] \displaystyle\int_{a}^{b} (f(s) - h_3)ds & \text{if } O(c_2(h_2)) > 0 \end{cases}$$

We thus have

$$O(b) = \begin{cases} \displaystyle\int_{c_2(h_2)}^{b} (f(s) - h_2)ds & \text{if } \displaystyle\int_{a}^{c_2(h_2)} (f(s) - h_2)ds \leq 0 \\[2em] \displaystyle\int_{a}^{b} (f(s) - h_3)ds & \text{if } \displaystyle\int_{a}^{c_2(h_2)} (f(s) - h_2)ds > 0 \end{cases}$$

or,

$$h_2 = \frac{1}{b - c_2(h_2)} \int_{c_2(h_2)}^{b} f(s)ds$$

where

$$f(c_2(h_2)) = \frac{1}{b - c_2(h_2)} \int_{c_2(h_2)}^{b} f(s)ds$$

if

$$\int_{a}^{c_2(h_2)} \{f_2(s) - \frac{1}{b - c_2(h_2)} \int_{c_2(h_2)}^{b} f_1(s)ds_1\}ds_2 \leq 0$$

Otherwise if the last condition is not met, use

$$h_3 = \frac{1}{b - a} \int_{a}^{b} f(s)ds$$

The question is how to easily discriminate between h_2 and h_3; we will show that if $O(c_2) > 0$, then $h_3 > h_2$. Thus the selection criterion is to pick the largest of the two.

Assume

$$O(c_2(h_2)) = \int_a^{c_2(h_2)} f(s)ds - \frac{c_2(h_2) - a}{b - c_2(h_2)} \int_{c_2(h_2)}^b f(s)ds > 0$$

then

$$\int_a^{c_2(h_2)} f(s)ds > \frac{c_2(h_2) - a}{b - c_2(h_2)} \int_{c_2(h_2)}^b f(s)ds$$

Now

$$h_3 = \frac{1}{b-a} \int_a^b f(s)ds = \frac{1}{b-a}\left[\int_a^{c_2(h_2)} f(s)ds + \int_{c_2(h_2)}^b f(s)ds \right]$$

$$> \frac{1}{b-a}\left[\frac{c_2(h_2) - a}{b - c_2(h_2)} \int_{c_2(h_2)}^b f(s)ds + \int_{c_2(h_2)}^b f(s)ds \right]$$

$$= \frac{1}{b-a}\left[\frac{c_2(h_2) - a + b - c_2(h_2)}{b - c_2(h_2)} \int_{c_2(h_2)}^b f(s)ds \right]$$

$$= \frac{1}{b - c_2(h_2)} \int_{c_2(h_2)}^b f(s)ds = h_2$$

Now we wish to show that

$$L(f,\epsilon) = \max (h_1, h_2, h_3)$$

$$= \max \left[\frac{1}{c_1(h_1) - a + \epsilon} \int_a^{c_1(h_1)} f(s)ds, \; \frac{1}{b - c_2(h_2)} \int_{c_2(h_2)}^b f(s)ds, \; \frac{1}{b - a} \int_a^b f(s)ds \right]$$

with the constants determined as above. We must examine the following cases.

(a) $h_1 > h_2 > h_3$
(b) $h_1 > h_3 > h_2$
(c) $h_3 > h_1 > h_2$

For these, $c_1(h_1) < c_1(h_2) < c_2(h_2) < c_2(h_1)$.

(d) $h_2 > h_1 > h_3$
(e) $h_2 > h_3 > h_1$
(f) $h_3 > h_2 > h_1$

For these, $c_1(h_2) < c_1(h_1) < c_2(h_1) < c_2(h_2)$.

Case (a). If $L(f,\epsilon)$ were equal to h_1 then

1. $O(c_1(h_1)) \leq h_1\epsilon$ by assumption
2. Since $h_2 > h_3$, $O(c_2(h_2)) \leq 0$, then

$$\int_{c_2(h_1)}^{b} (f(s) - h_1)ds \leq \int_{c_2(h_1)}^{b} (f(s) - h_2)ds \leq \int_{c_2(h_2)}^{b} (f(s) - h_2)ds \leq 0$$

where the first inequality holds since $h_1 > h_2$; the second inequality holds since $c_2(h_2) < c_2(h_1)$; and the third inequality holds by assumption.

Hence, all conditions are met.

Case (b) through (f). All handled similarly to Case (a) above.
This argument shows that $L(f,\epsilon) = \max(h_1, h_2, h_3)$. Note that

$$L(f,\epsilon) \geq \frac{1}{b-a} \int_{a}^{b} f(s)ds$$

Also we already know that $L(f,\epsilon) \geq f(b)$.

As a subcase, consider the function of Figure 8.23. Applying the general formula just derived above we obtain

$$L(f,\epsilon) = \max \left[\frac{1}{c_1 - a + \epsilon} \int_{a}^{c_1} f(s)ds, \frac{1}{b-a} \int_{a}^{b} f(s)ds \right]$$

as we would expect from the earlier calculation for Function Type B. Here $c_2(h_2) = b$ and $f(s)$ is less than both terms in the expression for the expression for $L(f,\epsilon)$.

Two examples are shown in Figure 8.24 and 8.25. In Figure 8.24 $h = 4$ is sufficient to guarantee $O(c_2) = 0$, however, $O(c_1) > h\epsilon$; in fact $h = 3.3$ is already sufficient to meet this constraint. $h = 4$ guarantees $O(c_1) \leq h\epsilon$, but $O(b) > 0$. $h = 7$ meets all requirements.

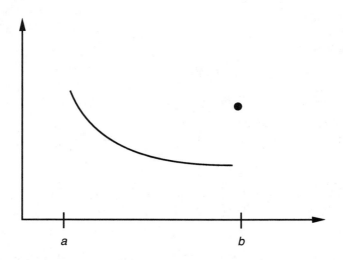

Figure 8.23 Subcase of Function Type D.

Function Type E

Assume that $f(s)$ has the general shape of Figure 8.16 Type E. We require

$$O(c_2(h_1)) = \int_{c_1(h_1)}^{c_2(h_1)} (f(s) - h_1)ds \leq h_1\epsilon$$

$$O(b) = \begin{cases} \int_{c_3(h_2)}^{b} (f(s) - h_2)ds & \text{if } O(c_3(h_2)) = 0 \\[2em] \int_{c_1(h_3)}^{b} (f(s) - h_3)ds & \text{if } O(c_3(h_2)) > 0 \end{cases}$$

with

$$O(c_3(h_2)) = \int_{c_1(h_2)}^{c_3(h_2)} (f(s) - h_2)ds$$

(with $O(c_3(h_2)) > 0$).
    We then have

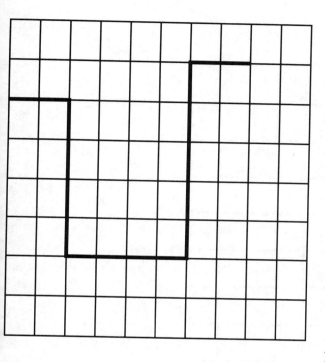

$a = 0$
$b = 8$
$c_1 = 2$
$c_2 = 6$

$$\frac{1}{8} \int_0^8 f(s)ds = 4.25$$

$$\frac{1}{2} \int_6^8 f(s)ds = 7.00$$

$\epsilon = 1$

$$\frac{1}{3} \int_0^2 f(s)ds = 4.00 \qquad L(f,\epsilon) = 7$$

$\epsilon = 2$

$$\frac{1}{4} \int_0^2 f(s)ds = 3.00 \qquad L(f,\epsilon) = 7$$

$\epsilon = 2$

$$\frac{1}{5} \int_0^2 f(s)ds = 2.40 \qquad L(f,\epsilon) = 7$$

$\varepsilon = 1$

t	$h = 4$	$h = 4.5$	$h = 7$
1	2.00	1.50	0.00
2	4.00	3.00	0.00
3	2.00	0.50	0.00
4	0.00	0.00	0.00
5	0.00	0.00	0.00
6	0.00	0.00	0.00
7	3.00	2.50	0.00
8	6.00	5.00	0.00

$O(t)$

Figure 8.24 Example of computation for Function Type D.

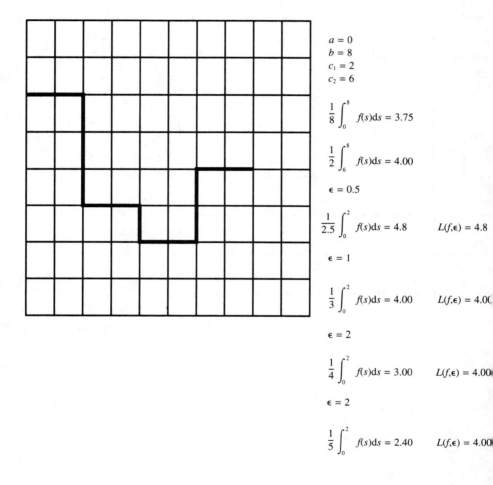

$a = 0$
$b = 8$
$c_1 = 2$
$c_2 = 6$

$$\frac{1}{8} \int_0^8 f(s)ds = 3.75$$

$$\frac{1}{2} \int_6^8 f(s)ds = 4.00$$

$\epsilon = 0.5$

$$\frac{1}{2.5} \int_0^2 f(s)ds = 4.8 \qquad L(f,\epsilon) = 4.8$$

$\epsilon = 1$

$$\frac{1}{3} \int_0^2 f(s)ds = 4.00 \qquad L(f,\epsilon) = 4.00$$

$\epsilon = 2$

$$\frac{1}{4} \int_0^2 f(s)ds = 3.00 \qquad L(f,\epsilon) = 4.00$$

$\epsilon = 2$

$$\frac{1}{5} \int_0^2 f(s)ds = 2.40 \qquad L(f,\epsilon) = 4.00$$

Figure 8.25 Second example of computation for Function Type D.

$$L(f, \epsilon) = \max\left[\frac{1}{c_2(h_1) - c_1(h_1) + \epsilon} \int_{c_1(h_1)}^{c_2(h_1)} f(s)ds, \ \frac{1}{b - c_3(h_2)} \int_{c_3(h_2)}^{b} f(s)ds, \ \frac{1}{b - c_1(h_3)} \int_{c_1(h_3)}^{b} f(s)ds \right]$$

where the constants are determined by

$$f(c_1(h_1)) = f(c_2(h_1)) = \frac{1}{c_2(h_1) - c_1(h_1) + \epsilon} \int_{c_1(h_1)}^{c_2(h_1)} f(s)ds$$

$$f(c_3(h_2)) = \frac{1}{b - c_3(h_2)} \int_{c_3(h_2)}^{b} f(s)ds$$

$$f(c_1(h_3)) = \frac{1}{b - c_1(h_3)} \int_{c_1(h_3)}^{b} f(s)ds$$

Note that by the nature of $f(s)$

$$\frac{1}{b - c_1(h_3)} \int_{c_1(h_3)}^{b} f(s)ds \geq \frac{1}{b - a} \int_{a}^{b} f(s)ds$$

Function Type F

Assume that $f(s)$ has the general shape of Figure 8.16 Type F. We require

$$O(c_1(h_1)) = \int_{a}^{c_1(h_1)} (f(s) - h_1)ds \leq h_1\epsilon$$

$$O(c_3(h_\bullet)) = \begin{cases} \int_{c_2(h_2)}^{c_1(h_1)} (f(s) - h_2)ds \leq h_2\epsilon \quad \text{if } O(c_2(h_2)) = 0, \text{ or } \int_{a}^{c_2(h_2)} (f(s) - h_2)ds \leq 0 \\ \int_{c_a}^{c_3(h_3)} (f(s) - h_3)ds \leq h_3\epsilon \quad \text{if } O(c_2(h_2)) > 0 \end{cases}$$

$$O(b) = \begin{cases} \int_{c_2(h_4)}^{b} (f(s) - h_4)ds \quad \text{if } O(c_2(h_4)) = 0, \text{ or } \int_{a}^{c_2(h_4)} (f(s) - h_4)ds \leq 0 \\ \int_{a}^{b} (f(s) - h_5)ds \quad \text{if } O(c_2(h_4)) > 0 \end{cases}$$

We then have (constants are obtained with the right hand side)

$$h_1 = \frac{1}{c_1(h_1) - a + \epsilon} \int_a^{c_1(h_1)} f(s)ds = f(c_1(h_1))$$

$$h_2 = \frac{1}{c_1(h_2) - c_2(h_2) + \epsilon} \int_{c_2(h_2)}^{c_1(h_2)} f(s)ds = f(c_1(h_2)) = f(c_2(h_2))$$

$$h_3 = \frac{1}{c_3(h_3) - a + \epsilon} \int_a^{c_3(h_3)} f(s)ds = f(c_3(h_3))$$

$$h_4 = \frac{1}{b - c_2(h_4)} \int_{c_2(h_4)}^b f(s)ds = f(c_2(h_4))$$

$$h_5 = \frac{1}{b - c_2(h_4)} \int_a^b f(s)ds$$

$L(f, \epsilon) = \max(h_1, h_2, h_3, h_4, h_5)$.

Function Type G

Assume that $f(s)$ has the general shape of Figure 8.16 Type G (from this point on we will not make specific reference on how to obtain the constants; these are obtained in the usual way as exemplified above). We require

$$O(c_2(h_1)) = \int_{c_1(h_1)}^{c_2(h_1)} (f(s) - h_1)ds \le h_1\epsilon$$

$$O(c_2(h_{\bullet})) = \begin{cases} \int_{c_3(h_2)}^{c_4(h_2)} (f(s) - h_2)ds \le h_2\epsilon & \text{if } O(c_3(h_2)) = 0, \text{ or } \int_{c_1(h_2)}^{c_3(h_2)} (f(s) - h_2)ds \le 0 \\ \int_{c_1(h_3)}^{c_4(h_3)} (f(s) - h_3)ds \le h_3\epsilon & \text{if } O(c_3(h_2)) > 0 \end{cases}$$

$$O(b) = \begin{cases} \int_{c_3(h_4)}^b (f(s) - h_4)ds & \text{if } O(c_3(h_4)) = 0, \text{ or } \int_{c_1(h_4)}^{c_3(h_4)} (f(s) - h_4)ds \le 0 \\ \int_{c_1(h_5)}^b (f(s) - h_5)ds & \text{if } O(c_3(h_4)) > 0 \end{cases}$$

Solve for h_1, h_2, h_3, h_4, h_5 and then $L(f, \epsilon) = \max(h_1, h_2, h_3, h_4, h_5)$.

Function Type H

Assume that $f(s)$ has the general shape of Figure 8.16 Type H. We require

$$O(c_1(h_1)) = \int_a^{c_1(h_1)} (f(s) - h_1)ds \le h_1\epsilon$$

$$O(c_3(h_\bullet)) = \begin{cases} \int_{c_2(h_2)}^{c_3(h_2)} (f(s) - h_2)ds \le h_2\epsilon \quad \text{if } O(c_2(h_2)) = 0, \text{ or } \int_a^{c_2(h_2)} (f(s) - h_2)ds \le 0 \\ \int_a^{c_3(h_3)} (f(s) - h_3)ds \le h_3\epsilon \quad \text{if } O(c_2(h_2)) > 0 \end{cases}$$

$$O(b) = \begin{cases} \int_{c_4(h_4)}^b (f(s) - h_4)ds \quad \text{if } O(c_2(h_4)) = 0 \text{ and } O(c_4(h_4)) = 0, \text{ or} \\[2mm] \qquad\qquad \int_a^{c_2(h_4)} (f(s) - h_4)ds \le 0 \text{ and } \int_{c_2(h_4)}^{c_4(h_4)} (f(s) - h_4)ds \le 0 \\ \int_{c_2(h_5)}^b (f(s) - h_5)ds \quad \text{if } O(c_2(h_5)) = 0 \text{ and } O(c_4(h_4)) > 0 \\[2mm] \qquad\qquad \text{and } \int_a^{c_2(h_5)} (f(s) - h_5)ds \le 0 \\ \int_a^b (f(s) - h_6)ds \quad \text{if } O(c_2(h_5)) > 0, O(c_4(h_4)) > 0 \end{cases}$$

Solve for $h_1, h_2, h_3, h_4, h_5, h_6$ and then $L(f,\epsilon) = \max(h_1, h_2, h_3, h_4, h_5, h_6)$.

Function Type I

Assume that $f(s)$ has the general shape of Figure 8.16 Type I. We require

$$(c_2(h_1)) = \int_{c_1(h_1)}^{c_2(h_1)} (f(s) - h_1)ds \le h_1\epsilon$$

$$(c_4(h_\bullet)) = \begin{cases} \int_{c_3(h_2)}^{c_4(h_2)} (f(s) - h_2)ds \le h_2\epsilon \quad \text{if } O(c_3(h_2)) = 0, \text{ or } \int_{c_1(h_2)}^{c_3(h_2)} (f(s) - h_2)ds \le 0 \\ \int_{c_1(h_3)}^{c_4(h_3)} (f(s) - h_3)ds \le h_3\epsilon \quad \text{if } O(c_3(h_2)) > 0 \end{cases}$$

$$O(b) = \begin{cases} \displaystyle\int_{c_5(h_4)}^{b} (f(s) - h_4)ds & \text{if } O(c_3(h_4)) = 0,\ O(c_5(h_4)) = 0 \\[2em] \displaystyle\int_{c_1(h_4)}^{c_3(h_4)} (f(s) - h_4)ds \le 0 \text{ and } \int_{c_3(h_4)}^{c_5(h_4)} (f(s) - h_4)ds \le \\[2em] \displaystyle\int_{c_3(h_5)}^{b} (f(s) - h_5)ds & \text{if } O(c_3(h_5)) = 0,\ O(c_5(h_4)) > 0 \\[2em] \displaystyle\int_{c_1(h_5)}^{c_3(h_5)} (f(s) - h_5)ds \le 0 \\[2em] \displaystyle\int_{c_1(h_6)}^{b} (f(s) - h_6)ds & \text{if } O(c_3(h_5)) > 0,\ O(c_5(h_4)) > 0 \end{cases}$$

Solve for h_1, h_2, h_3, h_4, h_5, h_6 and then $L(f, \epsilon) = \max (h_1, h_2, h_3, h_4, h_5, h_6)$.

Function Type J

Assume that $f(s)$ has the general shape of Figure 8.16 Type J. We require

$$O(c_1(h_1)) = \int_{a}^{c_1(h_1)} (f(s) - h_1)ds \le h_1\epsilon$$

$$O(c_3(h_\bullet)) = \begin{cases} \displaystyle\int_{c_2(h_2)}^{c_3(h_2)} (f(s) - h_2)ds \le h_2\epsilon & \text{if } O(c_2(h_2)) = 0, \text{ or } \int_{a}^{c_2(h_2)} (f(s) - h_2)ds \le 0 \\[2em] \displaystyle\int_{a}^{c_3(h_3)} (f(s) - h_3)ds \le h_3\epsilon & \text{if } O(c_2(h_2)) > 0 \end{cases}$$

$$O(c_5(h_\bullet)) = \begin{cases} \displaystyle\int_{c_4(h_4)}^{c_5(h_4)} (f(s) - h_4)ds \le h_4\epsilon & \text{if } O(c_2(h_4)) = 0 \text{ and } O(c_4(h_4)) = 0 \\[2em] \displaystyle\int_{a}^{c_2(h_4)} (f(s) - h_4)ds \le 0,\ \int_{c_2(h_4)}^{c_4(h_4)} (f(s) - h_4)ds \\[2em] \displaystyle\int_{c_2(h_5)}^{c_5(h_5)} (f(s) - h_5)ds \le h_5\epsilon & \text{if } O(c_2(h_5)) = 0 \text{ and } O(c_4(h_4)) > 0, \\[2em] \displaystyle\int_{a}^{c_2(h_5)} (f(s) - h_5)ds \le 0 \\[2em] \displaystyle\int_{a}^{c_5(h_6)} (f(s) - h_6)ds \le h_6\epsilon & \text{if } O(c_2(h_5)) > 0 \text{ and } O(c_4(h_4)) > 0 \end{cases}$$

$$O(b) = \begin{cases} \int_{c_4(h_7)}^{b} (f(s) - h_7)ds & \text{if } O(c_2(h_7)) = 0 \text{ and } O(c_4(h_7)) = 0, \text{ or} \\ \\ \int_{a}^{c_2(h_7)} (f(s) - h_7)ds \le 0 \text{ and } \int_{c_2(h_7)}^{c_4(h_4)} (f(s) - h_7)ds \le 0 \\ \\ \int_{c_2(h_8)}^{b} (f(s) - h_8)ds & \text{if } O(c_2(h_8)) = 0 \text{ and } O(c_4(h_7)) > 0 \\ \\ \int_{a}^{c_2(h_8)} (f(s) - h_8)ds \le 0 \\ \\ \int_{a}^{b} (f(s) - h_9)ds & \text{if } O(c_2(h_8)) > 0, O(c_4(h_7)) > 0 \end{cases}$$

olve for h_1, h_2, h_3, h_4, h_5, h_6, h_7, h_8, h_9 and then $L(f,\epsilon) = \max(h_1, h_2, h_3, h_4, h_5, h_6, h_7, h_8, h_9)$.

2.4 General Solution of $L(f,\epsilon)$

he previous solutions provide insight for a general solution for $L(f,\epsilon)$.

2.4.1 Critical Points of a Function $f(s)$

efore proceeding we need to define the *polynodality* of a function. We do this by defining he critical points R of $f(s)$. For simplicity we assume that $f(s)$ is differentiable everywhere [a,b]; if $f(s)$ is not differentiable, the critical points can still be defined but a more laborate formulation is required. In this section we define such quantity only when $f(s)$ differentiable; however, outside this section we assume that the set of critical points is lways defined. Let R be the roots of $f'(s) = 0$ and $|R|$ the cardinality of R. See Figure .26.

2.4.2 Polynodality of $f(s)$

efine $p(f) = |R| + 3$. The quantity $\chi(f) = |R| + 1$ represents the number of points of iterest internal to the interval [a,b]; $p(f) = \chi(f) + 2$ represents the number of points of iterest including the boundary points.

2.4.3 Grammar of Functions

further characterization of $f(s)$ is required to obtain $L(f,\epsilon)$. To this end we construct ie following language-theoretic grammar:

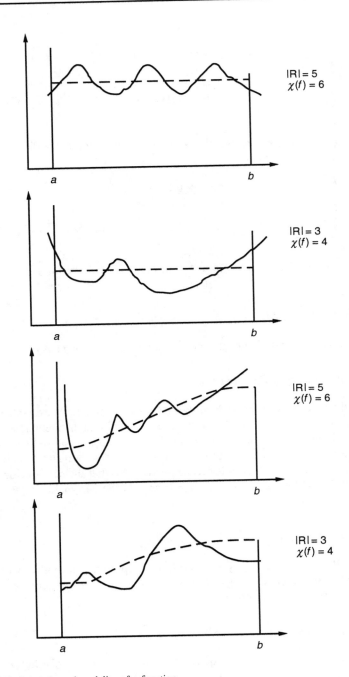

Figure 8.26 Defining the polynodality of a function.

Starting symbol: S
Non-terminal symbols: $V_N = \{R_1, R_2\}$
Terminal symbols: $V_T = \{u, n\}$
Productions: P: $S \rightarrow u\ R_1$
$S \rightarrow n\ R_2 u$
$S \rightarrow n\ R_2$
$R_1 \rightarrow nuR_1 | nu$
$R_2 \rightarrow unR_2 | un$

The grammar is

$$G = (V_N,\ V_T,\ S,\ P).$$

It is easily shown that the language $L(G)$ generated by G is

$$L(G) = \{u(nu)^j,\ u(nu)^j n,\ n(un)^j,\ n(un)^j u,\ j = 0,\ 1,\ 2,\ ...\}.$$

Define the functional

$$X: L(G) \rightarrow R+$$
$$X(u(nu)^j) = 2(j + 1)$$
$$X(u(nu)^j n) = 2(j + 1)$$
$$X(n(un)^j) = 2(j + 1) + 1$$
$$X(n(un)^j u) = 2(j + 1) + 1.$$

Finally define an isomorphism from the set of functions F to $L(G)$ as follows:

$\tau: F \rightarrow L(G)$

$\tau(f) = u(nu)^j$ if and only if $\chi(f) = 2(j + 1)$ and $f(s)$ is decreasing in a neighborhood of a

$\tau(f) = u(un)^j$ if and only if $\chi(f) = 2(j + 1)$ and $f(s)$ is increasing in a neighborhood of a

$\tau(f) = u(nu)^j n$ if and only if $\chi(f) = 2(j + 1) + 1$ and $f(s)$ is decreasing in a neighborhood of a

$\tau(f) = n(un)^j u$ if and only if $\chi(f) = 2(j + 1) + 1$ and $f(s)$ is increasing in a neighborhood of a

Figure 8.27 provides some examples.

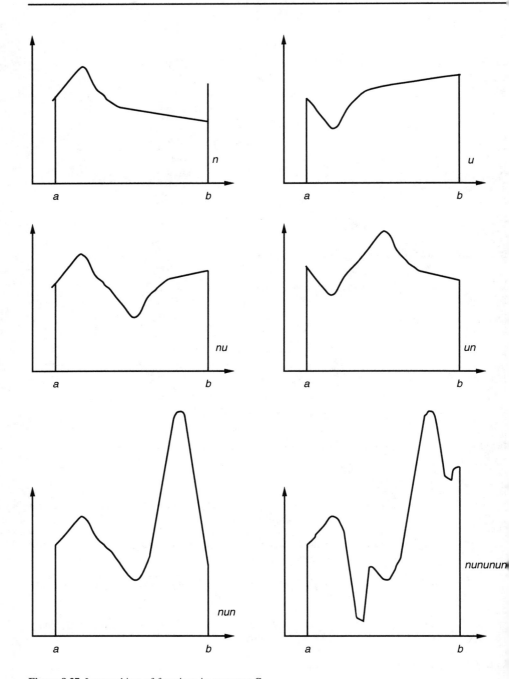

Figure 8.27 Isomorphism of functions in grammar G.

8.2.4.4 Closed Form Solution for Any Function

We are now ready to state the general closed form solution for $L(f,\epsilon)$. In every case we do not explicitly show the functionality of the constants c's (for notational convenience) on the respective hs; this functionality must be borne in mind when performing the actual calculation. Also, we do not explicitly state how to obtain the constants; this can be done as indicated in the previous section.

In each case we let

$$c_0 = a$$
$$c_{\chi(\bullet) + 1} = b$$

Notice that $\chi(f) = X(\tau(f))$, by definition.

8.2.4.4.1 $\tau(f) = u(nu)^j n$

Define

$$\Phi_f(z) = \begin{cases} \epsilon & \text{if } z \le \chi(f) \\ 0 & \text{if } z = \chi(f) + 1 \end{cases}$$

$$\Psi_f(z - 1) = \begin{cases} z - 1 & \text{if } z \le \chi(f) \\ \chi(f) - 1 & \text{if } z = \chi(f) + 1 \end{cases}$$

Then for

$$z = 1, 3, 5, \ldots, 2k + 1, \ldots, \chi(f), \chi(f) + 1$$
$$w = 0, 2, 4, \ldots, 2k, \ \Psi_f(z - 1)$$

define

$$h(z,w) = \frac{1}{c_z - c_w + \Phi_f(z)} \int_{c_w}^{c_z} f(s) ds$$

we have here $((j + 2)(j + 3)/2) + (j + 2)$ distinct equations, since $\chi(f) = 2(j + 1) + 1$.
Finally,

$$L(f,\epsilon) = \max_{z, w} h(z,w)$$

Stated equivalently, we need to find the maximum $h(\bullet, \bullet)$ with

$$h(z, w) = \frac{1}{c_z - c_w + \epsilon} \int_{c_w}^{c_z} f(s)ds$$

for $z = 1, 3, 5, \ldots, \chi(f)$ (since $\chi(f)$ was odd) and $w = 0, 2, 4, \ldots, z - 1$, and

$$h(\chi(f) + 1, w) = \frac{1}{c_{\chi(f)+1} - c_w} \int_{c_w}^{c_{\chi(f)+1}} f(s)ds$$

for $w = 0, 2, 4, \ldots, \chi(f) - 1$ (since $\chi(f)$ was odd)

8.2.4.4.2 $\tau(f) = u(nu)^j$

Define

$$\Phi_f(z) = \begin{cases} \epsilon & \text{if } z \leq \chi(f) - 1 \\ 0 & \text{if } z = \chi(f) + 1 \end{cases}$$

$$\Psi_f(z - 1) = \begin{cases} z - 1 & \text{if } z \leq \chi(f) - 1 \\ \chi(f) & \text{if } z = \chi(f) + 1 \end{cases}$$

Then for

$$z = 1, 3, 5, \ldots, 2,k + 1, \ldots, \chi(f) - 1, \chi(f) + 1$$
$$w = 0, 2, 4, \ldots, 2k, \ldots, \Psi_f(z - 1)$$

define

$$h(z, w) = \frac{1}{c_z - c_w + \Phi_f(z)} \int_{c_w}^{c_z} f(s)ds$$

(we have here $((j + 2)(j + 3)/2)$ distinct equations, since $\psi(f) = 2(j + 1)$).
Finally,

$$L(f, \epsilon) = \max_{z, w} h(z, w)$$

Stated equivalently, we need to find the maximum $h(\bullet, \bullet)$ with

$$h(z, w) = \frac{1}{c_z - c_w + \epsilon} \int_{c_w}^{c_z} f(s)ds$$

or $z = 1, 3, 5, \ldots, \chi(f) - 1$ (since $\chi(f)$ was even) and $w = 0, 2, 4, \ldots, z - 1$, and

$$h(\chi(f) + 1, w) = \frac{1}{c_{\chi(f) + 1 - c_w}} \int_{c_w}^{c_{\chi(f)+1}} f(s)ds$$

or $w = 0, 2, 4, \ldots, \chi(f)$ (since $\chi(f)$ was even).

3.2.4.4.3 $\tau(f) = n(un)^j$

Define

$$\Phi_f(z) = \begin{cases} \epsilon & \text{if } z \le \chi(f) \\ 0 & \text{if } z = \chi(f) + 1 \end{cases}$$

$$\Psi_f(z - 1) = \begin{cases} z - 1 & \text{if } z \le \chi(f) \\ \chi(f) - 1 & \text{if } z = \chi(f) + 1 \end{cases}$$

Then for

$$z = 2, 4, \ldots, 2k, \ldots, \chi(f), \chi(f) + 1$$
$$w = 1, 3, 5, \ldots, 2k + 1, \ldots, \Psi_f(z - 1)$$

define

$$h(z, w) = \frac{1}{c_z - c_w + \Phi_f(z)} \int_{c_w}^{c_z} f(s)ds$$

we have here $((j + 2)(j + 3)/2) + (j + 1)$ distinct equations, since $\chi(f) = 2(j + 1)$). Finally,

$$L(f,\epsilon) = \max_{z, w} h(z, w)$$

Stated equivalently, we need to find the maximum $h(\bullet, \bullet)$ with

$$h(z, w) = \frac{1}{c_z - c_w + \epsilon} \int_{c_w}^{c_z} f(s)\,ds$$

for $z = 2, 4, \ldots, \chi(f)$ (since $\chi(f)$ was even) and $w = 1, 3, 5, \ldots, z - 1$, and

$$h(\chi(f) + 1, w) = \frac{1}{c_{\chi(f)+1} - c_w} \int_{c_w}^{c_{\chi(f)+1}} f(s)\,ds$$

for $w = 1, 3, 5, \ldots, \chi(f) - 1$ (since $\chi(f)$ was even)

8.2.4.4.4 $\tau(f) = n(un)^j u$

Define

$$\Phi_f(z) = \begin{cases} \epsilon & \text{if } z \le \chi(f) - 1 \\ 0 & \text{if } z = \chi(f) + 1 \end{cases}$$

$$\Psi_f(z - 1) = \begin{cases} z - 1 & \text{if } z \le \chi(f) - 1 \\ \chi(f) & \text{if } z = \chi(f) + 1 \end{cases}$$

Then for

$$z = 2, 4, \ldots, 2k, \ldots, \chi(f) - 1, \chi(f) + 1$$
$$w = 1, 3, 5, \ldots, 2k + 1, \ldots, \Psi_f(z - 1)$$

define

$$h(z, w) = \frac{1}{c_z - c_w + \Phi_f(z)} \int_{c_w}^{c_z} f(s)\,ds$$

(we have here $((j + 2)(j + 3)/2)$ distinct equations, since $\chi(f) = 2(j + 1) + 1$.)
Finally,

$$L(f, \epsilon) = \max_{z, w} h(z, w)$$

Stated equivalently, we need to find the maximum $h(\bullet, \bullet)$ with

$$h(z, w) = \frac{1}{c_z - c_w + \epsilon} \int_{c_w}^{c_z} f(s)ds$$

for $z = 2, 4, \ldots, \chi(f) - 1$ (since $\chi(f)$ was odd) and $w = 1, 3, 5, \ldots, z - 1$, and

$$h(\chi(f) + 1, w) = \frac{1}{c_{\chi(f)+1} - c_w} \int_{c_w}^{c_{\chi(f)+1}} f(s)ds$$

for $w = 1, 3, 5, \ldots, \chi(f)$ (since $\chi(f)$ was odd)

8.2.4.4.5 An Example

We now develop an example to show how to apply the theory. In Section 8.2.3.6.9 we solved the $n(un)^1u$ problem. It required six equations. Here we wish to solve a $n(un)^2u$ problem. For this we apply the formulas of the previous section (Section 8.2.4.4.4). Here $j = 2$, and one expects $(j + 2)(j + 3)/2 = 10$ equations. One has $\chi(f) = 2(j + 1) + 1 = 7$.

z can take the values 2, 4, 6, 8. w takes odd values up to z. Applying the last set of equations in Section 8.2.4.4.4, the values of z and w shown in Table 8.4 emerge.

Table 8.4
z and w values

z	w
2	1
4	1, 3
6	1, 3, 5
8	1, 3, 5, 7*

*$c_8 = b$, as noted in
Section 8.2.4.4.

Then $L(f, \epsilon) = \max (h_i)$, $i = 1, 10$, with the h_i given below.

$$h(z, w) = h(2, 1) = h_1 = \frac{1}{c_2 - c_1 + \epsilon} \int_{c_1}^{c_2} f(s)ds$$

$$h(z, w) = h(4, 3) = h_2 = \frac{1}{c_4 - c_3 + \epsilon} \int_{c_3}^{c_4} f(s)ds$$

$$h(z, w) = h(4, 1) = h_3 = \frac{1}{c_4 - c_1 + \epsilon} \int_{c_1}^{c_4} f(s)ds$$

$$h(z, w) = h(6, 5) = h_4 = \frac{1}{c_6 - c_5 + \epsilon} \int_{c_5}^{c_6} f(s)ds$$

$$h(z, w) = h(6, 3) = h_5 = \frac{1}{c_6 - c_3 + \epsilon} \int_{c_3}^{c_6} f(s)ds$$

$$h(z, w) = h(6, 1) = h_6 = \frac{1}{c_6 - c_1 + \epsilon} \int_{c_1}^{c_6} f(s)ds$$

$$h(z, w) = h(8, 7) = h_7 = \frac{1}{b - c_7} \int_{c_7}^{b} f(s)ds$$

$$h(z, w) = h(8, 5) = h_8 = \frac{1}{b - c_5} \int_{c_5}^{b} f(s)ds$$

$$h(z, w) = h(8, 3) = h_9 = \frac{1}{b - c_3} \int_{c_3}^{b} f(s)ds$$

$$h(z, w) = h(8, 1) = h_{10} = \frac{1}{b - c_1} \int_{c_1}^{b} f(s)ds$$

8.2.5 The Filter of $f(s)$

So far we have described the level at which to size the system, $L(f,\epsilon)$, to satisfy the $f(s)$ requirement. One is also interested in the shape of the curve obtained by designing the system at this level, namely, the history of the work flow as a function of time. We can such actual work the *filter of $f(s)$*, $F(f,\epsilon)(s)$. Clearly the filter depends on the initial requirement $f(s)$ and on ϵ. Intuitively,

$$F(f,\epsilon)(s) = \begin{cases} L(f,\epsilon) & \text{where } O(s) > 0 \\ \min (f(s), L(f,\epsilon)) & \text{where } O(s) = 0 \end{cases}$$

See Figure 8.28. It is rather difficult to obtain $F(f,\epsilon)(s)$ in closed form, even for simple functions (functions taking finitely many values can be analyzed numerically).

Consider a monotonically decreasing function (Figure 8.16 B). We have shown that

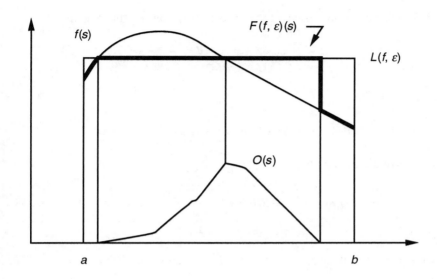

Figure 8.28 The filter of $f(s)$.

$$L(f,\epsilon) = \max \left\{ \frac{1}{b-a} \int_a^b f(s)ds, \frac{1}{c-a+\epsilon} \int_a^c f(s)ds \right\}$$

with $O(s)$ having a maximum at point c. We need to find $S = \{x|O(x) = 0\}$. Since $O(s)$ is not differentiable at the point where $O(s)$ crosses the x-axis, ζ,

$$\zeta = \inf x$$
$$O(x) = 0$$
$$x > c$$

because of the maximum term), we cannot consider $O'(x) = 0$. This would in fact lead to $f(x) = L(f,\epsilon)$ or $x = c$. Therefore, no general strategy to obtain $F(f,\epsilon)$ exists, and it must be secured by solving the integral equation above with the particular function at hand. For Function Type B, the point ζ may be obtained by noting that, at this point,

$$\int_a^\zeta (f(s) - L(f,\epsilon))ds = 0$$

Letting $G(x)$ be the antiderivative of $f(s)$, we obtain

$$G(\zeta) - \zeta L(f,\epsilon) = G(a) - aL(f,\epsilon).$$

This equation is now solved for ζ. Specifically consider the example

$$f(s) = -Ax + B$$
$$G(x) = (-A/2)x^2 + Bx$$

We need to solve

$$(-A/2)x^2 + Bx - L(F,\epsilon)\,x - G(a) + aL(f,\epsilon) = 0$$

This is a quadratic in x, with

$$x = \zeta = \frac{B - L(f,\epsilon) \overset{+}{\underset{-}{}} \sqrt{B^2 - 2BL(f,\epsilon) + L(f,\epsilon)^2 + 2Aa\,L(f,\epsilon) + A^2a^2 - 2AB}}{A}$$

We can now employ the exact value of $L(f,\epsilon)$ to obtain S and then $L(f,\epsilon)(s)$.

8.2.6 Stochastic RT Environment

8.2.6.1 Discrete Environment

Assume that with probability $p(i)$, the requests at time t is $f(i,t)$, $i = 1, 2, \ldots m$. Figures 8.29 and 8.30 depict examples for $m = 3$. Then clearly, the distribution of the engineering level is

$$\text{Prob } \{L(\bullet,\ \epsilon) = L(f(i),\epsilon)\} = p(i)$$

where $L(f(i),\epsilon)$ is computes as in Section 8.2.4. The "average" level at which one should engineer the system is then

$$\overline{L(f,\epsilon)} = \sum_{i=1}^{m} p(i)L(f(i),\epsilon)$$

One can also obtain

$$\overline{L(f,\epsilon)^2} = \sum_{i=1}^{m} p(i)L(f(i),\epsilon)^2$$

from which the variance of $L(\bullet,\ \epsilon)$ can be obtained. The tail of the distribution may be bounded using Tchbycheff's inequality.

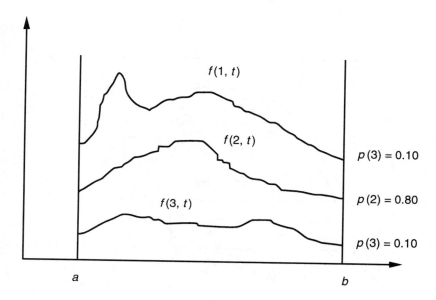

Figure 8.29 Discrete probability function.

8.2.6.2 Continuous Environment–Stationary Distribution

Assume that the p.d.f. of the service requests is $g(x)$, i.e.

$$\text{Prob}(\alpha \le S(t) \le \beta) = \int_{\alpha}^{\beta} g(s)ds$$

with S the amount of work at t. Note that we assume stationarity with respect to $g(s)$. See Figure 8.31. Then

$$\bar{L}(f, \epsilon) = \int_{-\infty}^{+\infty} uL(S(u),\epsilon)du$$

As above, one may obtain bounds on the tail of the distribution.

8.2.6.3 Continuous Environment—Nonstationary Distribution

Assume that the distribution of the service request is a function of time $g(t, s)$, that is,

$$\text{Prob }(\alpha(s) \le S(t) \le \beta(s)) = \int_{\alpha(t)}^{\beta(t)} g(t,s)ds$$

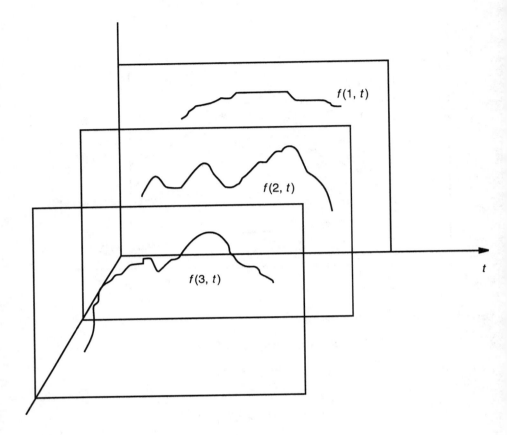

Figure 8.30 Another view of a stochastic requirement.

Then, again,

$$\overline{L}(f, \epsilon) = \int_{-\infty}^{+\infty} uL(S(u), \epsilon)du$$

8.2.6.4 Stochastic Examples

Discrete Case, m = 2. Consider the case of Figure 8.32. Using the theory above,

$$\overline{L}(f, \epsilon) = 4p(1) + 3(1 - p(1)) = p(1) + 3$$

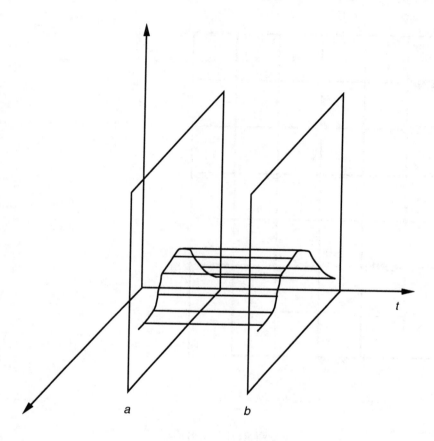

Figure 8.31 Stationary distribution.

Note that if $p(1) = 0$ this number is 3 which would equate to $L(f(2, t),1)$; if $p(1) = 1$, the number is 4, which equates to $L(f(1,t),1)$.

Discrete Case, $m = \infty$. Let $f(i,s) = e^{-is}$. Then

$$L(f(i),\epsilon) = \max \{(1/ib)(1 - e^{-ib}), \; 1/(i(b + \epsilon) + 1)\}$$

$$= (1/ib)(1 - e^{-ib})$$

Therefore if we let

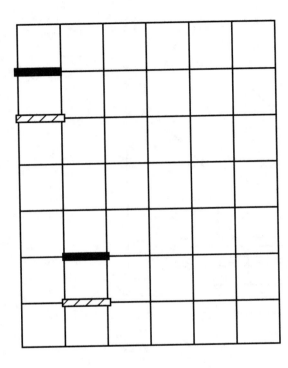

$$a = 0$$
$$b = 2$$
$$\epsilon = 1$$

$$f(1, t) = \begin{cases} 6 & 0 \le t < 1 \\ 2 & 1 \le t < 2 \end{cases}$$

$$f(2, t) = \begin{cases} 5 & 0 \le t < 1 \\ 1 & 1 \le t < 2 \end{cases}$$

$$\overline{L}(f,\epsilon) = 4p(1) + 3(1 - p(1)) = p(1) + 3$$

Figure 8.32 Example of computation for stochastic requirement.

$$\text{Prob } \{S(i,t) = f(i,t)\} = \frac{e^{-\lambda}\lambda^i}{i!}$$

then

$$\overline{L}(f,\epsilon) = \frac{1}{b}\sum_{i=1}^{\infty} \frac{e^{-\lambda}\lambda^i}{(i + 1)!}(1 - e^{-ib}).$$

8.2.7 Engineering Level in a Prioritized Environment

8.2.7.1 Introduction

Assume that there are two sets of service requests on the same facilities: $f_1(t)$, where service must be granted within ϵ_1, and $f_2(t)$, where service must be granted within ϵ_2. See Figure 8.33. Let $L(f_1, \epsilon_1, f_2, \epsilon_2)$ be the desired engineering level. Assume that $\epsilon_1 < \epsilon_2$ (if this is not true, simply rename the functions, so that it is then true). Clearly,

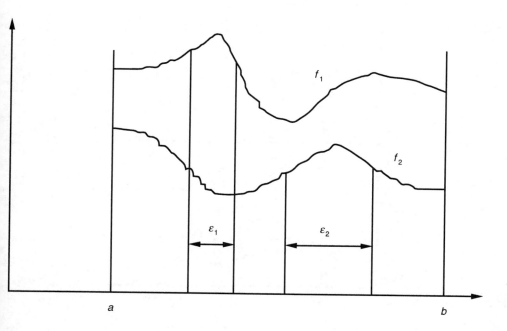

Figure 8.33 Prioritized environment.

$$L(f_1, \epsilon_1, f_2, \epsilon_2) \leq L(f_1 + f_2, \min(\epsilon_1, \epsilon_2))$$

and

$$L(f_1, \epsilon, f_2, \epsilon) = L(f_1 + f_2, (\epsilon))$$

Next we provide a general recursive formulation to obtain the engineering level in this prioritized environment. It is much more difficult to obtain closed form solutions similar to those derived in Section 8.2.4, since as Figure 8.34 indicates, even for the simplest functions, one must examine a large number of cases.

8.2.7.2 Definition of $L(f_1, \epsilon_1, f_2, \epsilon_2)$

For a sequence $v = \{x_i, i = 0, 1, ..., k\}$ contained in interval $[a,b]$, with $x_0 = a$, $x_k = b$, $\max d(x_i, x_{i+1}) = \Delta \leq \min(\epsilon_1, \epsilon_2)$, and h, define

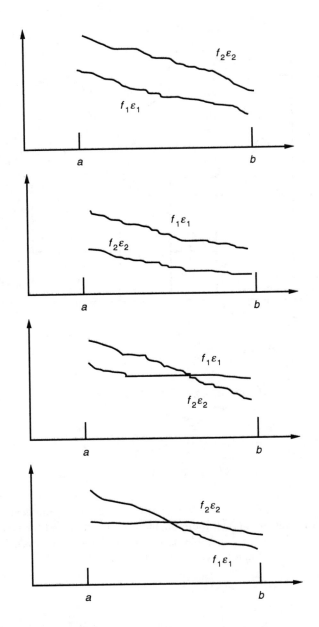

Figure 8.34 Multiple cases to be examined for two monotonically decreasing functions in order to derive closed-form solutions. Because of the renaming convention, eight combinations are reduced to these four cases.

$$S(\epsilon_1, \epsilon_2, h, V, \Delta) = \left[O_1(x_n), O_2(x_n) | x_n \epsilon V \right.$$

$$O_1(x_n) = \max\left(0, O_1(x_{n-1}) + \int_{x_{n-1}}^{x_n} f_1(s)ds - (x_n - x_{n-1})h\right),$$

$$O_2(x_n) = \max\left(0, O_2(x_{n-1}) + \int_{x_{n-1}}^{x_n} f_2(s)ds\right.$$

$$\left. - \max\left(0, (x_n - x_{n-1})h - O_1(x_{n-1}) - \int_{x_{n-1}}^{x_n} f_1(s)ds)\right)\right]$$

with $O_1(a) = O_2(a) = 0$.

Now define

$$L(f_1, \epsilon_1, f_2, \epsilon_2, \Delta) = \inf h$$
$$O_1(x_i) \leq h\epsilon_1 \text{ all } i$$
$$O_2(x_i) \leq h\epsilon_2 \text{ all } i$$
$$O_1(b) = 0$$
$$O_2(b) = 0$$

and

$$L(f_1, \epsilon_1, f_2, \epsilon_2) = \lim_{\Delta \to 0} L(f_1, \epsilon_1, f_2, \epsilon_2, \Delta)$$

Note that, if $f_2(s) = 0$, $O_2(\bullet) = 0$ and we only have the condition,

$$O_1(x_n) = \max\left(0, O_1(x_{n-1}) + \int_{x_{n-1}}^{x_n} f_1(s)ds - (x_n - x_{n-1})h\right)$$

which coincides with the definition when we have only one priority. If $f_1(s) = 0$, then $O_1(\bullet) = 0$ and we only have the condition

$$O_2(x_n) = \max\left(0, O_2(x_{n-1}) + \int_{x_{n-1}}^{x_n} f_2(s)ds - (x_n - x_{n-1})h\right)$$

since (a) the integral of f_1 is zero, $O_1(x_n) = 0$, and (b) the maximum term disappears since the term inside it is (now) positive. This coincides with the definition when we have only one priority.

8.2.7.3 Examples

In Figure 8.35 we show a general example. For $h = 4$ and 5 the constraint $O_2(x_n) \leq h\epsilon$ is violated. Now if $h = 6$, $O_2(6) = O_2(b) = 0$, therefore $L(f_1,\ \epsilon_1,\ f_2,\ \epsilon_2) \leq 6$ (a more refined calculation—not undertaken—may show that $h = 5.9$ might suffice). Note that if $b = 5$, then $h = 6$ would not suffice since $O_2(5) \neq 0$.

8.2.7.4 A Closed Form Expression: Special Case

To illustrate the general procedure required to obtain closed form expressions, we analyze the case of Figure 8.32 Top, shown in Figure 8.36 in more detail.

Constraint 1

We need $O_1(x_n) \leq h\epsilon_1$, for all x_n. The maximum of $O_1(x_n)$ occurs at c_1; therefore we need $O_1(c_1) \leq h\epsilon_1$,

$$\int_a^{c_1} f_1(s)ds - (c_1 - a)h_1 \leq h_1\epsilon_1$$

or

$$h_1 = \frac{1}{c_1 - a + \epsilon_1} \int_a^{c_1} f_1(s)ds$$

with c_1 obtained the usual way.

Constraint 2

We need $O_1(b) = 0$. We have

$$\int_a^b f_1(s)ds - (b - a)h_1 = 0$$

or

$$h_2 = \frac{1}{b - a} \int_a^b f_1(s)ds$$

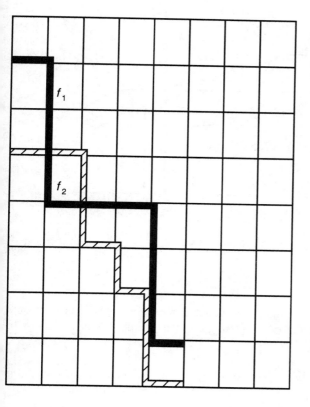

$a = 0$
$b = 6$
$\varepsilon_1 = 1$
$\varepsilon_2 = 2$

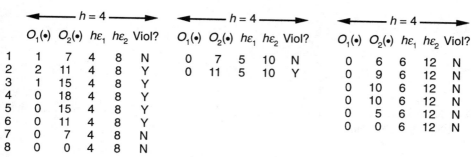

	$O_1(\bullet)$	$O_2(\bullet)$	$h\varepsilon_1$	$h\varepsilon_2$	Viol?
1	1	7	4	8	N
2	2	11	4	8	Y
3	1	15	4	8	Y
4	0	18	4	8	Y
5	0	15	4	8	Y
6	0	11	4	8	Y
7	0	7	4	8	N
8	0	0	4	8	N

$\longleftarrow h = 4 \longrightarrow$

$O_1(\bullet)$	$O_2(\bullet)$	$h\varepsilon_1$	$h\varepsilon_2$	Viol?
0	7	5	10	N
0	11	5	10	Y

$\longleftarrow h = 4 \longrightarrow$

$O_1(\bullet)$	$O_2(\bullet)$	$h\varepsilon_1$	$h\varepsilon_2$	Viol?
0	6	6	12	N
0	9	6	12	N
0	10	6	12	N
0	10	6	12	N
0	5	6	12	N
0	0	6	12	N

Figure 8.35 Calculating the engineering level in a two-class service case.

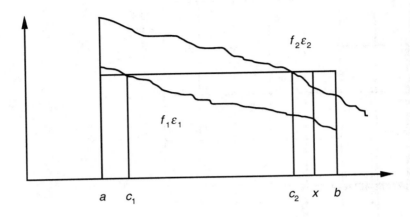

Figure 8.36 Closed form calculation.

Constraint 3

We need $O_2(x_n) \le h\epsilon_2$, for all x_n. As the figure above demonstrates this occurs at some point x greater than c_2, rather than at c_2 as one might initially think. We have $O_1(x) = 0$, or

$$\int_a^x f_1(s)ds - (x - a)h_3 = 0$$

Also, $O_2(x) \le h_3\epsilon_2$, or

$$\int_a^x f_2(s)ds = h_3\epsilon_2$$

We now have two equations in two unknowns (x and h_3) which must be solved simultaneously to obtain h_3.

Constraint 4

We need $O_2(b) = 0$. This leads to

$$h_4 = \frac{1}{b - a} \int_a^b (f_1(s) + f_2(s))ds$$

The desired engineering level is found by selecting the largest of the h's. That is, $L(f_1, \epsilon_1, f_2, \epsilon_2) = \max (h_1, h_2, h_3, h_4)$. Note parenthetically that $h_4 \geq h_2$.

Example. Consider the example of Figure 8.37 with $\epsilon_1 = \epsilon_2 = 11.5$ (although this example could be solved with the formulas of Section 8.2.4, we wish to demonstrate that the formula just derived works. Here

$$h_1 = \frac{1}{c_1 - a + \epsilon_1} \int_a^{c_1} f_1(s)ds = 12/(4 + \epsilon) = 12/15.5 \approx 0/8$$

$$h_4 = \frac{1}{b - a} \int_a^b f_1(s) + f_2(s)ds = 39/19 \approx 1.9$$

Now, solving simultaneously

$$hx - \int_0^x f_1(s)ds = 0$$

and

$$\int_0^x f_2(s)ds = h\epsilon$$

we easily obtain $h = 2$ and $x = 8$. Finally $L(f_1, \epsilon_1, f_2, \epsilon_2) = 2$.

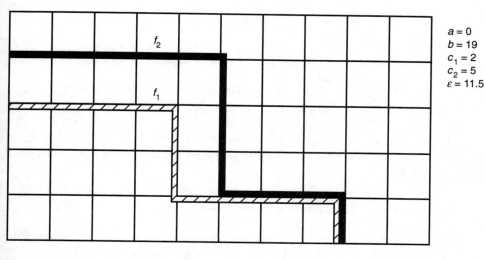

Figure 8.37 Example of a dual-class situation.

8.2.8 Approximations

In some cases one is interested in approximations to $L(f,\epsilon)$ rather than the exact solution.

8.2.8.1 Bounds for $L(f,\epsilon)$

We have already shown that

$$\frac{1}{(b-a)} \int_a^b f(x)dx \leq L(f,\epsilon) \leq \max_{[a,\ b]} f(s)$$

More generally let $x_i = i\Theta + a$, $i = 0, 1, \ldots, (b-a)/\Theta$, $\Theta \leq \epsilon$. By forcing $O(x_i) = 0$ (see Figure 8.38) we obtain

$$h_i = \frac{1}{\Theta} \int_{x_i}^{x_{i+1}} f(x)dx$$

Defining $z(\Theta) = \max (f(b), \max h_i)$, we see that

$$L(f,\epsilon) \leq z(\Theta) \leq \max f(s)$$

where the last maximum is over the interval $[a,b]$. Note that

$$\lim_{\Theta \to 0} z(\Theta) = \max_{[a,b]} f(s)$$

For the example of Figure 8.11, $h_1 = 5$, $h_2 = 4$, $h_3 = 0$, and $f(b) = 0$. Hence, $z(\Theta) = 5$. $L(f,\epsilon) = 3$. Hence the inequality holds.

The improvement (in most cases) of $z(\Theta)$-approach the over the maximum term is examplified by the case of Figure 8.39. In this case if we estimate $L(f,\epsilon)$ using the maximum we get $L(f,1) \approx 21$. Using $z(1)$ we obtain $L(f,1) \approx 11$. Note that $L(f,1) = 5.78$.

Engineering at $z(0)$ is the so-called busy-hour approach; here the hour having the highest traffic is selected (via the maximization over h_i) and the ensuing level is employed in the system design.

8.2.8.2 "Non-future" Approximation, Lower Bound

Assume that ϵ is relatively large compared with $b - a$, so that the constraint in engineering the system is not due to ϵ, but to the fact that present "vallies" cannot be filled with future work. Then if

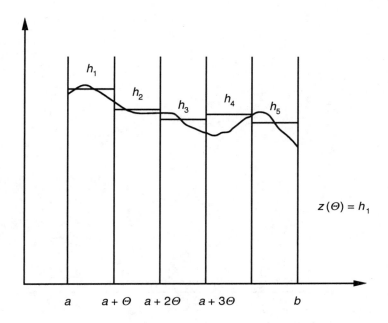

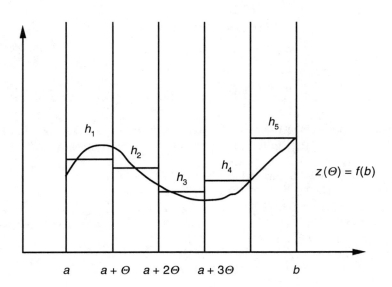

Figure 8.38 Approximation approach.

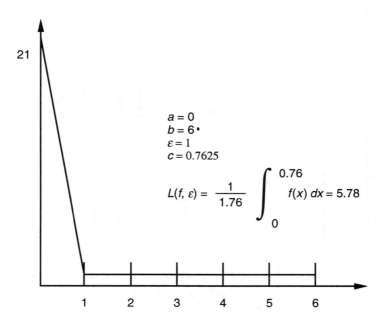

Figure 8.39 Example of approximation of calculation.

$$\Pi(v) = \frac{1}{(b-v)} \int_v^b f(x)\mathrm{d}x$$

and

$$\Pi = \max_{v\epsilon[a,b]} \Pi(v)$$

$\Pi(v)$ represents the average future work seen at v. Note that $L(f, b - a) = \Pi(a) \leq \Pi$. It follows that $L(f,\epsilon) \geq \Pi \geq \Pi(v)$ for all v in the interval $[a,b]$. In particular $L(f,\epsilon) \geq \Pi(a)$, where $\Pi(a) = A(f, b - a)$.

   For the example of Figure 8.11, $\Pi(0) = 3$, $\Pi(1) = 2$, $\Pi(2) = 0$, $\Pi(3) = 0$, $\Pi = 3$. Now we have $L(f,\epsilon) = 3 \geq \Pi = 3$.

   For the example of Figure 8.20, $\Pi(0) = 3$, $\Pi(1) = 3.22$, $\Pi(2) = 3.5$, $\Pi(3) = 3.57$, $\Pi(4) = 3.66$, $\Pi(5) = 3$, $\Pi(6) = 2$, $\Pi(7) = 1.66$, $\Pi(8) = 2$, $\Pi(9) = 1$, and $\Pi(10) = 1$. Now, $\Pi = 3.66 \leq L(f, 1) = 4.66$, and $\Pi = 3.66 \leq L(f, 2) = 3.66$.

REFERENCES

[1] D. Minoli, "A New Design Criterion for Store-and-Forward Networks", Computer Networks, 7(1983), 9–15.

Chapter 9

Relaxation Techniques: An Example of Quality-of-Service Management

This chapter applies the RT machinery developed in Chapter 8 to ATM QOS tradeoff situations. The purpose is to illustrate the use of the technique. The same technique can be used to study packet-switched networks, frame relay networks, and messaging networks, among others. As indicated in Chapter 8, there are numerous queueing/teletraffic models being applied to this problem (as a scan of the recent literature—not provided here—will indicate). RT is presented as *one possible alternative* or as a complement to these routine approaches. RT itself is independent of any application, and has been developed on its own merit.

9.1 APPLICATION

Figure 9.1 shows some typical ATM QOS results obtainable with RT methods. It is assumed that the switch (public or private) has 150 ATM terminations, each operating at STS-12c/OC-12. We take the unit-time to be 1 cell-time ($53 \times 8/622, 000, 000 = 424/622$ μs = 0.6816 μs). This means that one cell per 0.6816 μs can arrive on each port, for a maximum of 150 cells per 0.6816 μs from the entire population. The arrival profile used is contained in Appendix A; it is a possible, representative pattern that reflects periods with maximum levels of arrivals and medium levels of arrivals, as well as short periods of no arrivals (as long as a profile supports a similar mix, the results will be comparable even when using a different arrival profile). Table 9.1 depicts a summary of the results (the three detailed cases are shown in Appendix A).

One has $L(f, 1) = 132$; $L(f, 2) = 126$; $L(f, 4) = 114$; $L(f, 8) = 98$; and $A(f, 145) = 94.2$. Figure 9.1 plots the QOS (% of lost cells) as a function of the engineering level, which is parametrized on the allowed delay per cell. For example, if each cell can only

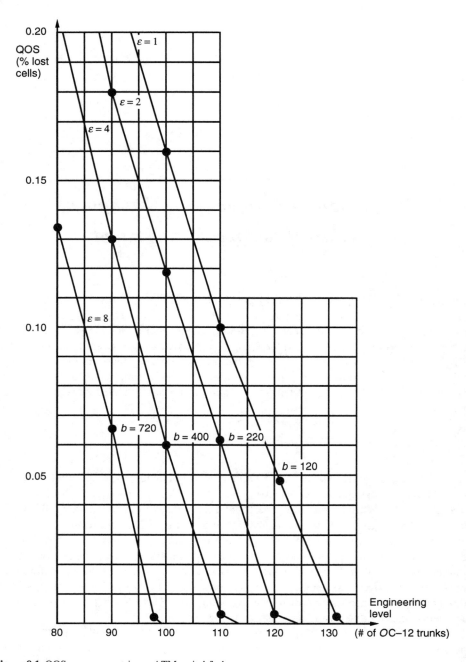

Figure 9.1 QOS management in an ATM switch/hub.

Table 9.1
QOS and Engineering Level Results

ϵ	h	Lost cells	QOS†	Actual Buffers	Theoretical Buffers*
1	80	4,036	0.29537	80	2,897
1	90	3,088	0.22600	90	1,627
1	100	2,190	0.16028	100	701
1	110	1,376	0.10070	110	521
1	120	664	0.04859	120	341
1	130	96	0.00703	130	161
1	131	40	0.00293	131	143
1	132 = $L(f, 1)$	0	0.00000	131	131
2	80	3,542	0.25922	160	2,897
2	90	2,516	0.18413	180	1,627
2	100	1,624	0.11885	200	701
2	110	864	0.06323	220	521
2	120	202	0.01478	240	341
2	125	2	0.00015	250	251
2	126 = $L(f, 2)$	0	0.00000	233	233
4	80	2,902	0.21238	320	2,897
4	90	1,792	0.13115	360	1,627
4	100	824	0.06030	400	701
4	110	162	0.01186	440	521
4	113	30	0.00220	452	467
4	114 = $L(f, 4)$	0	0.00000	449	449
8	80	2,257	0.16518	640	2,897
8	90	907	0.06638	720	1,627
8	97	30	0.00220	776	806
8	98 = $L(f, 8)$	0	0.00000	744	744

Note: Average $A(f, 145) = 94.2$
†Ratio of total cells (13,664) to lost cells.
*If aged cells are not flushed.

be delayed one cell-time ($\epsilon = 1$), then 120 OC-12 outgoing sharable trunks are required o achieve a 5% loss (all traffic is assumed to be directed to a single remote switch over a shared pool of bandwidth; the granularity is assumed to be cell-slots within SONET acilities). At least 120 buffers are needed to retain the cells during periods of congestion. A total of 132 trunks guarantee that no cell is lost, and 131 trunks provide a QOS of 0.00293. Appendix A shows that there are intervals when almost all interfaces present ells (149 cells arrive simultaneously); yet, because we allow a small, but bounded delay, ess than 149 trunks are needed.

If each cell could be delayed two cell-times ($\epsilon = 2$), then only 110 OC-12 outgoing runks would be required to achieve a 5% loss or better. However, more buffers are equired (in this case, 220). If each cell could be delayed eight cell-times ($\epsilon = 8$), then only 90 OC-12 outgoing trunks would be required to achieve a 5% loss or better. Again more buffers are required (in this case, 720).

Graphs such as these allow the designer to trade-off lost cells, delay, and buffers and pick the best combination for a given situation. Note for example, the slope of the curves in Figure 9.1. *For a 10% increase in the number of trunks one obtains a 100% improvement in the QOS* (e.g., at $\epsilon = 2$, the QOS improves from 0.12 to 0.6 when the size of the trunk pool increases from 100 trunks to 110 trunks).

9.2 OPTIMAL TRADEOFFS

Figure 9.2 depicts three engineering/design options.

If one assumes that the cost of each trunk is T and the cost of each $B = L(f, \epsilon) \times$ buffers is U, then the cost of servicing the total arriving Su_j cells in the case of strategy S3 would be

$$C = L(f, \epsilon) \times T + L(f, \epsilon) \times \epsilon \times U$$

(for a user supplying u_j cells, the prorated cost would be $(u_j/Su_j) \times C$).

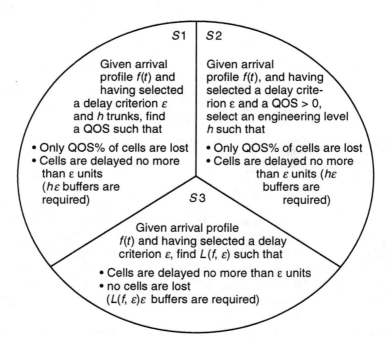

Figure 9.2 Controlling lost cells (QOS), buffer, or delay.

One approach is to charge s dollars per cell that is delivered within the stipulated delay criterion (for example, the private ATM switch may be ''owned'' by the corporate communications department, which in turn ''bills out'' customers for usage). Then, the total revenue is

$$R = s \times Su_j$$

and the revenue from user u_j would be $R_j = s \times u_j$.

Now, the profit P is equal to

$$P = R - C = s \times Su_j - L(f, \epsilon) \times T - L(f, \epsilon) \times \epsilon \times U$$

This discussion is about methodologies, and not actual values. However, some values are used here simply to illustrate how the methodology is applied.

For example, assume that $\epsilon = 2$; $L(f, \epsilon) = 126$; and $B = 233$, as per the study case of Table 9.1. Assume that an intraLATA OC-12 trunk that the user is putting in place costs $12,000 per month (presuming that a DS1 line costs as little as 6 DS0 lines, a DS3 line costs as little as 6 DS1 lines, and a STS-3 line costs twice as much as a DS3 line). Prorated to the 145 cell-interval of this illustrative example, one finds that

$$T = 12,000 \times [145/(22 \times 8 \times 3, 600 \times 1,000,000)] = 2.746 \times 10^{-6}$$

We also assume that the cost of a buffer is $1 per month amortized (e.g., $30 amortized in 30 months), or 2.746×10^{-9} per 145 cell-interval.

It is typical to assume that up to two hours/day of switched service is less expensive than a dedicated service. Thus, the per-hour cost could be $12,000/(22 \times 2) \approx 273, or 7.58×10^{-2} per second, or 11×10^{-6} per 145 cell-time units (note that this is about four times the stated cost). The cost per cell would be 7.58×10^{-8}.

$$C = 126 \times 2.746 \times 10^{-6} + 233 \times 2.746 \times 10^{-9} \approx 346 \times 10^{-6}$$

with the trunking cost dominating.

$$R = 13,664 \times 7.58 \times 10^{-8} = 1,035 \times 10^{-6}$$

Thus, $P = 689 \times 10^{-6}$. Now, the designer could choose to put in place less than $L(f, \epsilon)$ trunks, and lose some cells (strategy S1). This would mean loosing some revenue, however, the cost could also be much less. Therefore, for a particular value of T and U, the corporate communications department/carrier could find a value that maximizes the profit, as implied in Figure 9.3.

Assume that one engineered at a certain trunking level h. Given an arrival profile of $f(t)$, B_h buffers are needed (as depicted in Table 9.1). Then

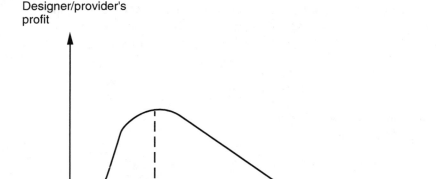

Figure 9.3 Choosing an optimal QOS.

$$C = hT + UB_h$$

The revenue would be

$$R = s(1 - QOS) \times Su_j$$

The profit would be

$$P = s(1 - QOS) \times Su_j - (hT + UB_h)$$

Table 9.2 reworks the numerical example above, assuming the number of buffer and QOS shown in Table 9.1. The profit increases as the carrier allows cells to be delaye a few units. The maximum profit is achieved at $\epsilon = 8$ and $h = L(f, 8) = 98$. For th chosen parameters, it happens that at a given e, the optimal profit is actually achieve by engineering at the level $L(f, \epsilon)$. This need not be true in general; for example, if th cost of buffering were higher, the optimum could be at values other than $L(f, \epsilon)$. In th example depicted in Table 9.3 (on page 274), the cost of buffering is increased 100-folc Note that now the maximum profit is achieved at $\epsilon = 1$ and $h = L(f, 1) = 132$; this occur because in the cases in which $\epsilon > 1$, the buffering cost becomes a dominating factor.

Table 9.2
Designer's Best Strategy Implies Trading-Off QOS, Trunk Bandwidth, and Delay

ϵ	h	Lost cells	QOS	Cost	Revenue	Profit
1	80	4,096	0.29	0.000220	0.000725	0.000505
1	90	3,088	0.22	0.000247	0.000802	0.000554
1	100	2,190	0.16	0.000275	0.000870	0.000595
1	110	1,376	0.10	0.000302	0.000931	0.000629
1	120	664	0.04	0.000330	0.000985	0.000656
1	130	96	0.00	0.000357	0.001028	0.000671
1	132	0	0.00	0.000363	0.001036	0.000673
2	80	3,542	0.26	0.000220	0.000767	0.000547
2	90	2,516	0.18	0.000248	0.000845	0.000597
2	100	1,624	0.11	0.000275	0.000913	0.000637
2	110	864	0.06	0.000303	0.000970	0.000668
2	120	202	0.01	0.000330	0.001020	0.000690
2	126	0	0.00	0.000347	0.001036	0.000689
4	80	2,902	0.21	0.000221	0.000816	0.000595
4	90	1,792	0.13	0.000248	0.000900	0.000652
4	100	824	0.06	0.000276	0.000973	0.000698
4	110	162	0.01	0.000303	0.001023	0.000720
4	114	0	0.00	0.000314	0.001036	0.000721
8	80	2,257	0.16	0.000221	0.000865	0.000643
8	90	907	0.06	0.000249	0.000967	0.000718
8	98	0	0.00	0.000271	0.001036	0.000764

As indicated, the optimum could be at values other than $L(f, \epsilon)$. This occurs when the cost of trunking is high. In the example in Table 9.4 (on page 275), the cost of trunking has been increased two-fold compared to the case above (the buffer cost is back to the initial value). As can be seen, there is a specific QOS that maximizes the profit for each value of ϵ. Interestingly, this value is around 6% for the numerical parameters used.

In a refinement of this design strategy, assume that the carrier wants to use a certain number of trunks h, but also wants to keep to some ϵ (by implication $h < L(f, \epsilon)$); this is done by allowing the QOS to degrade (strategy S2). In this case,

$$B = h\epsilon$$
$$C = hT + Uh\epsilon = h(T + U\epsilon)$$
$$R = s(1 - QOS)\, Su_j$$
$$P = R - C$$

.3 Conclusion

Cell relay service tariffs should become available in the next few years. Analyses similar to those discussed throughout this text will be required by the prospective end user in order to establish which corporate networks or subnetworks will benefit immediately from such service.

Table 9.3
Designer's Best Strategy Implies Trading-Off QOS, Trunk Bandwidth, and Delay

ϵ	h	Lost cells	QOS	Cost	Revenue	Profit
1	80	4,096	0.29	0.000242	0.000725	0.000484
1	90	3,088	0.22	0.000272	0.000802	0.000530
1	100	2,190	0.16	0.000302	0.000870	0.000568
1	110	1,376	0.10	0.000332	0.000931	0.000599
1	120	664	0.04	0.000362	0.000985	0.000623
1	130	96	0.00	0.000393	0.001028	0.000636
1	132	0	0.00	0.000399	0.001036	0.000637
2	80	3,542	0.26	0.000264	0.000767	0.000504
2	90	2,516	0.18	0.000297	0.000845	0.000548
2	100	1,624	0.11	0.000330	0.000913	0.000583
2	110	864	0.06	0.000362	0.000970	0.000608
2	120	202	0.01	0.000395	0.001020	0.000625
2	126	0	0.00	0.000415	0.001036	0.000621
4	80	2,902	0.21	0.000308	0.000816	0.000508
4	90	1,792	0.13	0.000346	0.000900	0.000554
4	100	824	0.06	0.000384	0.000973	0.000589
4	110	162	0.01	0.000423	0.001023	0.000601
4	114	0	0.00	0.000438	0.001036	0.000597
8	80	2,257	0.16	0.000395	0.000865	0.000469
8	90	907	0.06	0.000445	0.000967	0.000522
8	98	0	0.00	0.000484	0.001036	0.000551

Table 9.4
Designer's Best Strategy Implies Trading-Off QOS, Trunk Bandwidth, and Delay

ϵ	h	Lost cells	QOS	Cost	Revenue	Profit
1	80	4,096	0.29	0.000440	0.000725	0.000286
1	90	3,088	0.22	0.000495	0.000802	0.000307
1	100	2,190	0.16	0.000549	0.000870	0.000320
1	110	1,376	0.10	0.000604	0.000931	0.000327
1	120	664	0.04	0.000659	0.000985	0.000326
1	130	96	0.00	0.000714	0.001028	0.000314
1	132	0	0.00	0.000725	0.001036	0.000310
2	80	3,542	0.26	0.000440	0.000767	0.000327
2	90	2,516	0.18	0.000495	0.000845	0.000350
2	100	1,624	0.11	0.000550	0.000913	0.000363
2	110	864	0.06	0.000605	0.000970	0.000366
2	120	202	0.01	0.000660	0.001020	0.000361
2	126	0	0.00	0.000693	0.001036	0.000343
4	80	2,902	0.21	0.000440	0.000816	0.000376
4	90	1,792	0.13	0.000495	0.000900	0.000405
4	100	824	0.06	0.000550	0.000973	0.000423
4	110	162	0.01	0.000605	0.001023	0.000418
4	114	0	0.00	0.000627	0.001036	0.000408
8	80	2,257	0.16	0.000441	0.000865	0.000424
8	90	907	0.06	0.000496	0.000967	0.000471
8	98	0	0.00	0.000540	0.001036	0.000495

APPENDIX A
Illustrative Data Used in Analysis

In Table A.1, the first two columns display arrival rate. (All the results of Section 9.1 are based on this distribution.) The last two columns show results for $\epsilon = 2$, $h = 122$.

Table A.1
Baseline Arrival Rate Used to Derive Typical Results

Lost cells: 544
Total cells: 13,664
QOS (loss ratio): 0.03981

t	$f(t)$	$O(a)$	Lost cells
1	122	0.00	0.00
2	133	11.00	0.00
3	88	0.00	0.00
4	34	0.00	0.00
5	32	0.00	0.00
6	45	0.00	0.00
7	148	26.00	0.00
8	148	52.00	0.00
9	122	52.00	0.00
10	148	78.00	0.00
11	12	0.00	0.00
12	17	0.00	0.00
13	149	27.00	0.00
14	149	54.00	0.00
15	144	76.00	0.00
16	126	80.00	0.00
17	88	46.00	0.00
18	145	69.00	0.00
19	145	92.00	0.00
20	145	115.00	0.00

t	f(t)	O(a)	Lost cells
21	145	138.00	16.00
22	145	161.00	23.00
23	145	184.00	23.00
24	145	207.00	23.00
25	145	230.00	23.00
26	145	253.00	23.00
27	122	253.00	0.00
28	148	279.00	26.00
29	122	279.00	0.00
30	148	305.00	26.00
31	12	195.00	0.00
32	12	85.00	0.00
33	13	0.00	0.00
34	149	27.00	0.00
35	12	0.00	0.00
36	55	0.00	0.00
37	88	0.00	0.00
38	0	0.00	0.00
39	0	0.00	0.00
40	0	0.00	0.00
41	149	27.00	0.00
42	149	54.00	0.00
43	149	81.00	0.00
44	148	107.00	0.00
45	148	133.00	11.00
46	148	159.00	26.00
47	148	185.00	26.00
48	148	211.00	26.00
49	77	166.00	0.00
50	77	121.00	0.00
51	46	45.00	0.00
52	123	46.00	0.00
53	156	80.00	0.00
54	145	103.00	0.00
55	150	131.00	0.00
56	150	159.00	0.00
57	99	136.00	0.00
58	66	80.00	0.00
59	87	45.00	0.00
60	0	0.00	0.00
61	10	0.00	0.00
62	20	0.00	0.00
63	30	0.00	0.00
64	40	0.00	0.00
65	50	0.00	0.00
66	60	0.00	0.00
67	70	0.00	0.00
68	120	0.00	0.00

t	f(t)	O(a)	Lost cells
69	140	18.00	0.00
70	120	16.00	0.00
71	110	4.00	0.00
72	144	26.00	0.00
73	66	0.00	0.00
74	44	0.00	0.00
75	55	0.00	0.00
76	77	0.00	0.00
77	122	0.00	0.00
78	133	11.00	0.00
79	88	0.00	0.00
80	34	0.00	0.00
81	32	0.00	0.00
82	45	0.00	0.00
83	148	26.00	0.00
84	148	52.00	0.00
85	122	52.00	0.00
86	148	78.00	0.00
87	12	0.00	0.00
88	17	0.00	0.00
89	149	27.00	0.00
90	149	54.00	0.00
91	144	76.00	0.00
92	126	80.00	0.00
93	88	46.00	0.00
94	145	69.00	0.00
95	145	92.00	0.00
96	145	115.00	0.00
97	145	138.00	16.00
98	145	161.00	23.00
99	145	184.00	23.00
100	145	207.00	23.00
101	145	230.00	23.00
102	145	253.00	23.00
103	122	253.00	0.00
104	148	279.00	26.00
105	122	279.00	0.00
106	148	305.00	26.00
107	12	195.00	0.00
108	12	85.00	0.00
109	13	0.00	0.00
110	149	27.00	0.00
111	12	0.00	0.00
112	55	0.00	0.00
113	88	0.00	0.00
114	0	0.00	0.00
115	0	0.00	0.00
116	0	0.00	0.00

t	$f(t)$	$O(a)$	Lost cells
117	149	27.00	0.00
118	149	54.00	0.00
119	149	81.00	0.00
120	148	107.00	0.00
121	148	133.00	11.00
122	148	159.00	26.00
123	148	185.00	26.00
124	148	211.00	26.00
125	77	166.00	0.00
126	77	121.00	0.00
127	46	45.00	0.00
128	123	46.00	0.00
129	156	80.00	0.00
130	145	103.00	0.00
131	150	131.00	0.00
132	150	159.00	0.00
133	99	136.00	0.00
134	66	80.00	0.00
135	87	45.00	0.00
136	0	0.00	0.00
137	0	0.00	0.00
138	0	0.00	0.00
139	0	0.00	0.00
140	0	0.00	0.00
141	0	0.00	0.00
142	0	0.00	0.00
143	0	0.00	0.00
144	0	0.00	0.00
145	0	0.00	0.00

In Table A.2, the first two columns display arrival rate. (All the results of Section 9.1 are based on this distribution.) The last two columns show results for $\epsilon = 2$, $h = 122$.

Table A.2
Baseline Arrival Rate Used to Derive Typical Results

Lost cells: 122
Total cells: 13,664
QOS (loss ratio): 0.00893

t	$f(t)$	$O(a)$	Lost cells
1	122	0.00	0.00
2	133	11.00	0.00
3	88	0.00	0.00
4	34	0.00	0.00
5	32	0.00	0.00

t	f(t)	O(a)	Lost cells
6	45	0.00	0.00
7	148	26.00	0.00
8	148	52.00	0.00
9	122	52.00	0.00
10	148	78.00	0.00
11	12	0.00	0.00
12	17	0.00	0.00
13	149	27.00	0.00
14	149	54.00	0.00
15	144	76.00	0.00
16	126	80.00	0.00
17	88	46.00	0.00
18	145	69.00	0.00
19	145	92.00	0.00
20	145	115.00	0.00
21	145	138.00	0.00
22	145	161.00	0.00
23	145	184.00	0.00
24	145	207.00	0.00
25	145	230.00	0.00
26	145	253.00	9.00
27	122	253.00	0.00
28	148	279.00	26.00
29	122	279.00	0.00
30	148	305.00	26.00
31	12	195.00	0.00
32	12	85.00	0.00
33	13	0.00	0.00
34	149	27.00	0.00
35	12	0.00	0.00
36	55	0.00	0.00
37	88	0.00	0.00
38	0	0.00	0.00
39	0	0.00	0.00
40	0	0.00	0.00
41	149	27.00	0.00
42	149	54.00	0.00
43	149	81.00	0.00
44	148	107.00	0.00
45	148	133.00	0.00
46	148	159.00	0.00
47	148	185.00	0.00
48	148	211.00	0.00
49	77	166.00	0.00
50	77	121.00	0.00
51	46	45.00	0.00
52	123	46.00	0.00
53	156	80.00	0.00

t	f(t)	O(a)	Lost cells
54	145	103.00	0.00
55	150	131.00	0.00
56	150	159.00	0.00
57	99	136.00	0.00
58	66	80.00	0.00
59	87	45.00	0.00
60	0	0.00	0.00
61	10	0.00	0.00
62	20	0.00	0.00
63	30	0.00	0.00
64	40	0.00	0.00
65	50	0.00	0.00
66	60	0.00	0.00
67	70	0.00	0.00
68	120	0.00	0.00
69	140	18.00	0.00
70	120	16.00	0.00
71	110	4.00	0.00
72	144	26.00	0.00
73	66	0.00	0.00
74	44	0.00	0.00
75	55	0.00	0.00
76	77	0.00	0.00
77	122	0.00	0.00
78	133	11.00	0.00
79	88	0.00	0.00
80	34	0.00	0.00
81	32	0.00	0.00
82	45	0.00	0.00
83	148	26.00	0.00
84	148	52.00	0.00
85	122	52.00	0.00
86	148	78.00	0.00
87	12	0.00	0.00
88	17	0.00	0.00
89	149	27.00	0.00
90	149	54.00	0.00
91	144	76.00	0.00
92	126	80.00	0.00
93	88	46.00	0.00
94	145	69.00	0.00
95	145	92.00	0.00
96	145	115.00	0.00
97	145	138.00	0.00
98	145	161.00	0.00
99	145	184.00	0.00
100	145	207.00	0.00
101	145	230.00	0.00

t	$f(t)$	$O(a)$	Lost cells
102	145	253.00	9.00
103	122	253.00	0.00
104	148	279.00	26.00
105	122	279.00	0.00
106	148	305.00	26.00
107	12	195.00	0.00
108	12	85.00	0.00
109	13	0.00	0.00
110	149	27.00	0.00
111	12	0.00	0.00
112	55	0.00	0.00
113	88	0.00	0.00
114	0	0.00	0.00
115	0	0.00	0.00
116	0	0.00	0.00
117	149	27.00	0.00
118	149	54.00	0.00
119	149	81.00	0.00
120	148	107.00	0.00
121	148	133.00	0.00
122	148	159.00	0.00
123	148	185.00	0.00
124	148	211.00	0.00
125	77	166.00	0.00
126	77	121.00	0.00
127	46	45.00	0.00
128	123	46.00	0.00
129	156	80.00	0.00
130	145	103.00	0.00
131	150	131.00	0.00
132	150	159.00	0.00
133	99	136.00	0.00
134	66	80.00	0.00
135	87	45.00	0.00
136	0	0.00	0.00
137	0	0.00	0.00
138	0	0.00	0.00
139	0	0.00	0.00
140	0	0.00	0.00
141	0	0.00	0.00
142	0	0.00	0.00
143	0	0.00	0.00
144	0	0.00	0.00
145	0	0.00	0.00

In Table A.3, the first two columns display arrival rate. (All the results of Section 9.1 are based on this distribution.) The last two columns show results for $\epsilon = 1$, $h = 130$.

Table A.3

Baseline Arrival Rate Used to Derive Typical Results

Lost cells: 96
Total cells: 13,664
QOS (loss ratio): 0.00703

t	f(t)	O(a)	Lost cells
1	122	0.00	0.00
2	133	3.00	0.00
3	88	0.00	0.00
4	34	0.00	0.00
5	32	0.00	0.00
6	45	0.00	0.00
7	148	18.00	0.00
8	148	36.00	0.00
9	122	28.00	0.00
10	148	46.00	0.00
11	12	0.00	0.00
12	17	0.00	0.00
13	149	19.00	0.00
14	149	38.00	0.00
15	144	52.00	0.00
16	126	48.00	0.00
17	88	6.00	0.00
18	145	21.00	0.00
19	145	36.00	0.00
20	145	51.00	0.00
21	145	66.00	0.00
22	145	81.00	0.00
23	145	96.00	0.00
24	145	111.00	0.00
25	145	126.00	0.00
26	145	141.00	11.00
27	122	133.00	0.00
28	148	151.00	10.00
29	122	143.00	0.00
30	148	161.00	10.00
31	12	43.00	0.00
32	12	0.00	0.00
33	13	0.00	0.00
34	149	19.00	0.00
35	12	0.00	0.00
36	55	0.00	0.00
37	88	0.00	0.00
38	0	0.00	0.00
39	0	0.00	0.00
40	0	0.00	0.00
41	149	19.00	0.00
42	149	38.00	0.00

t	$f(t)$	$O(a)$	Lost cells
43	149	57.00	0.00
44	148	75.00	0.00
45	148	93.00	0.00
46	148	111.00	0.00
47	148	129.00	0.00
48	148	147.00	17.00
49	77	94.00	0.00
50	77	41.00	0.00
51	46	0.00	0.00
52	123	0.00	0.00
53	156	26.00	0.00
54	145	41.00	0.00
55	150	61.00	0.00
56	150	81.00	0.00
57	99	50.00	0.00
58	66	0.00	0.00
59	87	0.00	0.00
60	0	0.00	0.00
61	10	0.00	0.00
62	20	0.00	0.00
63	30	0.00	0.00
64	40	0.00	0.00
65	50	0.00	0.00
66	60	0.00	0.00
67	70	0.00	0.00
68	120	0.00	0.00
69	140	10.00	0.00
70	120	0.00	0.00
71	110	0.00	0.00
72	144	14.00	0.00
73	66	0.00	0.00
74	44	0.00	0.00
75	55	0.00	0.00
76	77	0.00	0.00
77	122	0.00	0.00
78	133	3.00	0.00
79	88	0.00	0.00
80	34	0.00	0.00
81	32	0.00	0.00
82	45	0.00	0.00
83	148	18.00	0.00
84	148	36.00	0.00
85	122	28.00	0.00
86	148	46.00	0.00
87	12	0.00	0.00
88	17	0.00	0.00
89	149	19.00	0.00
90	149	38.00	0.00

t	f(t)	O(a)	Lost cells
91	144	52.00	0.00
92	126	48.00	0.00
93	88	6.00	0.00
94	145	21.00	0.00
95	145	36.00	0.00
96	145	51.00	0.00
97	145	66.00	0.00
98	145	81.00	0.00
99	145	96.00	0.00
100	145	111.00	0.00
101	145	126.00	0.00
102	145	141.00	11.00
103	122	133.00	0.00
104	148	151.00	10.00
105	122	143.00	0.00
106	148	161.00	10.00
107	12	43.00	0.00
108	12	0.00	0.00
109	13	0.00	0.00
110	149	19.00	0.00
111	12	0.00	0.00
112	55	0.00	0.00
113	88	0.00	0.00
114	0	0.00	0.00
115	0	0.00	0.00
116	0	0.00	0.00
117	149	19.00	0.00
118	149	38.00	0.00
119	149	57.00	0.00
120	148	75.00	0.00
121	148	93.00	0.00
122	148	111.00	0.00
123	148	129.00	0.00
124	148	147.00	17.00
125	77	94.00	0.00
126	77	41.00	0.00
127	46	0.00	0.00
128	123	0.00	0.00
129	156	26.00	0.00
130	145	41.00	0.00
131	150	61.00	0.00
132	150	81.00	0.00
133	99	50.00	0.00
134	66	0.00	0.00
135	87	0.00	0.00
136	0	0.00	0.00
137	0	0.00	0.00
138	0	0.00	0.00

t	$f(t)$	$O(a)$	Lost cells
139	0	0.00	0.00
140	0	0.00	0.00
141	0	0.00	0.00
142	0	0.00	0.00
143	0	0.00	0.00
144	0	0.00	0.00
145	0	0.00	0.00

About the Author

Mr. Minoli has broad experience in the data communications and telecommunications fields. His responsibilities have included: fundamental research, advanced network planning, traffic engineering, network design, implementation, system integration, disaster recovery planning, communications quality control, standards work, user training, network management, and communications-related software development. Network designs have included: T1 backbone networks, channel extension, LAN interconnection, frame relay networks, cell relay networks, packet-switched networks, traditional SNA networks, voice networks, radio networks, satellite networks, and international networks.

In addition to extensive independent consulting, Mr. Minoli has worked for Bell Telephone Laboratories, ITT World Communications, and Prudential-Bache Securities. He has been a strategic data communications planner at Bell Communications Research (Bellcore) for the past seven years. His research at Bellcore has been aimed at (1) supporting the internal data processing/data communications needs of the Bell Operating Companies; (2) identifying data services that can be provided in the public network in the 1990s using the advanced intelligent network (AIN), integrated services digital network (ISDN), broadband ISDN (BISDN), and other platform-independent infrastructures; (3) undertaking network design functions for large end-user networks, in support of the Bell Operating Companies' responses to RFPs, and, more recently, (4) supporting cell relay/ATM signaling standards work.

Mr. Minoli has published five telecommunications books and approximately 200 technical and trade articles. In addition to this current book, he published the widely-distributed *Telecommunication Technologies Handbook* (Artech House, 1991), which is a comprehensive assessment of communications technologies and trends of the 1990s, including wireless, satellite, microwave and fiber transmission, metropolitan area networks, open systems interconnection standards and network security. His newly-published *Enterprise Networking* (Artech House, 1993) provides a detailed survey of network technologies such as fractional T1, T1, switched T1, T3, SONET, frame relay, cell relay, BISDN and SMDS. Another recently published book, *First, Second, and Next Generation*

LANs (McGraw-Hill, 1993) focuses on "gigabit LANs." Mr. Minoli also co-authored *Expert Systems Applications in Integrated Network Management* (Artech House, 1989). He has just completed a sixth book entitled *Multimedia—Technology, Communications, Applications*, which will also be published by Artech House.

Mr. Minoli is a frequent speaker and session chair at industry conferences. He is an Adjunct Associate Professor at New York University's Information Technology Institute, where he has educated more than 1,000 professionals over a period of eight years. Mr. Minoli has lectured at the Rutgers Center for Management Development for the past three years. He is on Datapro Research Corporation's Advisory Board for broadband networking. He has published over thirty key technology "Reports" over the past decade. Mr. Minoli is also a Contributor Editor of *Network Computing* magazine, with a circulation of 250,000. He ran a quarterly two-day seminar on *T1 Communication* for two years. In the past, Mr. Minoli has been a columnist for *ComputerWorld* magazine and a reviewer for the IEEE.

Index

The Artech House Telecommunications Library

Vinton G. Cerf, Series Editor

Expert Systems Applications in Integrated Network Management, E. C. Ericson, L. T. Ericson, and D. Minoli, editors

FAX: Digital Facsimile Technology and Applications, Second Edition, Dennis Bodson, Kenneth McConnell, and Richard Schaphorst

Fiber Network Service Survivability, Tsong-Ho Wu

Fiber Optics and CATV Business Strategy, Robert K. Yates et al.

A Guide to Fractional T1, J.E. Trulove

Handbook of Satellite Telecommunications and Broadcasting, L. Ya. Kantor, editor

Implementing X.400 and X.500: The PP and QUIPU Systems, Steve Kille

Inbound Call Centers: Design, Implementation, and Management, Robert A. Gable

Information Superhighways: The Economics of Advanced Public Communication Networks, Bruce Egan

Integrated Broadband Networks, Amit Bhargava

Integrated Services Digital Networks, Anthony M. Rutkowski

International Telecommunications Management, Bruce R. Elbert

International Telecommunication Standards Organizations, Andrew Macpherson

Internetworking LANs: Operation, Design, and Management, Robert Davidson and Nathan Muller

Introduction to Satellite Communication, Burce R. Elbert

Introduction to T1/T3 Networking, Regis J. (Bud) Bates

Introduction to Telecommunication Electronics, A. Michael Noll

Introduction to Telephones and Telephone Systems, Second Edition, A. Michael Noll

Introduction to X.400, Cemil Betanov

The ITU in a Changing World, George A. Codding, Jr. and Anthony M. Rutkowski

Jitter in Digital Transmission Systems, Patrick R. Trischitta and Eve L. Varma

LAN/WAN Optimization Techniques, Harrell Van Norman

LANs to WANs: Network Management in the 1990s, Nathan J. Muller and Robert P. Davidson

The Law and Regulation of International Space Communication, Harold M. White, Jr. and Rita Lauria White

Long Distance Services: A Buyer's Guide, Daniel D. Briere

Mathematical Methods of Information Transmission, K. Arbenz and J. C. Martin

Measurement of Optical Fibers and Devices, G. Cancellieri and U. Ravaioli

Meteor Burst Communication, Jacob Z. Schanker

Minimum Risk Strategy for Acquiring Communications Equipment and Services, Nathan J. Muller

Mobile Information Systems, John Walker

Narrowband Land-Mobile Radio Networks, Jean-Paul Linnartz

Networking Strategies for Information Technology, Bruce Elbert

For further information on these and other Artech House titles, contact:

Artech House
685 Canton Street
Norwood, MA 01602
(617) 769-9750
Fax:(617) 762-9230
Telex: 951-659

Artech House
6 Buckingham Gate
London SW1E6JP England
+44(0)71 630-0166
+44(0)71 630-0166
Telex-951-659